Classroom Discourse
and the Space of Learning

Classroom Discourse and the Space of Learning

Ference Marton, *Göteborg University*
Amy B. M. Tsui, *The University of Hong Kong*

With
Pakey P. M. Chik
Po Yuk Ko
Mun Ling Lo
Ida A. C. Mok
Dorothy F. P. Ng
Ming Fai Pang
Wing Yan Pong
Ulla Runesson

LAWRENCE ERLBAUM ASSOCIATES, PUBLISHERS
2004   Mahwah, New Jersey   London

Copyright © 2004 by Lawrence Erlbaum Associates, Inc.
All rights reserved. No part of this book may be reproduced in any form, by photostat, microform, retrieval system, or any other means, without prior written permission of the publisher.

Lawrence Erlbaum Associates, Inc., Publishers
10 Industrial Avenue
Mahwah, New Jersey 07430

Cover design by John Leung

Library of Congress Cataloging-in-Publication Data

Marton, Ference.
Classroom discourse and the space of learning / Ference Marton, Amy B. M. Tsui with Pakey P. M. Chik ... [et al.].
    p. cm.
Includes bibliographical references and index.
ISBN 0-8058-4008-7 (cloth : alk. paper)
ISBN 0-8058-4009-5 (pbk. : alk. paper)
1. Communication in education.   2. Learning.   3. Classroom environment.   I. Tsui, Amy.   II. Title.
LB1033.5.M265 2003
371.102'2—dc21
                                              2003047019
                                                    CIP

Books published by Lawrence Erlbaum Associates are printed on acid-free paper, and their bindings are chosen for strength and durability.

Printed in the United States of America
10 9 8 7 6 5 4 3 2 1

Contents

Contributors vii

Preface ix

Part I On Learning and Language

1 The Space of Learning 3
  Ference Marton, Ulla Runesson, and Amy B. M. Tsui

Part II On Learning

2 Variation and the Secret of the Virtuoso 43
  Po Yuk Ko and Ference Marton

3 Discernment and the Question, "What Can Be Learned?" 63
  Ulla Runesson and Ida A. C. Mok

4 Simultaneity and the Enacted Object of Learning 89
  Pakey P. M. Chik and Mun Ling Lo

Part III On Language

5 Questions and the Space of Learning 113
  Amy B. M. Tsui, Ference Marton, Ida A. C. Mok, and Dorothy F. P. Ng

6	The Semantic Enrichment of the Space of Learning *Amy B. M. Tsui*	139
7	The Shared Space of Learning *Amy B. M. Tsui*	165

Part IV   On Improving Learning

8	Toward a Pedagogy of Learning *Mun Ling Lo, Ference Marton, Ming Fai Pang, and Wing Yan Pong*	189
	Epilogue	227
	References	233
	Author Index	239
	Subject Index	241

Contributors

Ference Marton, Professor of Education, Faculty of Education, Göteborg University, Sweden, and Honorary Professor, Faculty of Education, The University of Hong Kong.

Amy B. M. Tsui, Chair Professor, Faculty of Education, The University of Hong Kong.

Pakey P. M. Chik, Student, Degree of Master of Philosophy, Faculty of Education, The University of Hong Kong.

Po Yuk Ko, Lecturer, Department of Curriculum and Instruction, The Hong Kong Institute of Education.

Mun Ling Lo, Head, Centre for Development of School Partnership and Field Experience, The Hong Kong Institute of Education.

Ida A. C. Mok, Assistant Professor, Faculty of Education, The University of Hong Kong.

Dorothy F. P. Ng, Teaching Fellow, Faculty of Education, The University of Hong Kong.

Ming Fai Pang, Assistant Professor, Faculty of Education, The University of Hong Kong.

Wing Yan Pong, Principal, Hong Kong Management Association, David Li Kwok Po College.

Ulla Runesson, Postdoctoral Fellow, Senior Lecturer, Faculty of Education, Göteborg University, Sweden.

Preface

This book is about learning in schools, and the role of language in learning. We have tried to capture its two main ideas in the title. Contained within the first idea is the premise that whatever you are trying to learn, there are certain necessary conditions for succeeding. Although you cannot be sure that learning will take place when those conditions are met, you can be sure that no learning will take place if they are not. The limits of what is possible to learn, we call "the space of learning." The second premise is that language plays a central role in learning: that it does not merely *convey* meaning, it also *creates* meaning. An understanding of how the space of learning is linguistically constituted in the classroom is best achieved through investigating "classroom discourse," which is what we aim to do here.

A teacher can never ensure that the intended learning will actually take place, but a teacher should try to ensure that it is *possible* for the students to learn what is intended. That is, the teacher should ensure that the space of learning allows for the intended learning to take place. For every educational aim, for every single thing that students are expected to learn, there are specific conditions necessary for that learning. In our view, finding out what these conditions are, and bringing them about, should be the teacher's primary professional task. A prerequisite for finding out these conditions is the realization that one's own way of teaching is not the only way. Such a realization can only be achieved by confronting different ways of teaching the same thing, by examining how the different ways are actually played out in the classroom and by comparing what is intended with what is enacted. And investigating the discourse in which the teacher and the students are engaged in the classroom is an essential part of this endeavor. It is, therefore, fundamentally important that teachers—and student teachers, for that matter—are given opportunities to observe different teachers teaching the same thing, and to analyze and reflect on how the classroom discourse in which they are engaged with the students maximizes or minimizes opportunities for learning.

This book is organized in four parts. In Part I, "On Learning and Language," we present the theoretical background, namely the theories that whatever you are trying to learn, there are certain necessary conditions for succeeding, and that language plays a central role in learning. Part II, "On Learning," comprises three chapters, each of which elaborates on one of the three core elements of our view of learning: variation, discernment, and simultaneity. Part III, "On Language," comprises three chapters as well, each of which deals with one of the three aspects of the role of language in classroom learning: the role of questions in constituting the space of learning, the semantic nature of the space of learning, and the joint constitution of that space. In Part IV, "On Improving Learning," we give three examples of teachers working together and using the very theoretical tools presented in the previous chapters.

Three features of this book distinguish it from similar books about learning in schools. First, it is a book about both theory *and* practice. It contains a detailed explication of the theory of learning that motivated the analyses of classroom teaching in the rest of the book. It presents detailed analyses of classroom teaching that were driven by classroom discourse data in a number of authentic cases of learning in school, and which will be of practical relevance to teachers.

Second, this book is more culturally situated than most other books about learning in schools. Most of the studies reported in this book have been carried out in Hong Kong. In every example, it is clearly demonstrated how the specific language, culture, and pedagogy molds what is happening in the classroom. At the same time, however, we would like to claim that it is also possible to generalize from the culturally specific examples and arguments presented in this book. We argue that whatever skills, whatever ways of thinking the students are expected to develop, there are necessary conditions for the development of these skills. These conditions are specific to every specific skill, to every specific way of thinking, and they must be met regardless of where the learning is taking place, and regardless of what other conditions there might be.

Third, this book—just like other books—is good for certain things and not so good for other things. As implied earlier, if you want to find out how certain specific capabilities (such as using elementary arithmetic in flexible ways, distinguishing between different tones in Cantonese, seeing bodies in motion in accordance with a Newtonian framework, realizing why green plants are essential for life on Earth) can be best developed, you will probably find this book useful. However, if you want to find out about generalizations that are universal, if they exist at all, such as how people become creative, what is the best arrangement for learning in general, the exact num-

PREFACE   xi

ber of intelligences or learning styles in humans, to what extent those intelligences or learning styles are biologically, economically, culturally, or linguistically determined, and so on, this book is probably not a very good source of inspiration. This book, we wish to emphasize, is not about universal generalizations about learning, nor is it about the development of specific capabilities per se. This book is about the *necessary conditions* for the development of any specific capability.

We would like to suggest that this book is best used in field practice for teacher education and in-service training for teachers. We feel that it will be of most practical use when read in conjunction with arrangements whereby teachers and student teachers have opportunities to observe different teachers teaching the same topic, and to investigate teacher–student discourse in light of the opportunities for learning that are afforded.

This book can, however, also be juxtaposed with other theoretical accounts of classroom learning. Dealt with in this way, it can be used, we believe, in advanced seminars in teacher education, and for courses at Master's level in educational studies.

ACKNOWLEDGMENTS

The research carried out in Hong Kong was made possible through a grant awarded to Professor Paul Morris (then Chair Professor of Education, The University of Hong Kong, now President of the Hong Kong Institute of Education) from the Standing Committee on Language Education and Research in Hong Kong (SCOLAR). We would like to express our sincere gratitude to Professor Morris, a brilliant scholar and a most generous colleague.[1]

Ference Marton and Ulla Runesson would like to acknowledge the support of The Tercentennary Foundation of the Bank of Sweden, and the Swedish Research Council, without which their work would not have been possible.

The authors of this volume would also like to thank the former Department of Curriculum Studies (now part of the Faculty of Education) at The University of Hong Kong, for providing the Departmental Research Fund, which allowed the authors to pay for expenses incurred in collaborating with Göteborg University and in securing linguistic editing assistance.

The research team included Dr. Tammy Kwan, whose contribution to this book is indicated by explicit references to her work. Vikki Weston has carried out a wonderful job of editing the language of the manuscript. Annie Chow, Miranda Cheung, and Winky Mok at The University of Hong Kong, as well as Lisbetth Söderberg and Barbro Strömberg at Göteborg University, have, in different but essential ways, helped us to put the manuscript in shape. We thank them all.

Two reviewers, Courtney Cazden of Harvard Graduate Schools and Gaalen Erickson of the University of British Columbia, have provided extremely useful and critical comments that have sharpened the focus of the book. We are very grateful to them. Finally, this book would never have materialized without the support of Naomi Silverman, Senior Editor, and Lori Hawver, Assistant Editor, of Lawrence Erlbaum Associates, both of whom have been most encouraging, accommodating, and efficient. To them we owe our deepest gratitude.

—Ference Marton
—Amy B. M. Tsui

ENDNOTE

[1]Part of the findings from this project have been reported previously in F. Marton & P. Morris. (Eds.). (2002). *What Matters: Discovering Critical Conditions of Classroom Learning.* Göteborg, Sweden: Acta Universitatis Gothoburgensis.

I

On Learning and Language

1

The Space of Learning

Ference Marton
Ulla Runesson
Amy B. M. Tsui

School is an institution with which all citizens in the industrial world have extensive familiarity, and one that frequently attracts considerable public and political attention. The discussions about school can be heated and the opinions polemic: "We should have less whole-class teaching," "We should have more project work," "We should have more peer learning," "We should have more problem-based learning," "By the year 2006, at least 20% of all learning in our school should be information technology (IT) supported," "Students should have more homework," "Students should have less homework," "We should do away with age grouping," "We should reintroduce age grouping," "We should have streaming," and so on.

All these opinions about what should be done assume, of course, that doing this or doing that is better than doing something else. But if we ask the question, "Better for what?" the answer is likely to be, "Better for learning, of course." "But for the learning of what?" "For the learning of everything?" These are the questions that must be addressed.

The point is that it is highly unlikely that there is any one particular way of arranging for learning that is conducive to *all* kinds of learning. In order to find effective ways of arranging for learning, researchers need to first address *what* it is that should be learned in each case, and find the different conditions that are conducive to different kinds of learning.

It is only when we have a fair understanding of what learners are expected to learn in particular situations, what they actually learn in those situations, and *why* they learn something in one situation but not in another, that pedagogy becomes a reasonably rational set of human activities. It is the aim of this book to provide such an understanding.

When people argue for a particular way of arranging for learning, or for a particular teaching method, such as working in groups or the use of pedagogical drama, they should make it clear what the particular arrangement, or the particular method, is good for and why. Pedagogical acts should take as their point of departure the capabilities they are supposed to contribute to developing. The point of schooling is not that students should or should not be grouped together in certain ways under certain conditions—such as being divided up according to age, ability level, or gender. Neither is the point that teachers should do certain things in certain ways, or that certain content should be covered. The point is that the students should develop certain capabilities.[1]

THE OBJECT OF LEARNING

Learning is always the acquired knowledge of something. And we should always keep in mind what that "something" is, that is, we should be clear about the object of learning.

In this book, the object of learning is a *capability*, and any capability has a general and a specific aspect. The general aspect has to do with the nature of the capability, such as remembering, discerning, interpreting, grasping, or viewing, that is, the acts of learning carried out. The specific aspect has to do with the thing or subject on which these acts are carried out, such as formulas, engineering problems, simultaneous equations, World War II, or Franz Kafka's literary heritage. In other words, the *general aspect* refers to acts (the *indirect* object of learning), whereas the *specific aspect* refers to what is acted upon (the *direct* object of learning). The learners' focus is normally on what they are trying to learn (the direct object of learning), whereas the teacher's focus should be on both; not only on that which the learners are trying to learn, but also on the way in which the learners are trying to master what they are trying to learn. We might assume therefore, that teachers are trying to work toward an *object of learning*. This object may be more or less conscious for the teacher and it may be more or less elaborated. But, whatever the circumstances, what teachers are striving for is the *intended* object of learning, an object of the teacher's awareness, that might change dynamically during the course of learning. This is the object of learning as seen from the teacher's perspective, and as such is depicted in this book as being evidenced by what the teacher does and says.

What is of importance for the students, however, is not so much how the teacher intends the object of learning to come to the fore, but how the teacher structures the conditions of learning so that it is possible for the object of learning to come to the fore of the learners' awareness. What the students encounter is the *enacted* object of learning, and it defines what it is possible to learn in the actual setting, from the point of view of the specific object of learning. There are obviously certain necessary conditions for

1. THE SPACE OF LEARNING 5

learning one thing or another. The enacted object of learning is the researcher's description of whether, to what extent, and in what forms the necessary conditions of a particular object of learning appear in a certain setting. The enacted object of learning is described from the point of view of a certain research interest and a particular theoretical perspective.

What is of decisive importance for the students, is what actually comes to the fore of their attention, that is, what aspects of the situation they discern and focus on. In the best case, they focus on the critical aspects of the object of learning, and by doing so they learn what the teacher intended. But they may also fail to discern and focus on some of the critical aspects, or they may discern and focus on other aspects. What they actually learn is the *lived* object of learning, the object of learning as seen from the learner's point of view, that is, the outcome or result of learning.

The Origin of Powerful Ways of Acting

Learning is the process of becoming capable of doing something ("doing" in the wide sense) as a result of having had certain experiences (of doing something or of something happening). Developing a learner's capability of handling novel situations in powerful ways is considered to be one of the most important educational aims. In order to address how this can be done, we have to reflect on the nature of powerful ways of acting, that is, ways of engaging in acts instrumental to achieving one's goals efficiently. Acting in powerful ways means, therefore, doing different things to achieve different aims, and doing different things in different situations. The powerfulness of one's acts is relative to one's aims and the situations.

Let us first consider the situations. As rational beings, we always try to act in accordance with any given situation, that is, the situation as we perceive it. What knowledge we might try to exploit depends on how we make sense of the situation. Our previous experiences affect the way in which we perceive the situation, but the way in which we perceive the situation also affects what experiences we see as relevant in that particular situation. We are trying to act in powerful ways, that is, we are trying to achieve our aims, not in relation to the situation in an objective sense, but in relation to the situation as we see it. Powerful ways of acting spring from powerful ways of seeing.

Let us take an example. Someone is standing in a lake with the water up to his knees and aiming at a fish in the water with a harpoon. He might aim at the fish where it appears to be, that is, where he actually sees it, or at a slightly adjusted angle, that is, where he thinks it should actually be if he takes the refraction of the light into consideration. These two different ways of acting are based on two different ways of understanding the situation and the latter is more powerful than the former. Let us take another example. Let us imagine that a sales tax of 10% is introduced in Hong Kong. One car dealer selling expensive cars simply increases the prices by 10%, while another adds only 5% on to the previous prices. The first car dealer assumes (wrongly) that sales tax must be added to the previous price and the buyer must always pay for it. However, the second one predicts (rightly) that demand will be adversely affected by the price increase and realizes that even if 10% of the net price has to be given to the tax authorities, a part of this sum has to be absorbed by the seller. (A similar example is elaborated in chap. 8). Again, there are two different ways of understanding the same situation and hence two ways of acting, one of which is more powerful than the other.

Let us look at some other examples that illustrate the thesis that powerful ways of acting derive from powerful ways of seeing. Let us take a very simple one to begin with. A word problem was given to some 7-year-old children. The problem is as follows: "I didn't have much money this morning when I went to school. Bob gave back 4 kronor that he had borrowed from me last week, and with that I could buy a green chocolate bar for 7 kronor. How much money did I have this morning when I came to school?"

Some of the children knew the answer almost instantly, whereas others struggled in vain. Was there anything that the former could do that the latter could not? Actually none of the children had ever seen a problem like this, nor did they remember any addition tables. Those who did not do too well saw the problem as one of addition; the child had some kronor to begin with and then he got 4 more, which made 7 altogether. But what then caused these children difficulty was the question: How can you add when you don't know what to add to? The children who did not find the problem difficult at all said something like this to themselves: "I can say that he had 7 kronor altogether and I know that he got 4 kronor from Bob. So I have to take away 4 kronor from 7 kronor." They continued, "One goes away: 6. Two goes away: 5. Three goes away: 4. And four goes away: 3. So he had 3 kronor this morning." Others might have said, "I have to look for the other part. I have to find out how many kronor I have to add to the 4 kronor I got from Bob, to get 7 kronor altogether. So the answer is 3." These children started with what they had got, which was 4, then they counted *three* units, 5, 6, 7, and visualized the "threeness" of those three units. Or others perhaps simply knew that 7 can, among other things, be broken down into 4 and 3. The children who could come up with the answer easily did not see the problem as an addition/subtraction problem but as a part–whole problem: the whole and one of the parts are given, the whole is 7 and the given part is 4; the missing part must then be 3. So the difference between the children who handled the problem easily and the others who did not was not so much what they *did*, but rather what they saw, that is, how they understood the problem. The children who could solve the problem saw it in terms of parts and whole, and therefore could solve it easily, whereas the children who could not solve the problem saw it in terms of the arithmetic operation, that is, addition, and therefore had difficulties solving it. The point here is that, in many cases, seeing sim-

1. THE SPACE OF LEARNING

ple arithmetic problems in terms of part–whole relations is a more powerful way of seeing them than seeing them in terms of arithmetic operations (Neuman, 1987) as already shown. The part–whole way of seeing works very well for *any* of the problems in which two parts are given and you have to find the whole, or when the whole and one of the parts are given and you have to look for the other part. For example,

$$a + b = \_$$
$$a - b = \_$$
$$\_ + b = c$$
$$a + \_ = c$$
$$\_ - b = c$$
$$a - \_ = c$$

Seeing the problem as a part–whole relation enables the child to act in a powerful way, in the sense of having a capability to deal with different problems.

Another well-known and more complex example of how "the capability of seeing" is of decisive importance, is de Groot's (1965) work on expertise in chess playing. "What is it that chess masters are especially good at?" de Groot asked, eager to find out whether it is true, as many people believe, that what chess masters are good at is being able to mentally visualize and try out a number of alternatives actions (and their consequences) in great depth.

However, this did not in fact turn out to be the case. The chess masters did not try more alternative courses of action than other players, or follow them up for longer. But the courses of action they considered were mostly more powerful ways of handling the situations than other courses of action would have been. So, what was it that enabled the chess masters to find more powerful ways of handling the situations? The most striking fact was that chess masters seemed to see the chessboard differently to other people:

> We know that increasing experience and knowledge in a specific field (chess, for instance) has the effect that things (properties, etc.) which, at earlier stages, had to be abstracted, or even inferred are apt to be immediately perceived at later stages. To a rather large extent, abstraction is replaced by perception, but we do not know much about how this works, nor where the borderline lies. As an effect of this replacement, a so-called "given" problem situation is not really given since it is seen differently by an expert than it is perceived by an inexperienced person. (de Groot, 1965, pp. 33–34)

Although de Groot also found that chess masters were much better at remembering positions on the board than novices, this was only true when the arrangements represented meaningful patterns, and was not the case when the arrangements were random configurations. In the latter case, the chess masters' memories were not significantly better than that of other people.

These findings were replicated by Chase and Simon (1973) who by examining the ways in which chess masters reconstructed configurations that they had briefly seen, and the errors that they made in doing so, arrived at the interpretation that chess masters can remember a great number of patterns of about eight pieces, and that they interpret every configuration on the board in terms of at most seven or eight such patterns. These patterns form a kind of gigantic alphabet comprising up to 10,000 letters, each one corresponding to a certain pattern (cited in Bereiter & Scardamelia, 1993).

The main difference between chess masters and less experienced players, according to this line of reasoning, has to do with the differences in ways of seeing the chessboard, and differences in ways of seeing various configurations as meaningful patterns. It is the chess master's way of seeing that enables the player to engage in powerful ways of acting. And there are other similar findings on the nature of expertise. Glaser and Chi (1988) showed that experts and novices differ as to the problems they see as similar and those problems they see as different. Physicists are able, for instance, to see that the problems of river currents, and the problems of headwinds and tailwinds in airplanes involve similar mathematical and physical aspects, such as relative velocities (Bransford, Brown, & Cocking, 2000). Similar findings originate from such diverse fields as electronic circuitry (Egan & Schwartz, 1979), radiology (Lesgold, 1988), computer programming (Ehrlich & Soloway, 1984) and teaching (Sabers, Cushing, & Berliner, 1991).

Relating these cases, Bransford et al. (2000) stated that expertise in a domain is characterized by sensitivity to patterns of meaningful information that might not be available to others dealing with the same problems within the same domains. In this book, we would like to assert that various degrees of expertise, that is, the capability of acting in powerful ways within a certain domain, is reflected in the various ways of seeing, that is, in the various meanings seen in a particular scenario or problem.

Thus it can be seen that people act not in relation to situations as such, but in relation to situations as they perceive, experience, and understand them. One of the most frequently recurring findings from our own research, as well as from others' research, is that whatever situation people encounter, they see it, experience it, and understand it in a limited number of qualitatively different ways (see Marton & Booth, 1997). In relation to particular aims, some ways of seeing are more powerful than others. Powerful ways of acting derive from powerful ways of seeing, and the way that something is seen or experienced is a fundamental feature of learning. If we want learners to develop certain capabilities, we must make it possible for them to develop a certain way of seeing or experiencing. Consequently, arranging for learning implies arranging for developing learners' ways of seeing or experiencing, that is, developing the eyes through which the world is perceived.

WAYS OF SEEING

What does it take to develop the learner's eyes? What is meant by "a way of seeing something?" Whatever we attend to is inexhaustible, in the sense that the information that can in principle be gained from it is unlimited. At the same time, as George Miller so aptly declared, almost 50 years ago, our capacity for processing information is seriously limited (Miller, 1956). The inevitable mechanism of selectivity originates from the contradiction between unlimited information and the highly limited capacity for processing this information with which humans are equipped.

Whenever people attend to something, they discern certain aspects of it, and by doing so pay more attention to some things, and less attention or none at all to other things.

If one person discerns certain aspects of something and another person discerns partly or wholly different aspects, we say that the two people see the same thing in different ways. So, a way of seeing something can be defined in terms of the aspects that are discerned at a certain point in time. The aspects are thus discerned (and attended to) at the same time rather than one at a time. A particular way of seeing something can be defined by the aspects discerned, that is, the critical features of what is seen.

An aspect of a thing corresponds to the way in which that thing might differ from, or be similar to, any other thing, that is, the way it is perceived to be, or the way that it is experienced by someone as different from, or similar to something else. The problem cited previously (about the child with 7 kronor) was understood, or experienced, by some children in terms of its part–whole structure. Some children noticed that it had the same whole in it (i.e., 7) as some other problem they had experienced, and in that respect it differed from problems in which the whole was other than 7. Furthermore, among those problems in which the whole was 7, it was similar to those in which one of the parts was 4 and different from those problems in which none of the parts was 4. Seeing the problem in terms of its part–whole structure means, we believe, seeing what the parts and the whole *are* and what they *are not*.

However, other children understood the same problem in terms of the arithmetic operation involved. They thought it was similar to other addition problems, and that it differed from problems about subtraction. Among addition problems, it was similar to those in which the second addend was 4, and different from those in which this was not the case. They probably also thought that it was similar to those additions in which the sum is 7, and different from those in which this was not the case. Seeing the problem in terms of the arithmetic operation involved required a thought process like this, we believe. The reason that some children could solve the problem and others could not was because they saw the same problem in different ways, that is, because they attended to different aspects. Attending to a certain aspect means comparing something we experience with other things that we have experienced earlier. The kinds of things brought into the comparison define the aspect that is attended to.

In Lo and Ko (2002), the English lessons of two primary Grade 4 classes are discussed. Evidence from the learning outcomes suggests that most children in one of the classes understood the "s" at the end of verbs as signaling third person singular, that is, that they "saw" the "s" in this particular way. This implies, we believe, that they made an implicit comparison of verbs where "s" was present with the same verb where "s" was absent. In the other class, most children did not seem to pay attention to the "s." They compared, we think, implicitly, the verbs with other verbs. The "s" has to do with the third person singular, that is, it has to do with grammar; whereas the comparison with other verbs—or other words—has to do with the meaning. The majority of the children in the first class seemed to attend to both the grammatical and the meaning aspects of the verbs, whereas most children in the second class did not seem to attend to the grammatical aspect of these verbs.

According to this line of reasoning, a way of seeing can be characterized in terms of the aspects discerned that are attended to simultaneously. This definition is very wide and very narrow at the same time. It is very wide because it refers to the meaning or appearance of almost anything. And it is very narrow because it simply aims at telling apart different ways of seeing in respects that are critical in relation to the efficiency of the acts that spring from those ways of seeing, those meanings, and those appearances.

DISCERNMENT

In order to see something in a certain way, a person must discern certain features of that thing. We should also be clear about the difference between *discerning* and *being told*. Medical students, for instance, might be advised by their professors to try to notice different features of their patients, such as the color of the lips, the moisture of the skin, the ease of breathing, and so on; this is being told. But in order to follow this advice, the students must experience those features, and the only way to experience them is to experience how they can vary. Noticing the color of a patient's lips, for example, would not mean very much if lip color was the same for everyone.

Similarly, *frame of reference* in physics only makes sense if we can think of more than one frame of reference. Even very abstract notions derive their meaning (in the sense of the experience of understanding) through variation. Historically, no one was aware of natural numbers, for instance, until there were other numbers such as negative numbers. At that point, the natural numbers could be identified as those that were not negative numbers. This is why in a sense we often know very little about our own country until we learn about other countries. And this is why teachers generally give a number of different examples in order to explain a new concept or principle. If teachers give one example only, they do so because they themselves consider the other alternatives to be obvious (which, however, they may not be for the students). In order to explain what a frame of reference is, it is not sufficient to point out that when we consider a moving body in the sky from the point of view of the ground, we consider it from a particular frame of reference. We also have to give other examples, such as considering it from the point of view of another body moving in the sky in parallel with the first one and at the same velocity.

By experiencing variation, people discern certain aspects of their environment; we could perhaps say that they become "sensitized" to those aspects. This means that they are likely to see future events in terms of those aspects; the physician will pay attention to the color of the patient's lips, the physicist will pay attention to the frame of reference from which a body in movement is considered. This is what we mean by learning to see certain things in certain ways. One main way of dealing with novel situations is to make use of previous experience. It is important to develop the capability for *professional seeing*, that is, seeing situations in terms of features that are generally critical within one's professional field. But it is equally important to be able to discern other features that are not critical in a general sense, but that may be critical in a specific case. Not only do you need to discern features that have proved to be essential in the past, but you must be able to discern new features when they are critical. This is in fact very central in research and it is very much how new discoveries are made. But we should remember that even the discernment of entirely new features depends on the variation you have encountered earlier.

The word "feature" has been used to stand for attribute, or aspect, such as color of lips, frame of reference, tallness, and so on, and we have pointed to the fact that human beings cannot discern a feature without experiencing variation in a corresponding dimension. However, we not only discern features, but also discern different qualities (i.e., values) in the relevant dimensions such as "blue," "ray of light," "very short," and so on.

Discernment and Context: Parts and Wholes

So far we have talked about the discernment of features and values within features. But it is also possible to think about discernment as a delimitation of wholes from their context and as a delimitation of parts within wholes (cf. Svensson, 1976).

Marton and Booth (1997) gave an example:

> What does it take to see a motionless deer among the dark trees and bushes of the night woods? To see it at all we have to discern it from the surrounding trees and bushes, we have to see its contours, its outline, the limits that distinguish it from what surrounds

it. We have to see, at least partially, where it starts and where it ends ... [but] not only do we have to discern it from its context, as a deer in the woods, but we also have to discern its parts, the way they relate to each other, and the way they relate to the whole. Therefore, on seeing the deer in the woods, in seeing its contours, we also see parts of its body, its head, its antlers, its forequarters, and so on, and their relationship in terms of stance. (pp. 86–87)

Discerning the relation of parts within wholes and discerning the whole from the context is an important aspect of discernment. Equally important is discerning the way wholes relate to the context. This is because the way the whole relates to the context shapes the discernment of the parts within the whole. What does this mean? Let us take some classroom data as examples.

Let us start with the role that context plays in determining the meaning assigned to a phenomenon. In a primary Chinese lesson on semantics, which is discussed in chapter 2, we see how one word took on a very different meaning when it was put in different contexts. In this lesson, the teacher told a story about how one word in Chinese *yao* (Putonghua) [要] (which can be translated literally as "want") was exploited by a barber, Afanti, to carry the diametrically opposed meanings, "give" (*gei*) (Putonghua) [给] and "keep" (*liu*) (Putonghua) [留] in order to take his revenge on a customer, Ahung, who kept refusing to pay for the service. In the story, the barber asked Ahung whether he "wanted" (*yao bu yao* (Putonghua) [要不要]) his eyebrows, whereupon Ahung replied that he "wanted" his eyebrows (*yao*), meaning he wanted to keep his eyebrows. Afanti shaved off Ahung's eyebrows and said, "You 'want' (*yao*) your eyebrows, so I'll give them to you!" Ahung was speechless because he had indeed said *yao*. After this, Afanti asked Ahung if he "wanted" his beard, and Ahung, who had a beautiful beard, immediately said, *bu yao* (Putonghua) [不要], that is, "don't want," meaning he did not want Afanti to shave off his beard. However, Afanti shaved off his beard all the same. Again, Ahung was speechless because he had indeed said *bu yao* ("don't want").

In this story, we see that the word *yao* was assigned different meanings in relation to different contexts. In the first instance, Ahung related it to the context of a barbershop where people had their hair and beard trimmed or cut, but would not typically have their eyebrows shaved off. Let us refer to this context as Context A. Therefore, when he said *yao*, he meant that he wanted to keep his eyebrows. However, Afanti deliberately related it to a different context where "want" (*yao*) can mean "give." Let us refer to this context as Context B. For example, in the context of making an offer, such as offering a drink, "Do you want a drink?" a positive reply from the addressee, *yao*, would entail the person making the offer actually giving a drink to the addressee. Then, in the second instance, when Ahung used *bu yao* to mean that he "did not want" his beard, he was relating *yao* to the context in which Afanti was operating in the previous exchange where *yao* meant "give," that is Context B. However, Afanti deliberately related *bu yao* ("don't want") to the context in which Ahung was operating previously, where *yao* meant "want" or "keep," that is Context A.

The story in this lesson suggests that the context to which something is related cannot necessarily be taken for granted. In classroom learning situations, it is very important that there is a mutual understanding (between teacher and students) of the context to which the teacher relates the object of learning in order to help learners discern its critical features.

Let us look at two lessons on writing a book report, for example, also reported by Chik (2002). In one lesson, the teacher (Teacher A) used genres of writing as the context for discussing the components that students should include in a book report. She specifically used narrative as a genre of writing and asked the students to think about the features that distinguish a book report from a narrative. In the other lesson, the teacher (Teacher B) used a different context for discussing a book report, that is, different ways of presenting a book report. Specifically, she cited the use of pictures to present a book report, a format with which students were also familiar.

Which is a more powerful context, in the sense of being more effective in bringing about learning? Which will help learners discern the critical features of a book report?

The answer to this question depends on the aspects of the book report on which the teacher wants to focus. In these two lessons, the object of learning is the essential components of a book report. One could argue that pictorial representation is one kind of format and that it can be contrasted with a written format. But there is nothing much that can be said apart from this, and it does not help the students to discern the components that are critical to a book report. On the other hand, other genres of writing, such as narratives, contain various components such as time, place, people, and sequence of events that are not found in book reports. What distinguishes one genre of writing from another is the components that they contain. In other words, the *genres of writing*, of which book reports are one instantiation and narratives another, provides the context to which the critical features of book reports relate.

Let us look at how Teacher A dealt with the components critical to a book report. She put eight components that were related to books on the board. They were: price of the book, date of reading, genre, call number, author, name of the book, summary, and commentary (impression after reading). Among them, the first four, although having to do with books, were not relevant to book reports. The teacher asked the students to take away those components that they felt should not be included in a book report. By asking the students to do that, the teacher was doing two things. First, she was attending to the internal relationship, a part–whole relationship, between the components and the book report. The components that remained on the board were author, name of the book, commentary, and summary. These four components were related to each other in the sense that they were constitutive of a book report in such a way that if any part was missing, it would no longer be a book report. For example, if the commentary was missing, the book report would become a piece of text in an annotated bibliography. Second, she was attending to the way in which the inclusion of parts that were not critical to a book report would affect the whole. For example, the inclusion of the price of the book and the publisher would constitute a whole that is no longer a book report, but another genre, for example, an advertisement.

The discernment of the critical components of a book report was brought about by discerning the book report as an instantiation of genres of writing. In other words, *genres of writing* was the context to which the book report was related. It is in relation to the book report as a genre, as opposed to other genres such as the *narrative*, that discernment of the parts was made possible. In other words, it is the discernment of how the whole relates to the context that enabled the discernment of the parts (of the whole).

VARIATION

We illustrate the significance of variation for the possibilities to learn by referring to some situations that will hopefully be easily recognizable to the reader.

Consider how we learn what coldness, tallness, or heaviness is. Saying that something is heavy does not mean anything to us unless we experience this against the background of a difference in weight, that is, weight that can vary. In the same way, for instance, knowing what red is presupposes the experience of other colors, that is, a variation in colors. Even knowing what color is presupposes an experienced variation of colors. Imagine for a moment that there was no variation of colors, that everything around us had the same color. It would be impossible for us to know what red, green, or yellow were, just as it would be impossible for us to discern color as a feature. If every object we encountered had the same color, this feature of the object would not be discerned.

The significance of variation for seeing something in a new way applies to abstract objects as well. Research on the way that young children solve simple arithmetic problems has reported that children who always solve simple additions (like $2 + 3 =$, $5 + 1 =$, $1 + 4 =$, etc.) by starting with the first addend, can suddenly change strategy and start with the biggest number. Instead of $2 + 3$, $1 + 4$ and so on, the order of the addends is changed, and the child adds $3 + 2 =$, $4 + 1 =$ (cf. Carpenter & Moser, 1984). In this situation, a variation of order of the addends is opened. You could say that an aspect that was taken for granted or was undiscerned became a discerned aspect. By this opening of variation, a feature of addition (that is, that the sum is independent of order of the addends) is discerned.

1. THE SPACE OF LEARNING

One of the main theses in this book is that the pattern of variation inherent in the learning situation is fundamental to the development of certain capabilities (see following text). An experimental study on motor learning (Moxley, 1979) demonstrated the importance of variation on learning. The experiment included children practicing to hit a target with a ball. Children in the control group always threw the ball at the target from the same direction, whereas children in the experimental group practiced throwing the ball at the target from different directions. When the two groups were compared trying to hit the target from a direction that was new to both groups, the group that had practiced hitting the target from different directions was then found to be superior to the group that had practiced hitting the target from the same direction all the time. It can be concluded that variation in direction seemed to be a critical feature of the practice and thus also critical for learning. However, we are not arguing for variation in general, and we are not saying that the more variation there is, the better the possibilities to learn. What we believe is that variation enables learners to experience the features that are critical for a particular learning as well as for the development of certain capabilities. In other words, these features must be experienced as dimensions of variation. Learning, for instance, to solve a problem in different ways requires experience of variation in solving strategies. Understanding the "manyness" of a number requires the experience of different numbers, just as the ability to throw a ball from different directions and still hit a target requires the experience of throwing an object from different angles, and realizing how a general principle can encompass different examples requires the experience of at least two different examples, and so on.

In mathematics, different strategies for solving problems, different numbers, and so on all make up dimensions of variation. One particular solving strategy is one value in a dimension of variation, whereas a different strategy is another value in this dimension. And thus the strategy as used in a specific example is an instance of that strategy. When we experience something, we discern aspects, or features, of the object and we experience values in the corresponding dimensions of variation. The experienced aspects are discerned as values in dimensions of variation. I experience the object on my table, for example, as a blue, cylindrical, ceramic mug with a handle (an instance). "Blue" and "cylindrical" are values in dimensions of variation (e.g., these are perceived in relation to the experience that they can vary). Features of the mug, such as the color, shape, material, and so on, are simultaneously discerned as a pattern of dimensions of variation (or to put it simply, as a pattern of variation), and these features constitute the particular object. In order to experience the object as a blue, cylindrical, ceramic mug, all of these aspects must be discerned and related to potential dimensions of variation. And because these aspects are necessary for defining the object in question, they are also called its *critical features*.

Patterns of Variation

According to the preceding line of reasoning, it is necessary to pay close attention to what varies and what is invariant in a learning situation, in order to understand what it is possible to learn in that situation and what not. In the different studies reported in this book, we are able to identify certain patterns of variation:

1. *Contrast.* As already mentioned, in order to experience something, a person must experience something else to compare it with. In order to understand what "three" is, for instance, a person must experience something that is not three: "two" or "four," for example. This illustrates how a value (three, for instance) is experienced within a certain dimension of variation, which corresponds to an aspect (numeriosity or "manyness").

2. *Generalization.* In order to fully understand what "three" is, we must also experience varying appearances of "three," for example three apples, three monkeys, three toy cars, three books, and so on. This variation is necessary in order for us to be able to grasp the idea of "threeness" and separate it from irrelevant features (such as the color of apples or the very fact that they are apples).

3. *Separation.* In order to experience a certain aspect of something, and in order to separate this aspect from other aspects, it must vary while other aspects remain invariant. This is how the "angle" aspect of hitting a target with a ball was developed in one group of children in Moxley's (1979) experiment, mentioned previously. The experiment could also be expanded by systematically varying the distance to the target, for instance, while other aspects were kept invariant; then systematically varying the weight of the ball, while keeping other aspects invariant, and so on. In this way the children could be prepared for various other situations, such as hitting targets from distances they have never thrown from, with balls of varying (and novel) weights, and so on.

4. *Fusion.* If there are several critical aspects that the learner has to take into consideration at the same time, they must all be experienced simultaneously. In everyday life, it is seldom that only one aspect of something varies at a time, and so the way in which we respond to a situation, such as hitting a target with a ball or a problem of human relations, spring from a more general holistic perception of the situation. We can compare this with a marriage counselor's professional way of seeing human relationship problems. The counselor is probably seeing different cases in terms of a limited number of analytically separated, but still simultaneously experienced, aspects. Our conjecture is that seeing a certain class of phenomena in terms of a set of aspects that are analytically separated but simultaneously experienced provides a more effective basis for powerful action than a global, undifferentiated way of seeing the same

class of phenomena. We believe that separating the aspects first and then fusing them together is more efficient (from the view of being able to adapt to changing conditions) than never taking the critical aspects apart. We also believe that this fusion will unavoidably take place through the simultaneous variation in the dimensions of variation corresponding to the critical aspects.

Another example of this type of fusion is presented in the comparison of two primary classes in Chinese language in chapter 4, whereby different aspects of the same word (form, meaning, pronunciation) are successfully fused in one of the classes, but not in the other. In chapter 8, there is a further example of this type, in the comparison of two groups of secondary economics classes. In this example, the elasticity of demand and the elasticity of supply are first separated and then fused in the classes in one group ("the learning study" group), but not in the other group ("the lesson study" group), in which they are only dealt with one at a time.

SIMULTANEITY AND AWARENESS

We have thus made the point that in order to discern a feature, a person must experience variation in that feature. For example, in order to experience a teenage girl as strikingly tall, we must have encountered teenage girls as typically being shorter or considerably shorter than this particular girl. The experience of tallness derives from juxtaposing what we see and what we remember; what we experience now and what we have experienced before. We have to be aware of both at the same time.

In general, to experience variation amounts to experiencing different instances at the same time. A particular color is experienced against the background of other colors that were experienced in the past; an act of kindness is experienced against the background of acts of kindness or cruelty that were experienced in the past. Variation is experienced very much as we experience a melody. Each tune is experienced in the context of other tunes. Of course, we would never experience a melody if we experienced each tone separately, one at a time. In the same way, we can never experience variation in any respect if we experience every instance one at a time. In order to experience variation in a certain respect, we have to experience the different instances that vary in that respect simultaneously, that is, we have to experience instances that we have encountered at different points in time, *at the same time*. We call this *diachronic* simultaneity. This is the simultaneous experience of different instances at the same time, which is necessary for experiencing variation in a certain dimension and for discerning the aspect of an instance corresponding to the dimension. However, you will remember that we have previously defined a way of seeing something as the discernment of various critical features of an instance simultaneously. This type of simultaneity, is called *synchronic simultaneity*, and is the experience of different co-existing aspects of the same thing at the same time.

Let us briefly return to Moxley's study of children practicing to hit a target with a ball. In the cited example, variation in the direction or angle of the throwing was compared to the absence of variation, in relation to a group's ability to perform the task of hitting the target from a direction that was new to both groups. As we mentioned, if the children were to learn to hit a target with any ball, from any direction, under any conditions, they would need to practice throwing the ball from different directions, with different balls (e.g. each one a different weight), under different conditions (e.g., different wind force). Mastering this capability would amount to being able to discern all of those features and being able to take them all into consideration at the same time (i.e., seeing ball-throwing situations in terms of features critical for hitting a target). Doing so amounts to experiencing the different aspects present at the same time simultaneously. In a metaphorical sense, we could talk about spatial integration or synchronic simultaneity at one particular point in time.

What does it take to experience different aspects of the same phenomenon? Clearly, the aspects must be discerned and the person must be focally aware of them. So simultaneity in the synchronic sense is obviously a function of discernment.

Experiencing variation is, however, as we have shown, contingent on the simultaneous awareness of instances that appear at different points in time. We would not be able to see a story as a story without the simultaneous awareness of other stories that we have come across in the past. This is a kind of temporal integration, a simultaneous awareness of what we are experiencing and what we have experienced before. Clearly, as well, in what we are experiencing, what we have experienced before must be or must have been discerned in order for us to experience it. In this respect, not only synchronic but also diachronic simultaneity is a function of discernment. Furthermore, there can be no experience of synchronic simultaneity without the experience of diachronic simultaneity, because in order to experience two aspects of the same thing together we must discern both separately, and that can only happen by having experienced variation in the dimensions of variation corresponding to each one of the aspects.

There is another form of the simultaneous experience in the synchronic sense, that is, one that is different from experiencing different aspects of the same thing at the same time. What we have in mind is the simultaneous experience of the whole and its parts; the whole being, for example, a deer in the forest (mentioned previously), a text we read in school, or basically anything that can be meaningfully divided into component parts.

In an example that appears in chapter 4, two teachers' ways of teaching Chinese are compared. Both teachers were trying to develop the students' vocabulary in the context of the same story. One of the teachers dealt with the story as a whole first, then with different paragraphs, sentences, and finally with individual words, taking each feature of the words (such as meaning, spelling, i.e., stroke pattern, and pronunciation) one at a time. In other words, the teacher dealt with the vocabulary items (words) sequentially and in isolation, instead of in context. The other teacher seemed to act in accordance with the view that the meaning of a character is modified by the word or phrase in which it occurs; that the meaning of the word or phrase is modified by the sentence in which it appears; and that the meaning of the sentence is modified by the text in which it forms a part. She tried to make sure that all of the different levels of the text (story, paragraph, sentence, word, character) were present in the students' awareness at the same time, by dealing with each level in the context of the next superordinate level. Furthermore, she dealt with different features of the characters in the context of each word, instead of dealing with each character as an individual unit as the other teacher had done.

Awareness

But, *where* are instances, aspects, parts, and wholes when they are experienced simultaneously? In a vivid sense they are present to us. They are not simply stored away somewhere deep down in our memory; we can hear them or see them, feel them, sense them or imagine them. They are in our awareness.

Awareness (we use the word as a synonym to consciousness) is the totality of a person's experiences of the world, at each point in time. It is all that is present on every occasion. Awareness changes dynamically all the time and every situation is experienced against the background of previous experiences. This occurs to varying degrees of course, but potentially, awareness is present against the background of a very, very great number of previous experiences. And to affect our experiences at this very moment, here and now, these previous experiences all have to be present at any one time. In a way, if we exaggerate things a little, we might say that we are aware of everything all the time, simply not in the same way. Actually there are very few things that we can be *focally*, that is, sharply, aware of at the same time, but a lot can affect the way in which we are aware of these things. In accordance with Gurwich's (1964) account, we might say that the characteristic of human awareness is that a limited number of objects, aspects of objects, or situations come to attract our attention (i.e., become focused), whereas a very great number of other things are there as background. It is against this background that we experience the things that we are focally aware of, that is, the things that are the focus of our attention. A generalized and ever changing figure–ground structure is thus characteristic for our awareness.

Discernment, Awareness and Simultaneity

Although learning can be viewed as the development of both capabilities and values, the focus of this book, as we stated earlier, is on learning as the development of capabilities. The kinds of capabilities we focus on are those that empower learners to deal with situations in powerful ways, that is, to simultaneously (in the diachronic sense) focus on features critical for achieving a certain aim. However, we can only experience simultaneously that which we can discern; we can only discern what we experience to vary; and we can only experience variation if we have experienced different instances previously and are holding them in our awareness simultaneously (in the diachronic sense). So the three (or rather four) key concepts of the theory are intimately linked, each of them being a function of another.

THE SPACE OF LEARNING

As we have already pointed out, nobody can discern a certain feature without experiencing variation in a dimension corresponding to that feature. Let us assume that two persons, A and B, are engaged in a conversaticn with a stranger, C, in a small cottage in a Nepalese mountain village. Afterward, it turns out that A had noticed that C spoke with a typical southwestern Nepalese dialect (actually all three of them did so), while B did not notice this at all. Why was it that B did not discern C's dialect whereas A did? What was varying, as far as dialects are concerned? As it was, nothing varied in the actual situation, but A had heard a lot of different Nepalese dialects previously and he related C's way of speaking to what he had experienced and noticed the similarity with a particular Nepalese dialect, and the difference when compared to other Nepalese dialects. B, on the other hand, had never been outside his village, had never watched TV or listened to the radio, and had actually never heard any other dialect. He could not discern the dialect because he did not know of any other. The variation experienced by A was a result of the memories of past events that A brought into the situation, and thus also into his encounter with C.

Now let us assume that C speaks a different dialect.

If this were the case, A would probably notice the fact, but also B would notice that C speaks in a way that is different from all the other people he has ever heard (he may even find it very difficult to understand C). At the same time, he would probably become conscious of the fact that he himself has a certain way of speaking.

In the first example, the only variation with respect to dialects was the fact that A had had previous experience of hearing other dialects, and that C's way of speaking was juxtaposed with this experience. In the second example, there is variation to be experienced in the actual situation. The insight that there are different ways of speaking can be derived from sim-

1. THE SPACE OF LEARNING 21

ply being exposed to them in this situation. There is a space created for gaining this insight in the second case. This space is created by challenging the taken-for-granted nature of the experience of people's ways of speaking in the person who has previously only been exposed to one way of speaking. *Creating a space* means opening up a dimension of variation (as compared to the taken-for-granted nature of the absence of variation). As our example illustrates, however, someone whose past experiences are sufficient for perceiving the necessary pattern of variation can experience variation without that space (i.e., the necessary pattern of variation) being constituted in the immediate situation. The *space of learning* refers to the pattern of variation inherent in a situation as observed by the researcher. This space is a necessary condition for the learner's experience of that pattern of variation unless the learner can experience that pattern due to what she has encountered in the past.

Now let us consider another type of variation. When we consider a moving body for example, we usually look at it from the point of view of the ground. We can say that the ground is taken as a *frame of reference*. But we could also look at the moving body from the point of view of another frame of reference; from our own moving body instead of the ground, for instance. And if we do that, we introduce variation in frames of reference. The very idea of frames of reference presupposes variation, as does the insight that looking at a body in movement from the point of view of rest (the ground) amounts to adopting a particular frame of reference.

In addition to looking at moving bodies from the point of view of rest, we also habitually look at them when they are under the influence of the gravitational force of the earth. So without being aware of this, we take the gravitational force for granted. In order to break this taken-for-granted nature of our awareness of the world, variation in the gravitational force must be introduced. This can be done by traveling in a space shuttle, or more easily, by looking at pictures from a space shuttle, by engaging in a simulation of the effects of varying gravitational force or simply carrying out a thought experiment. These two dimensions—gravity and frame of reference—form a *space of learning*. A *space of learning* comprises any number of dimensions of variation and denotes the aspects of a situation, or the phenomena embedded in that situation, that can be discerned due to the variation present in the situation. Variation that is not present in the situation can still be discerned, however, if variation is brought in by means of the learner's memory of previous experience. We should notice, here, that a space does not refer to the absence of constraints, but to something actively constituted. It delimits what can be possibly learned (in sense of discerning) in that particular situation.

But we are not interested in all types of variation. We must look at the situation from the point of view of a particular object of learning. And by doing so we can find out whether or not it is possible for the learner to appropriate that particular object of learning in that particular situation.

The Object of Learning

The *object of learning* can be defined by its critical features, that is, the features that must be discerned in order to constitute the meaning aimed for. The question we must ask therefore, is to what extent we find variation in the relevant respects. As learners can only discern that which varies, we must look for the pattern of variation necessary for developing the required capability. Unless there is variation in all the respects corresponding to the critical features, that is, the necessary pattern of variation is present, this capability cannot be developed. We are thus talking about the necessary pattern of variation. In order to develop a certain capability, the learner must encounter a certain pattern of variation, regardless of the arrangements for teaching that are made, and regardless of the way in which learning is organized (e.g., whether the learner participates in an authentic practice, or sits in a lecture hall with 300 students). The space of learning tells us what it is possible to learn in a certain situation.

In the light of a specific object of learning, the space of learning is a rather specific characterization of the interaction in the classroom. As already pointed out, the object of learning is there, to begin with, as an *intended object of learning* as seen from the teacher's perspective, then it is somehow realized in the classroom in the form of a particular space of learning. This is the *enacted object of learning* as seen from the researcher's point of view, constraining what is possible to learn.

We can see that the space of learning constituted in the classroom is the enacted object of learning. This is how the object of learning is constituted in the most concrete sense. And it is this that matters regarding opportunities to learn in school. Factors such as curriculum, teacher's intention, and so on, are mediated through the enacted object of learning.

The way that students see, understand, and make sense of the object of learning when the lesson ends and beyond, is the *lived object of learning*. The pedagogical situation and what the students actually learn can thus be described in the same terms. So now we can describe learning and teaching in relation to one another, from the point of view of learning, not as a relationship between cause and effect, but as a relationship between what is made possible and what possibilities are actually made use of.

The focus should thus be on learning in the first instance and on teaching in the second; the focus should be on what should be learned and what is actually learned. And what is actually learned should be understood in terms of the conditions of learning. If learning is actually taking place in the classroom, we should try to understand what the students learn in terms of what is taking place in the classroom. Whatever takes place in the classroom makes differing sense to different students. This is one of the most solid conclusions that can be drawn from our own research (Marton & Booth, 1997) or that of others. No conditions of learning ever *cause* learning. They

1. THE SPACE OF LEARNING

only make it possible for learners to learn certain things. And this, in our view, is exactly what pedagogy is about, especially the type of pedagogy of learning that we are putting forward in this book, that is, making learning possible. Let us consider two situations (two classroom scenarios) from the point of view of learning or developing a certain capability. We might describe what it is possible to learn with view of that capability in the two classrooms; we might describe what is taking place in each classroom in terms of the possibilities for learning that are brought about, and in terms of what kind of space of learning is constituted. The *space of learning* thus depicts the possibilities of learning in relation to the capability in question.

Throughout this book, when we talk about what it is possible to learn, we restrict ourselves to the kind of learning we have discussed in this chapter, namely learning to see certain things in certain ways. But even bearing this restriction in mind, there will undoubtedly be a great number of things that vary, and hence that will or could be discerned. The space of learning does not denote all that is possible to learn, even in the restricted sense of learning (i.e., learning to see). The space of learning captures only what it is possible to learn in a situation from the point of view of what is meant to be learned.

What is meant to be learned is the object of learning, which in our case is a capability of seeing something in a certain way. As we pointed out earlier, a certain way of seeing something can be characterized in terms of the aspects of a situation or phenomenon that are discerned and focused on simultaneously, or more precisely, the *critical* aspects of the situation or the phenomenon that are discerned and focused on simultaneously. Now the question is: How do we know what dimensions of variation we should look for? How do we know what critical features there are for a certain class of situations to be seen in a certain way? How can we characterize the nature of a certain capability?

Carlsson (1999) investigated "the anatomy of ecological understanding," comprising, among other things, the understanding of photosynthesis, recycling, and the conservation of energy. One of the critical features—actually the most critical feature of all of these component capabilities—was the idea of transformation, that is, that one thing turns into something qualitatively different: Sunlight and water are transformed into carbohydrates and oxygen in photosynthesis; material microscopic particles from human beings and animals, and so on, are for instance rearranged into soil, and soil rearranged into plants; and one form of energy, such as heat, can be turned into and stored in solid or liquid form through the conservation of energy.

In what sense is transformation a critical feature of ecological understanding and how can it be found or discovered? Is it by means of contemplating the concept of *ecological understanding*? Well, this was definitely not the way in which Carlsson found it. In Carlsson's study, this critical feature (transformation) appeared empirically, as a contrast to another frequent way of thinking that implied that certain things were perceived as consumed (e.g., sunlight, water, dead bodies, energy) and that other things were perceived as independently produced (e.g., coal, oil, or the chlorophyll in flowers and trees).

The *law of variation* applies thus to the researcher's work as well. It is not possible to discern a certain way of thinking about something without the contrast of other ways of thinking about the same thing. The *critical feature* is critical in distinguishing one way of thinking from another, and is relative to the group participating in the study, or to the population represented by the sample. For instance, if all the participants in Carlsson's study had embraced the idea of transformation, transformation may never have shown itself as a critical feature. The critical features have, at least in part, to be found empirically—for instance, through interviews with learners and through the analysis of what is happening in the classroom—and they also have to be found for every object of learning specifically, because the critical features are critical features of specific objects of learning.

The Space of Learning Is the Enacted Object of Learning

The *enacted object of learning* is the researcher's description of whether, to what extent and in what forms, the necessary conditions of a particular object of learning appear in a certain setting. The enacted object of learning is thus what we have also called the space of learning, thereby depicting what is possible to learn. What follows from this line of reasoning is that when we talk about learning, teaching, and other related matters, we should try to be explicit about what we have in our minds as far as the question of "What is learned?" (i.e., "What should be learned?" "What can be possibly learned?" "What is actually learned?") is concerned.

In this way, the space of learning, which comprises different dimensions of variation, is constituted by linguistic means in the interaction between teacher and students.

THE LINGUISTIC CONSTITUTION OF THE SPACE OF LEARNING

In the previous discussion, we described *learning* as the process of coming to experience the world in a certain way. We put forward the thesis that the space of learning is the space of variation, and that the dimensions of variation that *can* be opened up and those that are *actually* opened up contribute to qualitative differences between the way in which something *can be* experienced and the actual way in which it *is* experienced. The space of learning, therefore, is also an experiential space.

In talking about the space of learning as an experiential space, we are referring to experience not as an instantiation, but rather as a potential for experiencing, seeing, and understanding (see also Halliday & Matthiessen,

1999). It is in relation to this potential that learners can make sense of a particular object of learning. As such, this space is elastic; it can be widened if the teacher affords learners opportunities to explore the object of learning in a variety of ways.

Another thesis we put forward in this volume is that language plays a central role in the construal of experience, that it does not simply represent experience, as is widely perceived, but more importantly, it constitutes experience. Seen in this light, language plays a central role in learning, and understanding how the learning experience is being constituted by language is crucial to understanding how different ways of experiencing the object of learning are being brought about in the classroom.

Language and the Construal of Experience

Let us clarify what we mean by language and the construal of experience. The position that we are adopting is that the same phenomenon can be experienced in qualitatively different ways, and that the different construal of the experience will be reflected in the language used. For example, let us imagine that the janitor of a school locked the door of a computer laboratory and that two teachers were trying to open the door but could not. Teacher A said, "The janitor locked the door," whereas Teacher B said, "The door is locked." The same phenomenon was construed in different ways by these two teachers. For Teacher A, the janitor was the point of departure of the message, whereas for Teacher B, the door was the point of departure. Hence, for Teacher A, the message was about what the janitor did: that is, that he had locked the door. By contrast, for Teacher B, the message was about the state of the door, that is, that it was locked and therefore could not be opened.

The relationship between language and experience can be best seen by examining data on child language development. Halliday's (1973, 1975) seminal work on Nigel's language development shows that for children, learning language is also learning about the world through language. Halliday (1993) observed that

> When children learn language, they are not simply engaging in one type of learning among many; rather, they are learning the foundations of learning itself. The distinctive characteristic of human learning is that it is a process of making meaning—a semiotic process; and the prototypical form of human semiotic is language. (p. 93)

As the child experiences the world and as he learns how to mean (Halliday, 1973), his meaning potential is being reconstituted. The reconstitution of his meaning potential finds its realization in the way the child reconstructs his "grammar" so that it eventually shares the conventions of adult grammar.

Let us take for example child language development. At an early stage of language development, the child utters words as "annotations of experience" (Halliday 1993, p. 99). For example, on seeing a round object, a Cantonese speaking child will say "bo bo" [波波] (ball), no matter whether it is a round doorknob, a balloon, or a basketball. As adults comment on the child's annotations by saying, "Yes, it's a ball" or "No, that's not a ball; it's a doorknob," they are classifying things for the child. (In Cantonese, "bo" [波] (ball) is a generic term for all kinds of balls.) When the child appropriates the adult classification of a round object as "a ball," he is also implicitly classifying what is not a ball. In Halliday's terms, he is "outclassifying" (1993, p. 99).[2]

In other words, the child experiences variation among the round objects that he sees: Objects that are round and he can play with his mommy are called "balls," and objects that are round and are stuck on doors are "not balls." This experienced variation is realized in the language that the child uses to make a distinction between different kinds of round objects. Later, the child experiences variation within the class of "balls." He experiences balls that can be blown up into big ones, are light, and can rise into the air, and those that cannot. This kind of "ball" is called a "balloon." At this stage, the child is experiencing variation in the dimension of "ball," and there are three values in this dimension: "ball," "balloon," and "not ball." With this further distinction, the child's semantic system of "ball" changes. It is no longer a system with two terms, but with three terms. The meaning of "ball" changes as well. "Ball" no longer just means "not doorknob"; it means "not balloon" as well.

The relationship between language and experience is dialectic. The experienced variation enables the child to discern the distinctions that are realized in language, and the linguistic distinction enables the child to discern the variation. As Halliday (1978) observed, in this process:

> the construal of reality is inseparable from the construal of the semantic system in which the reality is encoded. In this sense, language is a shared meaning potential, at once both a part of experience and an inter-subjective interpretation of experience. (pp. 1–2)

This meaning potential is being reconstituted every time the child experiences language in use, and experiences what he can do with language.

Language and Distinctions

In order to make sense of what we have experienced, we need to be able to reduce the indefinitely varied phenomena of the world into a manageable number of phenomena of similar types. As Britton (1970) pointed out, objects in the world do not present themselves as readily classified. The classifications are given by humans in order to handle the world, and language is a principal means of doing this. We say "a principal means" because there are certain classifications that can be done without language. For example, if someone is asked to classify all the clothes in the wardrobe, he could put all the winter clothes in one pile, all the work clothes in another pile, and all the formal evening clothes in a third pile. However, in the majority of cases, it is not possible to make classifications without language. For example, how does one distinguish between a male human being who is related by blood to one's father and one who is not, by nonlinguistic means?

As Sapir (1961) pointed out,

> ... language is primarily a vocal actualization of the tendency to see realities symbolically ... an actualization in terms of vocal expression of the tendency to master reality not by direct and *ad hoc* handling of this element but by the reduction of experience to familiar forms. (pp. 14–15)

Adopting a similar stance to Sapir, Halliday (1978) proposed that

> Language has to interpret the whole of our experience, reducing the indefinitely varied phenomena of the world around us, and also of the world inside us, the processes of our own consciousness, to a manageable number of classes of phenomena: types of processes, events and actions, classes of objects, people and institutions, and the like. (p. 21)

We pointed out earlier in this chapter that the contradiction between the unlimited and inexhaustible amount of information available to us and the limited capacity of the human mind requires that we be selective in what we attend to. The things that we attend to are things that we discern as critical, not in a general sense, but critical in relation to a certain context. For this reason, the distinctions or classifications that we make in the process of reducing the indefinitely varied phenomena of the world into a manageable number of classes of phenomena are necessarily selective.

Let us take for example the way things are classified in different cultures. The famous British anthropologist Malinowski (1946) observed that societies classify their surroundings according to their needs and interests, and that this is done through language. For example, in Malinowski's study of primitive languages, it was found that the indigenous people of a primitive community tended to identify and differentiate the few objects that were useful to them and the rest were treated as an undifferentiated heap. A plant or a tree in a forest that was not connected to them traditionally or ritually, or that was not useful to them would be simply dismissed as "a bush." A bird that played no part in their tradition or was not part of their diet would be referred to as "just a flying animal" (1946, p. 331). However, if an object was useful, it would be named and its uses and properties described in detail, that is, it would be distinctly individualized. The fact that trees and birds were not named separately for their individual appearances does not mean that the people of this community could not see that the trees or birds were physically different. It simply means that to them the differences were not so critical in relation to the specific context of their everyday lives as to warrant making distinctions by linguistic means.

One of the most widely quoted examples is that Eskimos have seven words for "snow," each of which makes very fine distinctions between the size of the flakes of snow to indicate how heavy the snow is. The Sami language has almost 200 words for "snow," and each word indicates the condition of snow, that is, whether one can walk on it, or ski on it, what temperature it is, whether it will change quickly and how (see Vuolab, 2000). Language, therefore, encodes the distinctions made and the critical features of the distinctions; the distinctions are appropriated and maintained so as to make the discernment of the critical features possible.

Another example is the centrality of the family and the importance of rank according to generation in the Chinese culture. This is reflected in the complex kinship terms that make very fine distinctions between whether one is related to the father's side or the mother's side, and who is related to whom in the family tree. These distinctions are critical in Chinese culture because they indicate the place that one occupies in the family tree, and hence the status in the family (in the sense of the extended family). Because of these distinctions, it is possible to have a situation where a very young person has a higher rank than somebody who is considerably older, and therefore the younger person is addressed with a kinship term that indicates he or she is *zhang bei* (Putonghua) [長輩], that is, of a more senior generation in the extended family.

Distinctions that have been made to suit social purposes are not only encoded in the language but also maintained by means of language. In other words, the categories set up, and hence the distinctions made by language, not only express the social structure but also create the need for people to conform to the behavior associated with these categories. The complex kinship terms in Chinese are a realization as well as a means of maintaining the hierarchical human relations in Chinese societies. As Halliday (1978) pointed out, "By their everyday acts of meaning, people act out the social structure, affirming their own statuses and roles, and establishing and transmitting the shared system of value and knowledge" (p. 8).

Not only are distinctions made to suit social purposes, they are also made to serve specific needs at particular moments in time. Let us use, for example, color distinctions. The distinction between bright red and dark red is commonplace and most people would be able to distinguish a bright red car from a dark red car. Suppose you witnessed an accident between a dark blue car and a bright red car and you were asked by the police to provide an eyewitness account of what happened. You probably would say something like this: "A red car was going at full speed when a blue car coming from the op-

1. THE SPACE OF LEARNING 29

posite direction suddenly swerved into the opposite lane and collided head-on with the red car." You would not take the trouble to say "the bright red car" and the "dark blue car" because the distinction between and bright and dark colors is not critical. However, if it was a bright red car colliding with a dark red car, then the distinction between dark red and bright red would be critical. Of course, if there was only one car, there would be no need to describe the color at all. For example, if you saw a car crashing into a supermarket, your eyewitness account to the police would be something like this: "I saw a car crashing into the supermarket at 10:00 a.m. this morning," but not "I saw a bright red car crashing into the supermarket at 10:00 a.m." because the color of the car is not critical in relation to the event or the context. Critical to the event or the context is what happened.

In the context of a learning situation, such as the classroom, the language that is used by the teacher and the students to make distinctions in relation to the object of learning is often of critical importance. Let us use an example from a lesson that will be reported in greater detail in chapter 5. A science teacher, in the context of teaching how a reed relay[3] operates, asked the students what happened to the electrical resistance value when light was shone on a light-diode resistor[4] (LDR). One student replied, "Small." When the student used the adjective "small," she was making a distinction between the size of the resistance in the LDR before and after the light was shone on the LDR. In other words, she was describing resistance as a state. The teacher, however, was not happy with the description because her question was "What happened to the resistance?" In other words, she wanted the students to describe the change of state caused by light shining on the LDR, and "small" was therefore not an appropriate answer. She insisted that the student use the verb "decreases" instead of the adjective "small." This teacher was not nitpicking, but was making an important distinction between *a state* and *a change of state*. In other words, the two states were classified as two different phenomena. In other contexts, such a distinction may not have been important at all, but in the context of understanding a phenomenon in physics, specifically the operation of a reed relay, this was an important distinction (see chap. 5 for a more detailed explication of the reed relay).

Let us take another example from a classroom learning situation. Two Hong Kong primary teachers were teaching lessons about festivals. One of the objects of learning in both lessons was to help the students to indicate their preferences for the festivals, using the phrase "like best." Both teachers gave their students the same list of festivals. Teacher A asked the students to first indicate the festivals that they liked and then indicate which one they liked best. By doing this, the teacher opened up a dimension of variation in indicating preferences that included "like" and "like best," and presupposed the choice of "do not like." In other words, in the semantic system of "like," there were three choices: "do not like," "like," and "like best." By juxtaposing "like" and "like best," the teacher was able to help the students experience variation in their feelings toward these festivals and thereby discern the meaning of "like best" as the superlative form of "like." By contrast, Teacher B made no such distinction. She simply asked her students to indicate what they "liked best." Consequently, some of the students in this class took "like best" as having a similar meaning to "like."

Language and Structure of Awareness

In our discussion of simultaneity and awareness, we pointed out that awareness is the totality of our experience of the world and that we experience every situation against the background of a vast number of previous experiences. We further pointed out that the characteristic of human awareness is that only a limited number of things come to the fore and become focused, whereas the rest recedes to the background. We observed that the figure–ground structure of awareness is dynamic and ever changing.

In the discussion of language and the construal of experience, we pointed out that the encoding of previous experience by linguistic means enables us to make sense of what we are experiencing. We wish to further argue that language also plays an important role in not only representing the structure of awareness but also in changing it. Let us take the previously cited example of the janitor locking the door of the computer laboratory. If we say, "The janitor locked the door," the janitor becomes the theme or subject of the clause and is the grounding for the rest of the clause. That is, *what the janitor did* was the figure. However, if we say, "The door was locked by the janitor," the fact that the door was locked becomes the ground, and the janitor becomes the figure.

In classroom situations, it is very important that the teacher is able to bring critical features of the object of learning into students' focal awareness. That is to say, it is crucial that the teacher is able to bring out the figure and ground relationship. This is often achieved through linguistic means, and most obviously through the use of questions because the structure of all questions involves a figure–ground relationship. For example, the often cited question, "Have you stopped beating your wife?" presupposes that you have been beating your wife and queries whether you have stopped the action or not. In other words, "beating your wife" is ground, and "have you stopped" is figure. What the teacher presents as ground is what he assumes to be shared knowledge, and what he presents as figure is what he wants to be the focus of the students' attention. For example, let us see how different questions asked by different teachers can result in different learning experiences for students (this example is presented in more detail in chap. 5). Two primary English teachers in Hong Kong were teaching the determiner "some" to indicate inexact quantity. Both teachers used *Old MacDonald's Farm* as the context for teaching, and both showed the students a series of pictures with different kinds of animals and

1. THE SPACE OF LEARNING   31

different numbers of animals on the computer screen. Both teachers also started by showing one animal and asking the students what they could see so as to elicit the name of the animal shown. After this, the first teacher repeatedly asked the students, "How many (name of animal) can you see?" This elicited exact numbers, such as "three," "four," "five," and so on. The second teacher, however, repeatedly asked the students, "What can you see?" and did not ask "How many?" The question "How many cats can you see?" presupposes that the animals that the students can see are cats and queries the exact number of cats. Hence, the cats are the ground and the number of cats the figure. This question focuses the students' attention on the exact number. The question "What can you see?" presupposes that the students can see something (on the computer screen) and queries "what" it is that they can see. In other words, the exact number of animals they can see is not the figure. Their focus of attention is on whether there is only one or more than one animal. The students' performance in a test administered at the end of the lesson showed that the students taught by the first teacher did less well when using the determiner "some" to indicate inexact quantity than the students taught by the second teacher.

THE SEMANTIC DIMENSION OF THE SPACE OF LEARNING

So far, we have focused on the necessary conditions for learning, the necessary conditions being the discernment of critical features of the object of learning through experiencing dimensions of variation relating to this specific object of learning both diachronically and synchronically, and holding these critical features in focal awareness simultaneously. However, these necessary conditions may not be sufficient for powerful learning to take place.

Let us take for example some science lessons that will be explained in detail in chapter 6. Two science teachers explained the process of *neutralization* to their students. Both explained that *neutralization* is a reaction between acid and alkali that results in a pH value of 7. Both of the teachers used laboratory demonstrations to show what happens when neutralization occurs, by using a change of the color of the solution as the means of making the process visible. Both varied the proportion of acid and alkali, and the change of pH value to indicate the levels of acidity and alkalinity, to help students understand the concept of neutralization. However, one teacher used many everyday examples that were familiar to the students to help them make sense of neutralization (e.g., the use of alkaline ointment to sooth the itchiness caused by acids injected into the skin by mosquitoes, and the use of alkaline toothpaste to neutralize the acidic saliva when cleaning our teeth). The other teacher, however, dealt with neutralization very much as a process of mixing acids and alkalis in a laboratory experiment. By using examples that the students were able to relate to easily, the first teacher made available possibilities for students to assign a much richer meaning to the object of learning. For these students, neutralization was no longer just a process that took place in the laboratory, but a also a process that had a place in their daily lives.

The space of learning is constituted therefore not only by the possibilities for discernment of critical features of the object of learning, often brought about by linguistic means, but also by the examples and analogies that the teacher uses, the stories that the teacher tells, the contexts that the teacher brings in, and so on. It is constituted by the meanings that learners assign to these examples, analogies, stories, and contexts, as well as by the previous experience that they bring in as they try to make sense of the object of learning. All of this constitutes the semantic dimension of the space of learning in which the critical features of the object of learning are interpreted and understood. A space of learning that is semantically rich allows students to come to grips with the critical features of the object of learning much more effectively than one that is semantically impoverished.

THE SHARED SPACE OF LEARNING

In order for us to discern critical features of the object in question, we need to be able to make sense of what we are experiencing in relation to what we have experienced before; this is the diachronic dimension of our awareness. As we pointed out before, we cannot talk about tallness unless we have also experienced shortness; we cannot say what bright red is unless we have experienced other shades of red. In other words, what learners have experienced before is crucial to how they make sense of their current experience. In order to make it possible for learners to discern critical features of the object of learning, teachers must be aware of whether learners can make sense of these critical features through their previous experience. The teacher must also be aware of how much is shared between himself and the learners. In other words, what the teacher presents as ground should be shared common ground between himself and the students, so that what he presents as figure can be made sense of by the students in relation to the ground. In this sense, the space of learning is a shared space of learning.

Language is the key means by which this shared space is constituted. We have illustrated this point in the previous discussion on teachers' questions. The following is a further example. In a study of some mathematics lessons of Brazilian kindergarten children, in which the teacher was teaching addition and the concepts of *more* and *less*, Cestari (2001) found that the use of unclear deictic reference and the lack of an explicit indication as to which realm the teacher was moving in confused the students and made them unable to answer her questions.

1. THE SPACE OF LEARNING

The lesson was a mathematics lesson at kindergarten level and the students were around 5 or 6 years old. The teacher was teaching addition and was helping the students to understand not only addition but also the mathematical concepts of more and less.

The teacher put three boxes on one side and two boxes on another. She then asked the students whether there were the same number of boxes on both sides, which side had more, and which side had less. The teacher had no problems getting the students to indicate that the side with three boxes had more. However, when she asked the students about the side with two boxes, confusion set in. The following is an excerpt from the lesson:

1.1 [Cestari, 2001]

5	T:	Which side has more?
6	S:	3
7	T:	(The side) of how many?
8	Ss:	Of 3!
9	T:	Which has 3. And this side, which has 2?
10	S:	2.
11	T:	Hmm?
12	S:	2.
13	T:	This side has more or less? (pointing to the side with 2 boxes)
14	S:	More!
15	T:	Hmm?
16	Ss:	More! Ss: Less!
17	T:	Why less? It is because there are only …
18	Ss:	More!
19	T:	2, and here there are more because there are …
20	Ss:	Less!
21	T:	Here there are more because how many are there?
22	Some Ss:	3!
23	T:	3, then 3 is bigger than …?
24	S:	2!

In line 9, when the teacher asked the question, "And this side, which has 2?" one student simply reported the number of boxes on the other side (line 10), and the same answer was given when the teacher asked for the answer again with an interrogative interjection (line 11). The teacher then repeated her question in a slightly fuller form that included the quantitative comparative notion "more or less." She also gave a more explicit indication of which side she was referring to by pointing to the side with two boxes (line 13). This, however, did not meet with much success. The class was split between "more" and "less" (see line 16). In line 17, even though the teacher provided the linguistic scaffolding to help the students to justify why one side was less than the other side, and tried to get them to fill in the blank with "two," she still failed to elicit the correct answer. It was not until she made the justification very explicit by stating the quantitative comparative notion "more" and the number "how many are there" (line 19 and line 21) that she finally succeeded in getting the correct answer.

Cestari (2001) identified the source of confusion as emanating from the absence of a definite reference in the incomplete interrogative in line 9, and observed that even though the teacher tried to repair the communication gap by pointing to the side with two boxes and explicitly asking whether it had more or less, the confusion remained. The confusion has very much to do with the fact that the teacher was trying to establish a correspondence between the number of boxes and the mathematical notion of "more" and "less," and the fact there was a lack of common ground, or mutuality, between her and the students with regard to whether she was moving in the realm of quantity of boxes, or in the realm of the mathematical notion of "more" and "less." In line 9, when the teacher asked the cryptic question "And this side, which has 2?" she was moving in the realm of the mathematical notion of "more" and "less," and trying to get the students to extrapolate from the question what she wanted them to tell her, which was whether the side with two boxes had more or less boxes than the side with three boxes. The students, however, were moving in the realm of the quantity of boxes.

When the teacher then tried to get the students to justify why one side had less, she was moving in the realm of the quantity of boxes and was trying to get the students to complete the justification by supplying the number of boxes (line 17 and line 19). Yet, the students were moving in the realm of the mathematical notion of "more" or "less." It was only when she made the relationship explicit between the mathematical notion of *more* and the *quantity* of boxes (line 21) and said, "Here there are *more* because *how many* are there?" that the students were able to answer the question. This example illustrates nicely that unless the teacher and the learners share a common ground in relation to the object of learning, it is not possible for the learners to make sense of the object of learning.

There is a further sense in which the space of learning is a shared space. We have already pointed out that previous experience is the frame of reference against which current experience is interpreted or made sense of, but that the current experience also modifies the way in which the previous experience is construed. This is an ever-changing and interactive process in which the features that we discern in a situation and what we discern as critical keep being revised. One crucial means in which this is done is by talking over events with people and by reflecting on the events after they have occurred (Britton, 1970). Language not only plays a crucial role in the modification of each other's understanding and perception of the world but also becomes part of the experience itself. The modification of the learners' and teacher's understanding of the world is what classroom teaching and learning is all about. This process is brought about jointly by the teacher and the learners through interaction in which meaning is negotiated and co-constructed. In this sense, the space of learning is a shared space of learning. In chapter 6, we see how the students modify each other's understanding of the world by engaging in collaborative talk. In chapter 7, we see how the teacher and the students together co-construct an understanding of the function of a "clan" (a community in which all members have the same surname) in a history lesson.

TOWARD A PEDAGOGY OF LEARNING

The expression *pedagogy of learning* may strike the reader as vaguely odd. Pedagogy is about teaching and upbringing after all; and teaching and upbringing is much about learning, so is the pedagogy of learning not a tautology?

Well, it could have been, but it is not. We set out at the beginning of this chapter by pointing to the fact that discussions about pedagogy are, as a rule, not phrased in terms of learning but in terms of the conditions of learning, and that they often lack precise statements about the ways in which those conditions facilitate learning and what kind of learning they would facilitate. It is often simply assumed that the conditions argued for would facilitate all kinds of learning.

When we use the expression *pedagogy of learning,* we do not refer to the process whereby the conditions of learning are taken as the point of departure and it is simply assumed that these conditions embody "the art of teaching all things to all men." The pedagogy of learning means taking learning as the point of departure and exploring the conditions that might be conducive to bringing that learning about.

As learning is always the learning of something, there are severe limits to discussing learning in general, without reference to what is learned. What is learned is the object of learning and we argue that a pedagogy of learning must take as its point of departure the very object of learning.

Most of the studies reported in this book follow the simple design of comparing how the same object of learning was dealt with in two or more different classrooms. We have used this model because we believe that the way in which the object of learning is dealt with in the classroom is of decisive importance, and that we can only find out how the object of learning is dealt with in the classroom by comparing it with another way of dealing with the same object of learning (this follows from the theory of variation discussed in this chapter). In this book, we describe much of what we found about differences in the ways in which the same objects of learning were dealt with.

In all studies reported in this book, we transcribed verbatim everything that was said in the classroom and carried out our analyses on the transcripts. We have also used some of the transcripts or parts thereof (without identifying the school, class, or the teacher) in seminars and workshops. Frequently we let the workshop participants—educational researchers, school administrators, teacher educators, and teachers—read through the transcripts and then address our initial question: "We have here two classes dealing with the same topic (content or object of learning). What would you say you find the most striking difference between the two?"

Very rarely did we hear comments on the way in which the object of learning was handled in the two classes, that is, what it was possible for the student to learn in one case and what it was possible for the student to learn in the other. Most comments concerned whether there was a case of whole-class teaching or group work, whether the teaching was teacher-centered or student-centered, whether or not audiovisual tools, IT, manipulatives were used, and so on.

We do not deny that the way in which the learning situation was arranged in each class was of importance for the possibility to learn. For instance, we agree with the argument that the opportunity for communication in the classroom is of importance for students' learning, and with the argument that the way in which the learners are able to participate in the constitution of the object of learning is also important. However, we claim that what students are communicating and what they are interacting about is just as significant as how they interact and communicate.

Let us use an example from a study of a mathematics lesson reported by Voigt (1995, pp. 173–174) to show that there can be features of the learning situation other than interaction that are also important for students' learning. Voigt described how two students, Jack and Jamie, went about solving a group of arithmetic tasks:

1. $50 - 9 = 41$
2. $60 - 9 = 51$
3. $60 - 19 = 41$
4. $41 + 19 = 60$
5. $31 + 29 = 60$
6. $31 + 19 = 50$
7. $32 + 18 = \_$

Let us take a look at how problem 7 was talked about by the boys.

Jack:	Uh-huh, that's 18, not 19.
Jamie:	Yeah, but that's 32 not 31.
Jack:	Oh yeah!
Jamie:	They're the same thing.

1. THE SPACE OF LEARNING

Researcher:	What's the same thing?
Jamie:	These two. [He points to the 31 + 19 = 50 and 32 + 18 = _]
Researcher:	Hang on, I was asking Jack. Which ones? We've got 31 and 19.
Jack:	Makes 50.
Researcher:	Yeah.
Jack:	And look, 32 and 18. See, its just one more than that [points to the task], and that's one higher than that.

It can be seen from the excerpt that the last task was solved by a compensation strategy, a strategy that the boys actually had not used in the previous tasks. So, this task was handled differently from the previous ones. In other words, the boys learned to handle the problem in a new way. Voigt (1995) used the notions "negotiation of mathematical meaning" and "meaning taken as shared" (p. 174) for understanding and explaining students' learning. He argued that without the interaction between the boys, this new strategy never would have emerged. Undoubtedly, the interaction was of importance for the students' learning in this case. However, can this new way of handling the task, and hence the students' learning, be explained by the interaction and the negotiation of meaning *only*? We believe we must also understand what it is possible to learn in the situation in order to account for what the participants actually learn.

If we take a closer look at the problems, it is possible to look at this other side of learning; that is, *what* it was possible to learn. To us as authors, it is obvious that the way in which this group of problems was composed affected what it was possible to learn. In this group of problems, there was a particular variation present. Something varied, whereas other things were invariant between the problems. First of all, there was a variation between addition and subtraction (problem 1 through 3 and 4 through 7, respectively). Further, if we first analyze problems 4 and 5 in detail, we will find another variation, namely that the tenths changed both in the first and the second addend (from 41 to 31, and from 19 to 29, respectively). Both these additions have the same total sum (i.e., 60), but they have a different part–part–whole relation. Let us now look at problems 6 and 7. Problem 6 involves and combines numbers from problems 4 and 5. The first addend is the same as the first addend in problem 5 and the second addend is the same as the second addend in problem 4. In problem 7, there is a change of the ones in both the addends (i.e., increasing from 31 to 32 and decreasing from 19 to 18, respectively). Obviously, there was a very systematic variation in the composition of the problems. We would say that a particular pattern of variation was afforded to the students to experience. And from the excerpt just cited we interpret that the students did discern a pattern of variation. For instance, one of the boys said: "See, it's just one more than that [points to the problem], and that's one higher than that." So, we want to conclude that the afforded variation was a feature of the learning situation that was also significant for students' learning.

In these examples, we have tried to point out a variation that was present in the learning environment, a variation that it was possible for the learners to experience. What we argue for in the following chapters is that this afforded variation is a critical feature in relation to the way in which the intended learning is brought about, as well as being a critical feature for students' learning. The thesis of this book is that the differences in what the students learn is to a large extent a function of what they can possibly learn. What they can possibly learn is a space of learning constituted by that which it is possible to discern.

In the aforementioned example, there is certainly an interaction taking place that contributes to constituting the space of learning. But the series of problems also contributes to constituting the space of learning. Without the particular pattern of variation that is embodied in the problems, the students would not have been able to come up with the idea of compensation, not in that particular situation, at least. In several places in this book, we give examples of how the space of learning is constituted in the interaction. In chapter 5, chapter 6, and chapter 7, for instance, we see how the teacher and the students jointly constitute the space of learning as the teacher takes on the students' responses and opens them up for inquiry and further development. We also see how students interacting in groups, jointly constituted the space of learning by bringing in their own cultural and daily experiences to make sense of the object of learning. For example, in chapter 6, when students discuss how the appearance of the sloth should be described, several of them think that all eyes are black and that therefore there is no need to include the color of the sloth's eyes. In other words, they are not able to discern the color of its eyes as a critical feature. However, one student draws the group's attention to the fact that a rabbit's eyes are red, thus showing that not all eyes are black. Another student agrees with his observation. The group finally agrees on including the color of the sloth's eyes in the description. What is happening here is that through collaborative interaction, the students are able to bring in dimensions of variation that might otherwise be neglected if students are not afforded the opportunity to interact among themselves.

We are not denying that the space of learning may in part, or entirely, be constituted in the interaction between students. However, the point we would like to make is that reference is frequently made to interaction (student centeredness, activity approach, task-based learning, etc.) as something that is inherently conducive to learning, without relating the interaction to what is learned. And that the lived object of learning is—as a rule—not explained in any precise way. Interaction, student centeredness, and so on, are assumed to be good for learning in some very general, but rather vague sense, and for their own sake.

In this book, we try to establish the precise link between learning and conditions of learning. This link is established by means of the relationship between the object of learning and the space of learning, where the enacted object of learning is identical to the space of learning, both of which refer to the object of learning as it realized in the classroom. It is the object of learning that the students encounter, and the object of learning that they can possibly learn, or learn about, making it into a part of themselves. If we are interested in how students learn to see certain things in certain ways, we must ask ourselves what critical features of the object of learning students can possibly discern in a particular classroom situation. Nobody can learn to see certain things in certain ways without experiencing certain patterns of variation. This statement is true in general as far as this kind of learning (learning to see something in a certain way) is concerned, and it implies that very specific patterns of variation are necessary conditions for the learning of—or learning about—specific objects of learning.

Having said that, we do not wish to imply that it does not matter whether the teaching is whole class, or whether students work in groups; whether students are engaged in task-based or problem-based learning, or in project work; whether teaching is student centered; whether IT is used; or whether there is a joyful atmosphere in the classroom or not. Differences in the way in which the conditions of learning are organized may undoubtedly constrain or facilitate the constitution of the space of learning necessary for the development of a certain capability. But in order to understand how these differences inhibit or facilitate the development of a certain capability, we have to understand how they constrain or facilitate the constitution of the specific space of learning necessary for developing that specific capability. And this understanding can never be derived from a general way of organizing the conditions of learning. For this reason, we can never truthfully argue that one way of organizing the conditions of learning is, in general, better than another way.

In this book we try to develop a theoretical perspective and a conceptual framework for understanding learning in schools in terms of what it is possible to learn in schools. If we know what the students should learn, and if we know what conditions are necessary for them to learn, then we could reasonably work toward creating those necessary conditions. It must be remembered, however, that for each specific capability (of seeing something in a certain way), there are necessary, *specific* conditions. Even if we know in general that there must be a certain space of learning that comprises dimensions of variation that correspond to the critical features defining this specific way of seeing a specific phenomenon, we do not know what these critical features are in every specific case.

This "blessed ignorance" is a weakness that can be turned into a strength by engaging the teachers themselves in finding the missing insights that are needed for achieving different particular educational aims, and for developing specific capabilities and particularly powerful ways of seeing particular phenomena. Teachers focusing on the same object of learning can do so together by finding the critical features in each case, creating what are believed to be the necessary conditions for developing that capability, checking what the students learn and whether the conjectures were justified, revising the framework if necessary, checking again, documenting the process as well as the outcomes, and sharing it with other teachers.

Teachers could in this way participate in the collective construction of professional knowledge, not only as a part of their own professional development but also as scientific research that may yield new insights. Several examples of such an enterprise are outlined in chapter 8 of this book.

ENDNOTES

[1] To be fully accurate, of course, we should say, "develop certain capabilities *and values*." However, although not wishing to place more importance on one rather than the other, the focus of this book is on the development of capabilities rather than values, as this has been the focus of our studies.

[2] The pronoun "he" is used in a sex neutral sense to avoid awkward use of "he or she."

[3] A *reed relay* is a device that will change a weak electrical current into a very strong current when it is connected to electric circuits. Reed relays are used in many electrical appliances that require large currents for operation, such as elevators, motors, and so on.

[4] A *light diode resistor* (LDR) can prevent an electric current from passing through an electric circuit because of its great resistance. Light diode resistors are sensitive to light. When exposed to bright light, the resistance reduces, thus allowing the electric current to pass through.

II

On Learning

2

Variation and the Secret of the Virtuoso

Po Yuk Ko
Ference Marton

MAKING SYSTEMATIC USE OF VARIATION

In chapter 1, we argued that whatever object of learning learners, try to appropriate, certain critical features of that object have to be discerned, that is, learners must learn to see certain situations in certain ways. But learners can never discern anything without experiencing variation. The experience of patterns of variation specific for different objects of learning is a necessary condition for appropriating those objects of learning. If this is true, then successful teachers must be good at constituting such necessary conditions in the classroom, that is, the specific patterns of variation. One of the main points of this book is that we have managed to identify a critical factor in teaching, a factor that distinguishes between teaching that makes a certain learning possible and teaching that fails to achieve this. The empirical comparisons in chapter 3 and chapter 4 demonstrate this in greater detail.

In any instance of teaching, there are things that are repeated and there are things that vary. One of the features of good practice and powerful pedagogy is the efficient use of variation and repetition, whether it be consciously or less consciously. Let us look at an example.

Kwan, Ng, and Chik (2002) offered a portrayal of an innovative teacher's way of transforming the intended object of learning into an enacted object of learning in the course of a double lesson in Chinese (the class was a primary Grade 2 class in Hong Kong).

The intended object of learning could be split into two intertwined aspects that were not to be dealt with separately, but at the same time. The students were expected to become better at the following skills: (a) describing animals, and (b) using the four language skills in an integrative manner.

The double lesson built on the previous lesson in which the students had learned to discern different aspects of a panda, such as its appearance (body, head, four limbs, color) and its movement. As the point of departure for the double lesson, a 3-minute film sequence was shown to the class. In the film sequence, the students saw a young sloth, who according to the narrator had lost its mother. The students saw the sloth climb down from a tree in search of a new home, swim across a nearby river, and climb up another tree where it encountered another sloth—which was luckily friendly—and thus the young sloth found a new home.

The students first watched the video with the narration, then watched it again without the narrative (seeing, listening). Next they focused on the sloth's appearance by discussing its various features (body, head, four limbs, color) and its movement (speaking, listening). Then the students wrote down their descriptions on overhead transparencies and showed them to the rest of the class (writing, reading). Finally they appointed a member of the group who came to the front of the class and acted as narrator and read aloud their description while the muted film sequence was replayed on the video (speaking, listening).

During the lesson, a highly complex pattern of variation was jointly constituted by the teacher and the students. Let us look at some interesting patterns of variation and invariance.

To begin with, the students were expected to shift their attention between two aspects of the animal: its appearance and its movement. We cannot say that these two aspects varied, but the students themselves were asked to vary the focus of their attention between the two different aspects and the four different parts of the animal. This shows that variation can thus be experienced by experiencing variation generated by the environment (e.g., focusing on different animals) or by varying one's attention or imagination (e.g., focusing on different aspects of the same animal). Furthermore, variation is always experienced against the background of what is invariant. So therefore we speak of "patterns of variation and invariance." In our specific case we have the following:

Variation	*Invariance*
different aspects	same animal

and

Variation	*Invariance*
different parts	same aspect (appearance)

By generating two kinds of variation in relation to the same animal, different aspects and different parts can be discerned. But is this specific to this ani-

2. VARIATION AND THE SECRET OF THE VIRTUOSO

mal? In order to generalize the acts of discernment, they have to be applied to more than one animal. As the same exercise was also carried out in relation to a panda during the previous lesson, this condition was actually met.

Variation	*Invariance*
different animals	same acts of discernment
(panda and sloth)	(between aspects, and between parts)

So far we have been dealing with the first of the two intended objects of learning: being capable of describing an animal. What about the second intended object of learning, using the four language skills in an integrative manner? As a matter of fact, the two intended objects of learning can be brought together by applying them to the same task: that is, describing animals in speech and in written form, and taking part in the description by listening and reading. The students talked about the appearance and movement of the sloth, they wrote down their observations, they read each others' observations, they commented on the film sequence when the sound was off, and they listened to each others' comments.

Variation	*Invariance*
different	same thing described
communicative acts	(the sloth)

We can see here the double functions of variation, that is, that differences between the different acts can be discerned when their object is the same. This is what we referred to as *separation* in the previous chapter. It is the dimension of communicative acts that is being separated from other aspects of the relationship between the describer and the described, that is, between the students and the story about the sloth. But because the object of these acts is the same, commonalities are brought out as well: words, expressions, and sentences. Different acts are discerned and brought together at the same time. A third pattern of variation present in the lesson makes it possible for the students to arrive at the insight that the same task can be carried out in different but equally correct ways. However, the different ways of doing something only become visible if they are perceived as being different ways of doing *the same thing* (otherwise different acts and different tasks co-vary and cannot be separated from each other). This is exactly the case in the lesson discussed here; the sloth is described in different ways, that is, by means of different communicative acts.

The teacher in this example is a Chinese teacher from Hong Kong. In fact, almost all of the examples in this book are about Chinese teachers, and most of them are from Hong Kong. Stigler and Hiebert (1999) emphasized that teaching is a cultural activity and argued that teachers in different cultures follow different scripts. If so, is it the case that there is a specific Chinese pedagogy, a Chinese script that is characterized, among other things, by an elaborate use of patterns of variation and invariance?

Is it reasonable at all to expect a specific Chinese pedagogy? Trying to find out whether there is one or not would be an impossibly large undertaking because of the sheer vastness and variability of the Chinese culture. An easier question to address—and one that for our purposes is actually more interesting—is this: What are the pedagogical practices considered to be exemplary in China? This was the question addressed by one member of our team (Ko, 2002), and the following section builds on her work.

A LESSON ON SEMANTICS

In this section, we present a lesson taught by an expert teacher in the People's Republic of China (PRC; the lesson was referred to briefly in chap. 1). The teacher is a "Special Rank Teacher," and the winner of a prestigious state-granted teaching award. The double lesson is a demonstration lesson that was audiotaped, transcribed, and published (Qian, 1985), in order to disseminate the teaching expertise of the teacher as a model lesson for his counterparts to follow. It allows us to see what is considered to be good pedagogy in the PRC.

The sample lesson is a reading lesson based on a prescribed text called "Semantics," which is a piece of expository writing about the lexical meanings of words. In the lesson, the teacher aimed to introduce several linguistic concepts on semantics, including the scope of meaning of words; the level of generality of words; homonyms, synonyms, and antonyms, and their usage. In the following, we first describe the lesson and then analyze the variational pattern.

Summary of the Lesson

Instead of introducing the linguistic knowledge directly, the teacher started with a story aiming to illustrate that the meaning of words can vary according to the context, and that it is important to be aware of the complexity of the meaning of words.

> Afanti was a hairdresser. There was one customer, Ahung, who always went to Afanti's place to have his hair cut but never paid for the service. It made Afanti very angry. He wanted to play a trick on Ahung. One day Ahung came to Afanti's again. Afanti first cut Ahung's hair. Then he began to shave Ahung's face, and asked, "Do you want your eyebrows?" Ahung replied, "Of course! Why ask!" Then, quick as a flash, Afanti shaved off Ahung's eyebrows and said, "You wanted your eyebrows, so I will give them to you!" Ahung was too mad to say anything; because he had indeed said he "wanted" his eyebrows. Meanwhile Afanti asked, "Do you want your beard?"

2. VARIATION AND THE SECRET OF THE VIRTUOSO 47

Ahung had a beautiful beard, and he immediately said, "My beard? No, no! I don't want my beard!" But again Afanti proceeded to shave off his beard. Ahung stood up and saw an egg-like head in the mirror. [Both the teacher and students laugh.] Furiously, Ahung reproved Afanti, "Why did you shave off my eyebrows and beard?" "I was only following your orders, sir!" Afanti answered calmly. There was nothing Ahung could say to that!

After telling the story, the teacher asked questions to help the students to unravel the ambivalence of the meaning of "want" (in Chinese, *yao* (Putonghua) [要]):

2.1

T: After listening to this story, do you know what kind of trick Afanti played on Ahung?

Ss: Afanti played a trick using the word "want."

T: What did Afanti mean by asking "Do you 'want' your eyebrows?"

Ss: It meant "to give."

T: Exactly! It meant "to give." You want them, then I shave them off and give them to you. Then what is the meaning of the word "want" in "Do you want your beard?"

Ss: "To keep."

T: Yes, it means "to keep." But how did Ahung interpret the word? He still thought it was to "give" him his beard. That's why he immediately answered, "I don't want it." And he fell into the trap. So you see, the word "want" has two meanings. It can mean this, or it can mean that. Afanti exploited the ambiguity of the meaning of "want" to trap Ahung. This story tells us it is important to master the meaning of a word and its scope of meaning [Teacher writes on the blackboard: meaning, scope of meaning].

In the story, the word "want" (*yao* (Putonghua) [要]) had two meanings—either "to keep" (*liu* (Putonghua) [留]) or "to give" (*gei* (Putonghua) [给]) according to different contexts. Afanti exploited the ambiguity of the meaning of "want" (homonyms) to trap Ahung. When Ahung interpreted "want" as meaning "to keep," Afanti deliberately interpreted the "want" as meaning "to give," and vice versa. As a result, Ahung lost his eyebrows and his beard. In the teacher-led discussion that immediately followed the reading, the teacher did not use metalanguage (i.e., the term *homonyms*) to illustrate the semantics concept, but simply highlighted the complexity of the meaning of words.

Next, the teacher showed the class some books and asked students to name them.

2.2

T:	... I first want you to look at some things and name them [holding up a book]. What is this?
Ss:	A Chinese book.
T:	[holding up another book] What is this?
Ss:	An English book.
T:	[holding up two books together] If we put them together, what do we call them?
Ss:	Books.
T:	Narrow down the scope.
Ss:	Textbooks.
T:	[holding up a dictionary] What is this?
Ss:	A dictionary.
T:	Is it a book?
Ss:	Yes, it is.
T:	What kind of book?
Ss:	Reference book?
T:	What are these three all together?
Ss:	Books.
T:	That's right. Chinese book, textbook, book, the scope of the meanings becomes bigger and bigger ...

In this excerpt, we see that the teacher started with specific kinds of books and then asked the students to provide a general word that could cover both kinds of books. But we also see that the teacher tried to help the students to see the difference in scope of meaning by showing how one kind of book subsumes another kind of book, such that language books are a kind of textbook and textbooks are in turn a kind of book, just as a reference book is also a kind of book.

On one hand, the teacher cleverly juxtaposed books at the same level of specificity—a Chinese language book and an English language book—and showed that it is only necessary to go one level up in order to subsume both books, namely by using the word "textbook." Hence, there is no need to subsume them both under the very general term *books*. The teacher then juxtaposed textbook and reference book, which are also at the same level of specificity, and showed that the next level up to subsume both would be "books." The class were therefore presented with three levels of generality, and the relationship between the examples was a hierarchical structure, that is, with one subsuming the other.

2. VARIATION AND THE SECRET OF THE VIRTUOSO

In order to help the students see the relationship between words of different levels of generality, which is denoted by the word relation known as *hyponyms*, the teacher varied the combination of the specifics and the levels of generality. As pointed out, the combination of the Chinese language book and the English language book can be subsumed precisely under "textbooks," which is at a more general level, but less precisely under "books," which is at a yet more general level. However, when the combination is of various types of books (i.e., text books and reference books), the use of the word "books" is the most appropriate.

The teacher helped the students understand the semantic features of a book by considering what is not a book (i.e., by using *contrasts*, mentioned in chap. 1):

2.3

T: ... [holding up pieces of newspaper] Is this a book?

Ss: No, that's newspaper.

T: Why is it not a book?

Ss: Because there's not enough [pages].

S: Even a pile of newspaper can't be called a book. A book has a cover, a newspaper doesn't.

S: Not exactly. If I have a book, and I tear off the cover, the book is still a book. Pictorials also have covers, but they aren't called books.

S: A book is a composition bound by a cover.

T: [holding up an exercise book] This also has a cover, hasn't it? But we don't call that a book. A book is a literary composition bound by a cover. You can see that with dictionaries, right? [students nodded their heads] To be a book, it has to be bound by a cover, and at the same time it has to fulfil another requirement: that of being a composition. Books are bound compositions. This is the definition of the word. Now can you give me the definition of a textbook?

S: A textbook is a composition used for teaching, bound in a cover.

T: Right! Then please give me the definition of this Chinese book.

S: A composition used for teaching Chinese, bound by a cover.

T: Very good! We put in more limits here. From the example above we can see that, from "book" to "textbook" to "Chinese book," what happens to the scope of meaning?

Ss: It becomes narrower.

T: Then how about the meaning? Does it become more specific, or more general?

Ss:	Specific!
T:	Again, you have discovered a rule: the smaller the scope of the meaning, the ... what ... the meaning becomes?
Ss:	The more specific the meaning becomes.
T:	Then how about, the bigger the scope?
Ss:	The more general the meaning becomes.

The teacher varied the examples of "not a book" and looked at the features they had in common and those that differed. Having a cover, for example, is certainly not a critical feature because although a magazine and an exercise book both have covers and a newspaper does not, all three of them are not books. The definition of the semantic features of a book paved the way for defining more specific kinds of books, for example, the language textbook. By getting students to define what a language textbook is, the teacher demonstrated that as the scope of meaning gets narrower, the meanings of the words get more specific.

The teacher also tried to relate scope of meaning to levels of generality. From book to textbook to language book, the scope becomes smaller and smaller. From book to textbook to language book, the level of generality becomes more and more specific.

The teacher used several different contexts to illustrate how words at different levels of generality should be used in relation to different contexts:

2.4

T:	So, I'd like to ask, should we be more specific or more general when we make choices of words in writing an essay?
S:	Sometimes it is better to be specific, but sometimes it is better to be general.
T:	Any examples?
S:	If somebody asks, "How many books do you have?" And you answer, "I have one math, one Chinese, one English, one physics and one chemistry book, so five books in total." That would be very clumsy. We would just say, "I have five books."
T:	Any other comments?
S:	Sometimes we should be more specific. For example, if that is a rabbit, we should not just give a general answer and only say that it is an animal.
T:	Very good. In writing and speaking, how should we choose our words? More specific ones or more general ones? It depends on the need of individual expressions. Be specific when necessary. The same applies to being general. Your biggest problem when

2. VARIATION AND THE SECRET OF THE VIRTUOSO

choosing words is that you tend to be too general and vague when you need to be specific. You saw a rabbit, but you say you saw an animal. So people don't know what you actually saw. Could you give me some examples of using words with vague meanings? ...

After dealing with levels of generality, the teacher dealt with another type of word relation: synonyms. To bring out this kind of word relation, the teacher contrasted it with homonyms, which had already been covered in the story of Afanti. Although *homonyms* are words with two meanings, *synonyms* are the opposite; that is, the same meaning denoted by different words. In other words, synonyms are understood in the context of the relation between meaning and word; synonyms being one kind of meaning word relationship and homonyms being another kind of meaning word relationship.

2.5

T: ... So, now we come to another question. In the story we mentioned, the word "want" used by Afanti has two meanings. But there are other situations where one meaning can be expressed by a number of words. Can you give me some examples?

S: For example "see," we sometimes use different words like "look up at," "glance at," "look down," etc. All these basically mean the same as "see."

T: Very good. These are the different interpretations of the word "see." Now, I'd like you to find some more examples of different words representing the same meaning.

S: Father, daddy, papa.

T: You learned a noun in the "Poem of Mulan" recently. What was it?

S: *Pater.*

T: Father, daddy, papa, and pater are all in the same semantic scope. Let us illustrate the scope of meaning by circles. For example, book, textbook, and Chinese book [teacher draws a circle on the board]. If this circle indicates "book," then where should we put the word "textbook?"

Ss: Inside the circle.

T: [drawing another circle] Then, how about the circles of pater, father, daddy, and papa?

Ss: They are of the same size.

T: All these four circles are overlapping. We call these four words synonyms. We also consider them equivalent as they share the same meaning....

Because the teacher contrasted these different examples, the students became aware of the two different relationships between words and meanings, that is, the difference between homonyms and synonyms.

Following this, the teacher drew the students' attention to the use of synonyms. Different examples were used to illustrate that different synonymous words should be used in different contexts for example: formal versus informal ("father" vs. "daddy" or "papa"); technical versus nontechnical ("sodium chloride" vs. "salt"); and different degrees of politeness ("wrinkly old fellow" vs. "Grandpa").

The teacher then revisited the different levels of generality.

2.6

T: S, please read out the first and second paragraph. [The student reads it out] Which sentences have you marked?

S: I have marked the last sentence in both paragraphs. The two that talk about the concepts of "ship" and "paper."*
[*The last sentences in the two paragraphs are: "The concept that 'ship' as a kind of marine transportation vehicle is generalized from the common properties that all ships share," and "The concept of 'paper' is also generalized from the common properties shared by all paper."]

T: Now I ask you, how does the general concept of "book" come about?

S: It comes from the common properties that are shared by different kinds of books.

T: Then what are the common properties of books?

Ss: They are bound by a cover.

T: And ... ?

Ss: They are compositions bound by a cover.

T: These are the common properties that every book has. With these, we can generate the concept of book. The concepts of "ship" and "paper" are also generated like this. Thus, we can understand the creation of a concept. S, could you please read the following paragraph? [continues to read, from "Comrade Mao Zedong" to "these two books"] What sentences have you marked?

Ss: [most students] This one: "In selection of words, one must be clear about the meaning and the scope of meaning in order to choose an accurate and suitable word."

T: Have you noticed what Comrade Mao said? This remark is interesting. According to our theory, have you seen the word "men?"

Ss: [some] Yes, we have. [some] No, we haven't, not according to the book.

2. VARIATION AND THE SECRET OF THE VIRTUOSO 53

T: None of you have seen the word "men." "Men" is an abstract concept. What we see are Cheung, Lee, Wong, Chiu, and so on. They are concrete, real people. What is the relation between the concept "men" and all real people?

S: All real people have general properties.

T: —The common properties generate a concept. Have you seen the word "building?"

Ss: No.

T: We see the words "teaching block," "classroom," and "our own flats," which are our "homes." All these are the solid "buildings" that we can really touch.

In this excerpt, the teacher referred back to the discussion about "books" and asked students to name the common properties of different kinds of books. Then the teacher gave a further illustration of the concept of the different level of generality of words. For example, "building" is at a higher level of generality or abstraction than "teaching block," which refers to a specific building. After clarifying the concept, the teacher guided the students to apply the knowledge to an exercise in the textbook.

In the last part of the lesson, the teacher introduced another word relation in semantics, that is, *antonyms*. He first asked students to suggest words with contrastive meanings (eminent–mediocre, clever–stupid, arrogant–modest). By searching for examples to exemplify antonyms, students focused on the critical features of these types of words—contrast in meaning.

2.7

T: Now we will discuss another phenomenon in semantics—contrast in meaning. Could you please tell me, what is the term for words with contrastive meaning?

Ss: [all] Antonyms.

T: Can you give me some examples of antonyms?

S: Eminent and mediocre.

S: Clever and stupid.

S: Arrogant and modest.

T: It seems quite easy for you to give examples for antonyms. What I really want you to focus on is how much understanding antonyms can help in presenting our ideas? For example, when we grasp the pair "arrogant" and "modest," how can we present our understanding of these antonyms? Comrade Mao has stated ...

S: "Modesty helps you improve, arrogance makes you decline."

T: You see, we express our ideas from both the positive and negative point of view. What is the advantage of doing this?

S: We can present our ideas comprehensively.

S: Thoroughly.

T: Comprehensive, thorough, are both correct. An additional point I want to make: Language presented in a thorough way requires our own thorough thinking. It is better to consider a problem from both the positive and negative sides. Thus, mastering rich antonyms can also help us to consider a problem thoroughly. I will write some words below and I want you to tell me their antonyms. Then, please use these antonyms to compose a sentence in order to show the meaning of these words.
[Teacher writes *praise, arrogant, good*. Students state the antonyms: *condemn, modesty, bad,* and the teacher writes them down on the board.]

T: Now, please use these words to make sentences. Remember, present them in a thorough way.

S: It is good to be praised. However, it would be bad if we became arrogant.

T: Good! Then what should we do after being praised?

S: The more praise we receive, the more modest we should be. We not only learn from criticism, we also appreciate praise.

T: You see, after learning these antonyms, we can tackle a problem thoroughly, and present our ideas meticulously. OK, we will stop here. I hope we have a good command of antonyms—helping us toward a detailed presentation; the more antonyms we master, the more complete will be our meaning. After school, please read the rest of this intellectual short essay, "Semantics 1," and mark the important sentences.

The Systematic Use of Variation in the Lesson

At the beginning of this chapter, we proposed that a systematic use of variation might be a specific feature of Chinese pedagogy, or at least of what is regarded as good teaching in China. The lesson "Semantics," which was taught by a state-selected expert teacher, exemplified that the teacher used variation systematically to create an optimal space of learning for the students.

There are several different patterns of variation–invariance in the lesson. For example, the story of Afanti highlighted a variation between word and meaning: that is, the concept that one word ("want") signifies two meanings ("keep" and "give") was illustrated by making the word ("want") invariant while varying the meanings ("keep" and "give"). This allowed students to discern a split between word and meaning (cf. "separation," mentioned in chap. 1). When introducing the concept of *synonyms*, the variation of word and meaning was used again. The concept of *synonyms* was highlighted by keeping the meaning (e.g., "see") invariant and varying the words used to refer to this meaning (e.g., "see," "look up," "glance at," "look down"), which allowed students to see that the same meaning could be represented by different words. By varying the relationship between word and meaning, students were guided to discern the complex relationship and also to discern the difference between homonyms and synonyms.

Homonyms:
    Variation   *Invariance*
    meaning   word

Synonyms:
    Variation   *Invariance*
    word   meaning

The awareness of the level of generality of words was highlighted by another set of variation, namely "books" as a category, and different types of books (e.g., Chinese book, reference book, and textbook). When the teacher guided students to compare the lexical meaning of "book" with categories that were within the scope of meaning of "book," students discerned that there were different levels of generality within the same category of words.

    Variation   *Invariance*
    level of generality   category ("books")

Another pattern of variation was used to illustrate the relationship between words and contexts. The teacher drew students' attention to different synonyms and their level of generality. This was done by keeping the words (the different synonyms) invariant and varying the contexts. Students' attention was drawn to focus on the match or mismatch between words and the different contexts, and they were also made aware of the importance of the usage of words in relation to the contexts. What is interesting is the way in which the teacher tried to simultaneously bring into the students' awareness what was covered in the previous episode, that is, a kind of word relation that pertained to levels of generality, and the critical semantic features of a word or a phrase.

Variation	Invariance
context	synonyms (i.e., one synonym at a time)

When the distinction between the synonyms was clarified by means of showing their appropriateness to one context but not to another, the teacher also demonstrated that the appropriate synonyms varied with context. This is an example of "fusion" as described in chapter 1 (i.e., fusion between synonym and context).

The teacher constructed the lesson coherently by means of correlated variation. The linguistic concepts in this lesson were not introduced discretely; but were closely linked together by the teacher's use of the same word as example or counterexample. For instance, the word "books" was used to illustrate concepts that have different but related meanings. It was also used to illustrate the difference between narrow and wide scope of meaning (Chinese book, reference book, and books, respectively). And in the latter part of the lesson concerning synonyms, the examples book, textbook, and Chinese book were referred to again, as a contrast to a new set of examples, pater, father, daddy, and papa, in order to illustrate that the latter shared the same scope of meaning. Likewise the word "want" was used in the story of Afanti to illustrate that the word meaning relation can be ambiguous, and was later used again as a counterexample of synonyms.

This analysis shows that the teacher used variation constantly and systematically to raise students' awareness of the richness of the meaning of words, as well as the higher order structure of words, such as homonyms, narrow–wide scope of meaning, specific–general meaning, synonyms, generic and specific reference, and antonyms.

ANOTHER THEORY OF VARIATION

In chapter 1, we presented a theory of learning that revolves around the concept of *variation*. In this chapter, we described two different examples of teaching carried out by Chinese teachers who both made pedagogically sophisticated use of variation. Basing our assessment on the aforementioned theory, both teachers are doing a good job and can be expected to make use of variation in pedagogically powerful ways. It should be noted that another theory of learning based on variation was presented long before our own, by a mathematics educator from Shanghai, Gu Lingyuan (Gu, 1991). Interestingly, unlike our theory, which was derived from our characterization of learning in the educational context, Gu developed his theory inductively by observing cases of good practice, that is, cases of teaching that resulted in good learning. So, in a way, Gu's theory of variation is itself a depiction of features of good Chinese pedagogy.

Gu's theory is more psychologically oriented than ours (which is an experiential theory), insofar as Gu is characterizing learning—notably the

2. VARIATION AND THE SECRET OF THE VIRTUOSO

learning of mathematics in terms of three consecutive, hierarchically organized levels of functioning, or educational goals. The following brief account of some parts of his theory is admittedly colored by the fact that one theory (Gu's) is here seen through the lenses of another theory (our own). What follows is our understanding of Gu's theory on the way in which the mastery of the levels of mathematical insights can be achieved by means of constituting different patterns of variation.

1. Understanding the Procedures or Principles

This section is about the ways in which it can be made possible for students to discern the critical features of a certain concept or principle. Due to the fact that Gu developed his theory within the field of geometry and only subsequently generalized it to other fields of mathematics and to other school subjects, we use the geometrical illustrations from Gu's original publication.

a. *Widening of the concept, by blocking out features erroneously assumed by students to be critical features of the concept.* For instance, students mostly think in terms of standard figures, tacitly (and erroneously) assuming that the differences between standard and nonstandard figures represent critical features (see Fig. 2.1).

In this case, the variation builds on the teacher's understanding of the students' understanding of the concept prior to the instructional sequence.

b. *Making it possible for the students to discern what is tacitly understood, by means of contrasting noninstances.* Figure 2.2 is an example.

c. *Making it possible for the students to make distinctions between cases that they treat as members of the same set.* Here, contrasting cases are intro-

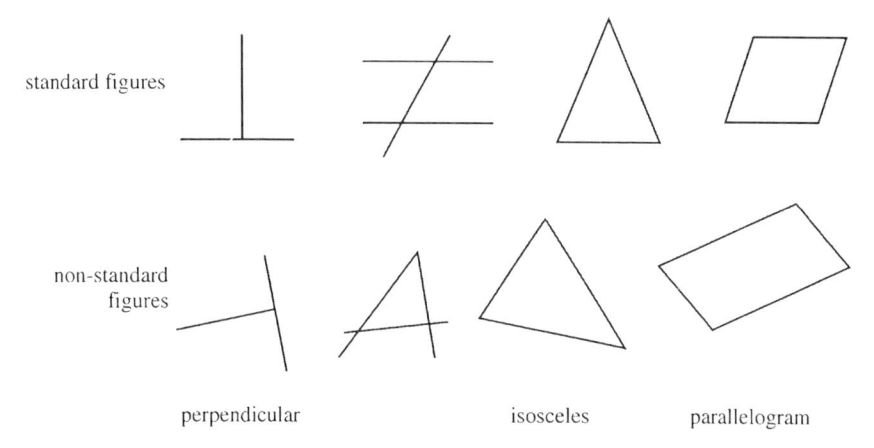

FIG. 2.1. Distinguishing between essential and nonessential features by contrasting standard and nonstandard figures. From L. Gu (1991), *Xuehui Jiaoxue* [Learning to teach], p. 68. Beijing, PRC: People's Education Press. Copyright © 1991 by Gu Ling Yuan. Reprinted with permission.

duced in order to make the distinctions possible. Two examples are shown in Fig. 2.3.

All three of these different ways of contributing to make it possible for the students to discern the critical features of the concept or principle in question, presuppose that the teacher has a good understanding of the students' preconceived ideas and of their habitual ways of dealing with the concept. The first pattern of variation corresponds to *generalization* and the two other patterns to *contrast* as defined in chapter 1.

2. Understanding the Process of Forming the Procedures or Principles

This section has to do with Gu's observation that students frequently have difficulties discerning the figure–ground structure of geometric forms, that is, with the question of discernment of wholes and parts of particular instances rather than the discernment of features across instances. This is very much like the discernment (or delimitation) of the deer and its parts discussed in chapter 1.

The distinction between the discernment of features and the discernment (or delimitation) of parts and wholes reminds us that the latter was introduced by Svensson (1976) to characterize differences in the understanding of the same text. (Svensson argued that readers differ as to how they delimit the wholes and parts and therefore make different senses of the same text.)

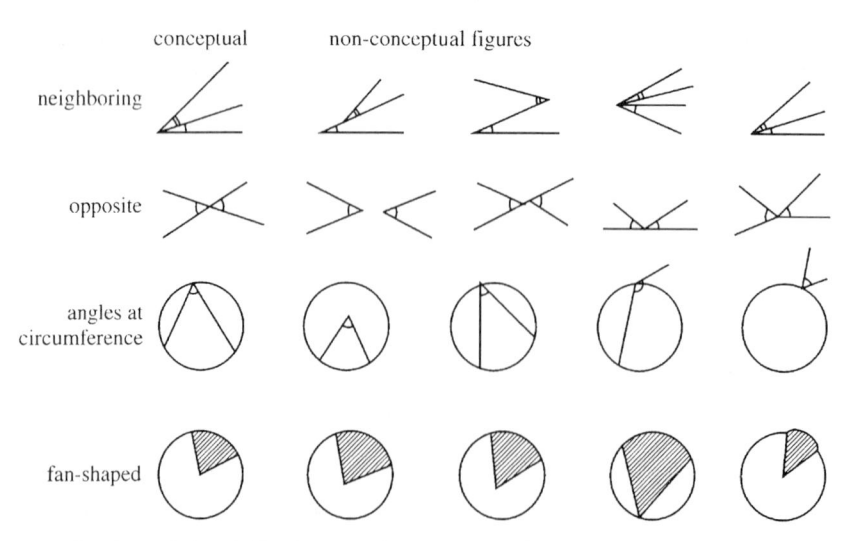

FIG. 2.2. Distinguishing between the presence and absence of essential features by contrasting conceptual and nonconceptual figures. From L. Gu (1991), *Xuehui Jiaoxue* [Learning to teach], p. 69. Beijing, PRC: People's Education Press. Copyright © 1991 by Gu Ling Yuan. Reprinted with permission.

2. VARIATION AND THE SECRET OF THE VIRTUOSO 59

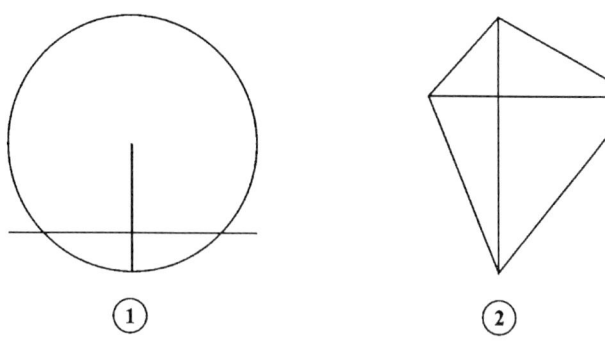

① Is the line perpendicular to the radius of the circle, a tangent of that circle?

② Is a quadrilateral with two perpendicular diagonals a rhombus?

FIG. 2.3. Focusing on essential features by omitting them. From L. Gu (1991), *Xuehui Jiaoxue* [Learning to teach], p. 70. Beijing, PRC: People's Education Press. Copyright © 1991 by Gu Ling Yuan. Reprinted with permission.

This distinction between the two forms of discernment is discussed in more detail in chapter 3.

The kind of variation that Gu proposes to make it possible for the students to discern the part–whole (and figure–ground) structure, is the transformation of the same figure through rotation and otherwise (see Fig. 2.4).

The students can in this way discern how complex figures are comprised of simple figures. Another example can be seen in Fig. 2.5.

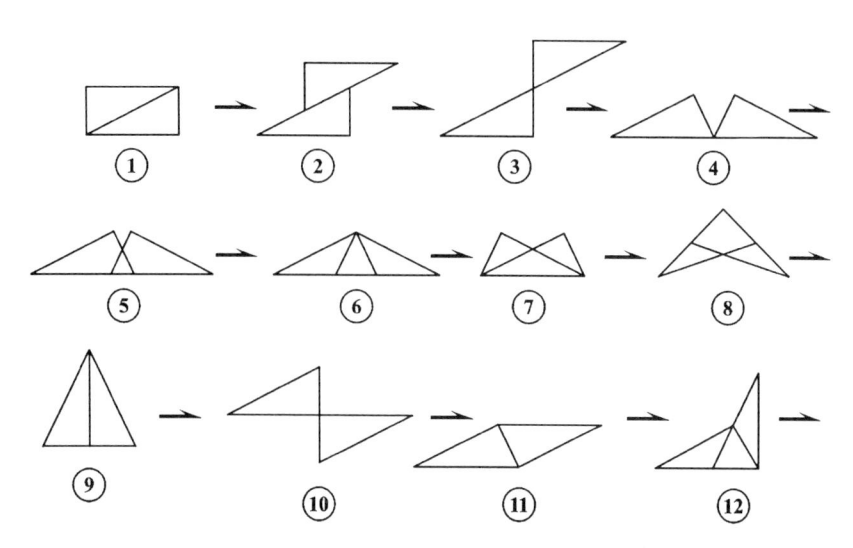

FIG. 2.4. Separating geometrical targets from complex backgrounds by variation. From L. Gu (1991), *Xuehui Jiaoxue* [Learning to teach], p. 73. Beijing, PRC: People's Education Press. Copyright © 1991 by Gu Ling Yuan. Reprinted with permission.

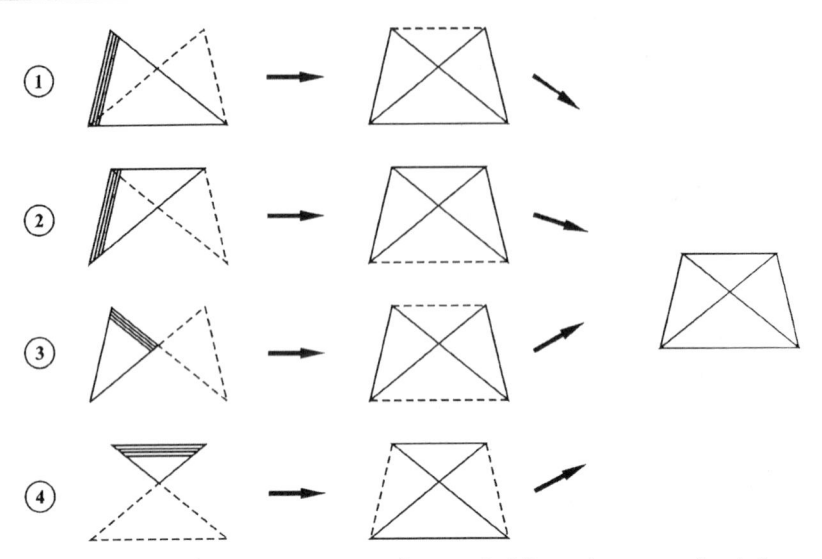

FIG. 2.5. Separating component parts of geometrical figures by structural variation. From L. Gu (1991), *Xuehui Jiaoxue* [Learning to teach], p. 74. Beijing, PRC: People's Education Press. Copyright © 1991 by Gu Ling Yuan. Reprinted with permission.

3. Discovering New Procedures and Principles by the Students Themselves

This is the third form of variation in the sense that here the students produce variation, or open their minds to variation (rather than encountering variation), within constrains posed by questions. This type of variation is illustrated in chapter 3, when we look at the open-ended problem of "the postman's route."

VARIATION WITH REPETITION—THE FEATURE OF GOOD TEACHING IN CHINA

Until recently, teaching in mainland China was mostly described as conservative, textbook-oriented, and characterized by teacher-centered rote learning (e.g., Cleverley, 1985; Seybolt, 1973). Some researchers, such as Leung (1991), claimed that the conservative features mainly stemmed from two traditions: the Confucian pedagogical tradition, and the Soviet mode of instruction. This resulted in a hybrid pattern of teaching and learning that was more or less textbook-based, teacher-centered, and content-overloaded. The predominance of drilling and repetition in Chinese classrooms suggested that Chinese teachers believed that repetition skill development should precede interpretation (Gardner 1989).

2. VARIATION AND THE SECRET OF THE VIRTUOSO

Some studies, as represented by Paine's (1990) work, described the distinctive teaching practice in modern China as being a "virtuoso model"—hence the title of this chapter. In China, direct whole-group instruction and teacher talk were found to be prevalent in classrooms. Paine (1990) observed that "It is this flair—a special timing, an elegance of language, a power of expression—that distinguishes the great teacher from the ordinary one" (p. 69).

She recognized the shortcomings of this model in the sense that the teacher plays an active role whereas the students have a passive role; the teacher is the actor, the students the audience. She comments that

> Although teachers in China frequently voiced concern about reaching the students academically, the literature and interviews with teachers suggest that the main intellectual thrust of teaching centers on the teachers' performance and minimizes or inadvertently neglects the interactional potential of classroom experience. Adapting teaching to particular audiences, though clearly the mark of a good teacher, is not a necessary requirement of the fine classroom performer, given the dominant conception of the teacher's role. (Paine, 1990, p. 68)

However, Paine admits that despite the negative implication of this model, the emphasis on teaching as a virtuoso performance incorporated both a recognition of the importance of knowledge and an acknowledgment of the role of personal, humanistic qualities of aesthetics, affection, and commitment in teaching.

Cheng (1992) had similar views on the practice of teaching in China, and used the metaphor of "drama" to describe it:

> Sometimes, I think, to teach a lesson in China is to be like an actor performing a drama. Everything should be planned in detail; every action should follow the script. There is no room for any mistakes. The lesson plan is just like the script of a drama. (p. 107, in Chinese, our translation)

Cheng (1992) believed that the emphasis on strict lesson planning may have an undesirable effect, as it reduces the opportunities for students to contribute to the planning of the lesson. However, Cheng points out that the emphasis on serious lesson planning reflects the conscientious attitude of teachers in China that contributes to maintaining the quality of the teaching profession in the country.

It should be noted that there is also other—mostly more recent—literature that portrays the Chinese classroom as interactive and effective. These works argue that the whole-class instruction method commonly found in Chinese classrooms allows each child to have the maximum opportunity to benefit from the teacher, and to enhance conceptual understanding; and that it is this that contributes to the excellent performance of Chinese students in international academic campaigns (Stevenson & Lee, 1997). These researchers have also found that Chinese classrooms are active, and that students participate in thought-provoking tasks or questioning (Cortazzi 1998; Cortazzi & Jin, 2001). Some researchers are also interested in tracing the historical origin of some of the distinctive perceptions of teaching and learning in Chinese classrooms. They identify the impact of Confucian views of teaching and learning on education in China and some other East Asian countries, as the Confucian-heritage-culture (CHC) learner phenomenon (e.g., Biggs, 1996; Ho, 1991). These researchers try to associate some of the dominant learning approaches adopted by students in the East Asian countries with the Confucian culture. They point out that although Chinese classrooms are apparently full of rote learning, the repetition is used by the learners as a means to enhance understanding. These researchers argue that the emphasis on repetition and memorization should not simply be dismissed as conservative, as Chinese teachers also emphasize recitation with reflection, and memorization with understanding (Biggs, 1996; Lee, 1996).

By using a combination of the variation theory of learning presented in chapter 1, and Gu's theory of variation as a conceptual framework, Huang (2002) recently characterized mathematics teaching in China (more precisely in Shanghai) as being both highly teacher-centered and highly student-centered (if we use "teacher-centered" in the sense of the enacted object of learning being close to the intended object of learning, and "student-centered" in the sense of the students owning the space of learning, that is, that they participate in bringing it about). Those lessons that are considered to be good in China are planned, choreographed, and well thought-out lessons. But their elaborate design nevertheless still offers plenty of space for the students' own independent and spontaneous ideas. The students are highly active and they pay attention to the teacher. In a similar way, the teacher, having thoroughly orchestrated the lesson, can fully focus on the various ideas the students come up with. By using her previous experiences and her knowledge of the ways that the students often think about the specific objects of learning, the teacher is able to anticipate what the students are going to come up with spontaneously. The mathematics lesson from a Shanghai classroom described in chapter 3, is another example of this way of teaching. As we already mentioned, Paine (1990) argued that in the Chinese classroom, the teacher is the performing actor whereas the students make up the passive audience. A more accurate metaphor would be, we believe, to see the teacher as the director, and the students as the actors playing in accordance with a script that they have never seen.

3

Discernment and the Question, "What Can Be Learned?"

Ulla Runesson
Ida A. C. Mok

In chapter 2, the primary focus was on variation. In this chapter, the focus is mainly on *discernment*. In accordance with the theory put forward in chapter 1, we argue that a certain way of learning, of understanding or "seeing" a particular phenomenon, means that certain critical features must be discerned and held in our awareness simultaneously. Hence, the possibility for the learner to discern or focus on these features is a necessary condition for learning something in a certain way. We illustrate this theory using different examples from mathematics lessons.

DISCERNMENT, EXPERIENCE, AND MEANING

In chapter 1, examples were given that illustrated how different professionals must pay attention or must be sensitive to certain aspects of a situation in order to handle the situation in a certain way. The ability to handle a situation could be described in terms of the way in which the situation is seen or experienced; in other words, the origin of powerful ways of acting is powerful ways of seeing.

The way in which a situation is seen or experienced depends on the features of the situation that are discerned. In every situation, we can attend to all the different aspects of the situation. However, this is not what happens. We do not attend to all these aspects and we do not attend to them at the same time. Instead, we pay particular attention to some aspects—that is, some features of the situation are discerned, whereas others are not. The features that we discern are in the fore of our attention, or put differently, they are held in our focal awareness; and they are held in our awareness at the same time. We can say therefore, that a certain way of experiencing could be characterized in terms of the aspects that are discerned simultaneously.

The particular way in which the individual experiences a situation—or a phenomenon—is the way the individual understands it. Experiencing implies experiencing the object as something, thus experiencing a meaning. When we use the concept *a way of experiencing something* and describe how something is experienced, we describe the meaning that this something has for the individual. That which appears to be the same thing could have a different meaning for different individuals. It could also have different meanings for the same individual at different times. What meaning it has for the individual could be understood in terms of which aspects of the object are discerned and held in the focal awareness simultaneously. One way of experiencing implies the simultaneous discernment of certain features, whereas another way of experiencing implies the simultaneous discernment of other features.

We learn to experience by discerning aspects of the object to which we direct our awareness. In order to gain a certain understanding of a phenomenon, we must be able to discern certain critical features. Following this line of reasoning, if we, as educators, want our students to gain a particular way of understanding, or to develop a particular capability, we must make it possible for them to discern features that are critical for that particular learning.

DISCERNING CRITICAL FEATURES OF WHAT IS TAUGHT

What do we mean by *critical features*? And how can different ways of handling these critical features in the learning situation provide different possibilities for learning? Learning what a square is—and what it is not—for instance, takes the discernment of the critical features of that geometrical shape. Consequently, if the teacher aims at making the learner understand what a square is, he or she must start with what it takes to know and recognize the critical features of a square, in order to make learning possible. In this case, the critical features are the size of the angles, the number of sides, and the relations between them, and it must be possible for the learners to discern these features. However, simply pointing out these critical features to the learners is not enough.

We illustrate this point with a thought experiment. Let us imagine two different classrooms with two different teachers, both intending to help their students learn what a square is. They both talk about the characteristics of a square and refer to a picture of a square. In that respect the lessons are similar. But let us imagine that the first teacher simply points to the angles, stating that they are four right angles; points to the four sides, show-

3. DISCERNMENT AND "WHAT CAN BE LEARNED?" 65

ing the relation between the sides (i.e., equal); and finally gives a definition of a square. The second teacher similarly points out—or focuses on—the angles, the sides and the relation between them, but also introduces a variation of these aspects. For instance, she draws a picture of a rhombus beside the square and draws the students' attention to the difference between the angles of the square and the angles of the rhombus respectively. Next she compares the number of sides in a square with the number of sides in a triangle. In the same way, she contrasts the relation between the opposite sides of a square and a rectangle. Finally, the teacher points to squares of different sizes.

If we take a closer look at how that which was taught was handled, and what it was possible to learn, we find that the same critical features of the square were focused on in both lessons (angles, number of sides, and the relation between them). However, whereas the second teacher indicated that the size of the angles, the number of sides, and the relation between the sides could be different between what is a square and what is not a square, her counterpart did not. In this way, a variation of the critical features was brought to the attention of the students by means of contrasts. The teacher also gave examples of different squares (i.e., squares with different area). In this way, the geometrical shape was constant, but the size of the shape was varied. In the lesson taught by the first teacher, however, such variation was not introduced. It was not possible for the learners to experience the fact that the size of an angle could vary. Neither was it possible for them to experience the fact that the same shape could have different sizes, but still be called a square.

According to the theoretical framework laid down in chapter 1, that which varies is likely to be discerned. For instance, it is necessary to know what a right angle is not, in order to learn what it actually is. And it takes the experience of (at least) two different examples of squares (i.e., variation of the area) to understand what a square is. So, in other words, the space of variation afforded or constituted—partly with the learners—is critical for the possibility to discern these critical features. A certain pattern of variation is necessary for a certain learning to happen. So, in answer to the question, "How can learning best be promoted for my students?," we would say, "Take as your point of departure the capabilities you want them to develop. What do you want your students to learn? What is critical for this learning and for this way of understanding? Make it possible for the learners to discern those features that are critical for that learning."

However, we must stress that we are not saying that what is taught is necessarily what is learned by the students. From our point of view, there is no causality between teaching and learning. That is, there is no guarantee that a particular learning will take place simply because teachers act in a certain way, or structure the learning situation in a particular way. But, what teachers can accomplish is to create the possibility of learning something in a certain way. It is not possible to say conclusively how the teacher affects what students learn simply by looking at the way in which the teacher teaches the lesson. However, it is possible to say what students are afforded to learn in that particular learning situation to account for differences in possibilities for learning, and to show how these are reflected in what students actually learn.

STUDENTS' ACHIEVEMENTS AND POSSIBILITIES FOR LEARNING

In 1992, Stevenson and Stigler published some remarkable findings in their book, *The Learning Gap*. These findings indicated more or less that previous speculations—that is, that a learner's achievement is affected by differences in what it is possible to discern—seemed to be correct. In two studies, Stevenson and Stigler (1992) compared achievement in mathematics in primary Grade 1 and primary Grade 5 students from a number of schools in Sendai, Taipei, and Minneapolis; and in Sendai, Taipei, Beijing, and Chicago, respectively. Although the American students already seriously lagged behind the Asian students in primary Grade 1, by the time they reached primary Grade 5, the gap had widened so much that there was basically no overlap; the performance in the best American schools was weaker than the performance in the weakest of the Asian schools.

Several other comparative studies (e.g., the Third International Mathematics and Science Study [TIMSS], 1999; see Mullis et al., 2000) have demonstrated that Japanese students, and Chinese students from Hong Kong and Taiwan, do much better in mathematics than American students.

There were serious attempts to account for such differences. One of these was the TIMSS-video study, in which a great number of mathematics lessons in Germany, Japan, and the United States were recorded and intensely scrutinized. Stigler and Hiebert followed up *The Learning Gap* (Stevenson & Stigler, 1992) by publishing their book, *The Teaching Gap*, in 1999 (Stigler & Hiebert, 1999). Their way of describing the typical Japanese lesson and the typical American lesson offers a potential explanation of the observed differences in achievement between Japanese and American students.

In a typical Japanese lesson, after having reviewed the previous lesson, the teacher introduces the problem of the day: a problem complex enough to be used as a framework for the entire lesson and for elaborating different ideas and procedures. As a rule, the students first work on the problem individually and in a number of different ways, and then continue the work in groups. Eventually different groups present their solutions and these are compared. The teacher—and the students as well—comment on the strength and weaknesses of different approaches. Finally, the teacher summarizes the work and points to the most powerful ideas that have come up during the lesson.

In a typical American lesson, the teacher also starts by reviewing the previous lesson. Then the teacher may introduce definitions, terms and, above all, a method for solving a certain kind of problem. After the demonstration, the students are given a relatively large number of problems of the same kind to practice on. After they have practiced these, another type of problem may be introduced. The method for solving this kind of problem is demonstrated by the teacher, and the students are given a further set of problems of this other kind to practice on.

Mathematics lessons in China have been described in similar terms as Stigler and Hiebert described the Japanese lesson (see Stevenson & Stigler, 1992). And to a certain extent, it would be true to say that the differences just illustrated could potentially provide an explanation of the differences in achievement between Asian and American students.

If we simplify things somewhat, we can argue that an important difference between Chinese and Japanese mathematics lessons on one hand, and American lessons on the other, is that in the former, the students mostly face one problem to which they are asked to find different solutions, whereas in the latter, the students are presented with one method for solving one kind of problem, which they then practice by solving different problems of the same kind.

In each case, the students were afforded different possibilities for what could be learned. In one type of lesson, students were given the possibility to learn how to find solutions to a problem, whereas in the other, they were afforded the possibility to learn how to make use of a particular solution.

In these studies, comparisons were made using lessons with different mathematical contents. Thus, the comparison was made on a general level. In the following example, two lessons that aimed to teach the same specific content are compared in relation to what was possible to learn.

LEARNING THE OPERATOR ASPECT OF THE FRACTIONAL CONCEPT

Runesson (1999) studied five mathematics lessons, all teaching fractional numbers and percentages. In many respects, the lessons were very similar. For instance, four of them used the same textbook, and the classroom work was organized in a very similar way. The aim of Runesson's study was to investigate the various ways in which teachers handle content, in this case, fractional numbers and percentages. Let us take a closer look at two of the teachers.

In both lessons, the content being taught was the operator aspect of the fractional concept (e.g., how to find 1/3 of 12). In both cases, the discussion took place in a whole-class setting. The lessons were audiorecorded and transcribed verbatim. The dialogue is presented alongside our analysis:

3.1 [Mathematics Lesson / Fractions/ Secondary Grade 1]
Teacher A

T: OK. Here I have a piece of string. It's 90 centimeters long. [Teacher holds up a piece of string] Three people have to share that equally. How do you go about that? Fair share? Tell me, Sylvia.

The teacher introduces the problem. A manipulative aid is used. A strategy for solving the problem (1/3 of 90) is introduced.

S1: Well ... divide by three.

T: Yeah, each one will get a third. But let's say one of them wants to have more than the others. The string is still 90 centimeters long and I want 2/3. How could we figure that out? 2/3 of a piece of string that is 90 centimeters long? Thomas?

The nominator is changed; 1/3 is changed to 2/3 (2/3 of 90).

S2: [inaudible]

T: Right. First you figure out the length of a third and then take another one ... and together that makes ... ? What did you say? 60 centimeters? Yes. So, first you have to figure out the length of 1/3. Measure that, and then take another one. [The teacher first marks 1/3, then 2/3 of the whole length of the string].

The teacher elucidates the strategy and illustrates with the manipulative aid. (1/3 of 90 = 90/3 = 30)

T: OK. Let's take a look at this piece of string. [The teacher is holding up a shorter piece of string] This is only 40 centimeters long. I would like to have one fifth of 40 centimeters. [Writing on the blackboard: 1/5 of 40 cm]

A new problem (1/5 of 40) is introduced. A manipulative aid is used.

Written representation

3. DISCERNMENT AND "WHAT CAN BE LEARNED?" 69

S2:	8 centimeters.	
T:	Yes, each fifth is 8 centimeters. But let's say we want 3/5. How do you figure that out? Tell me, Lisa.	*The nominator is changed (3/5 of 40). The teacher asks for an appropriate strategy.*
S3:	Three times 8.	
T:	OK. First we must figure out how much 1/5 is. So, you divide 40 by 5, and you get 8. And three fifths must be three times as much. Three such pieces. That's 24. But let's say that the piece of string is 60 centimeters instead. [Writes 60 cm on the board]. One of you should have 3/5, and another one 2/5. How much will the person who gets 3/5 have? ... OK. How do we go about this? The whole piece of string is 60. I should have 3/5, then I must figure something out first, what ... ? Martin.	*The teacher elucidates the strategy.*

The whole is changed (3/5 of 60). Written representation

The teacher asks for the appropriate strategy. |
S4:	5 divided by 60	
T:	Well, now you said it the other way around—60 divided by 5. What's that?	
S5:	12	
T:	OK. 12. So now we know that 1/5 is 12. Then how much is 3/5?	

If we analyze this data in terms of the aspects focused on, it is apparent that the focus was on the strategy for solving the problem (i.e., calculating the length of a fractional part of a piece of string). This is the aspect that the teacher tried to draw the students' attention to. But only one strategy or procedure was presented, and hence the strategy was not varied. This particular aspect was focused on, but was kept invariant. However, the teacher did change the parameters in the problem. After introducing the first problem and presenting an appropriate solving strategy, the teacher changed the length of the piece of string (i.e., the whole) as well as the size of the fractional part (1/5 of

40). In the following example, the numerator was changed (3/5 of 40), and finally in the last example, the whole (i.e., the length of the string) was changed. Thus, the strategy was invariant, while the numbers varied in a systematic way. (1/3 of 90, 2/3 of 90, 1/5 of 40, 3/5 of 40, 3/5 of 60)

Let us now contrast this approach with that of Teacher B, whose teaching also dealt with the operator aspect of fractional numbers. The day before this lesson, the students had been working on a particular problem in which they had to mark 3/7 of a rectangle with a size of 7 × 8 squares, as shown in Fig. 3.1.

3.2 [Mathematics/Fractions/Primary Grade 6]

Teacher B

	The rectangle is shown on an OHT. To begin with the teacher asks Lena to tell the class how she marked 3/7 of the rectangle.	*A manipulative aid is used.*
S1:	If you just take seven squares from the whole, and then take three of those ... If you count "one, two, three," and mark them.	*In each group of seven squares, three are marked.*
T:	Why?	*The teacher asks for an argument.*
S1:	Well it is 3/7 of the small pile. And then I continue: one, two, three, four, five, six, seven, go on like that. I keep counting to seven and marking three of them.	*The student is explaining her strategy.*

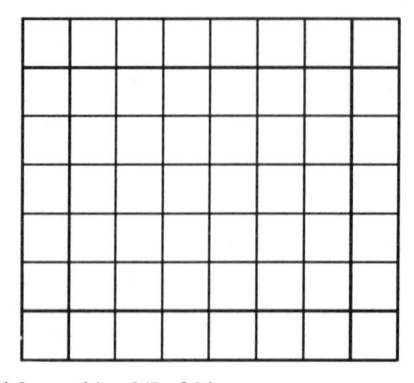

FIG. 3.1. The grid for marking 3/7 of 56.

3. DISCERNMENT AND "WHAT CAN BE LEARNED?" 71

T:	Oh yeah. I understand! You counted one, two, three, four, five six, seven, and then you marked three of them. And then one, two, three, four, five, six, seven, and you marked them. In other words, you do it like this [pointing at the projection on the board] one, two, three, four, five, six, seven. You can mark the last ones like that. How do you go on? In the same way?	*The teacher elucidates Lena's strategy.* *A manipulative aid is used.*
S1:	Yes.	
T:	Well did anyone do it differently? Did you all do it like that?	*The teacher asks for alternative strategies.*
Ss:	No.	
T:	Well what about you ... Sophie?	
S2:	Well, I just divided it into seven parts.	*Another student explains her strategy, which is different from the previous one.*
T:	OK. You just counted all the squares and divided them into seven. OK, Maria what about you?	*The teacher asks for alternative strategies.*
S3:	Well I tried different numbers like that until I got seven parts.	*Yet another student explains her strategy, which is different from the previous one.*

Here, Teacher B focused on the solving strategy in a similar way to Teacher A. Thus, the focused aspects were the same in both lessons. But, we can observe that Teacher B asked the students to come up with different solving strategies to the same problem (3/7 of 56). The variation in the students' solving strategies was made explicit when the teacher asked: "Did you all do it like that?" The students' responses showed that they had come up with different ways of solving the problem. Lena solved the problem by counting seven squares in each column and then marking three of them. Sophie divided the 56 squares into seven parts (and multiplied six by three). And finally, Maria tried different numbers, which multiplied by three equals

56. So, in B's lesson, the solving strategy varied, whereas the parameters of the problem were the same (i.e., 3/7 of 56), and hence were invariant.

The different ways in which the students chose to solve the problem imply that they had different interpretations of the operator aspect of fractional numbers. The way that Lena solved the problem implies that she interpreted 3/7 of 56 squares by arranging the 56 squares into groups of seven and then taking three out of seven in each group (stretcher/shrinker interpretation; Behr, Harel, Post, & Lesh, 1993) as illustrated in Fig. 3.2.

The other two strategies both imply another interpretation, namely dividing 56 squares into seven groups and then taking three groups out of the seven groups (duplicator/partition-reducer interpretation) as illustrated in Fig. 3.3.

In Lesson B, the variation in solving strategies that were presented by and to the students also involved a variation in the semantic interpretation of the operator aspect of fractional numbers. Thus, in this situation, a variation of the semantic interpretation of the concept was introduced.

Now let us take a close look at the two lessons. What is the main difference between the two teachers' ways of dealing with the same content (a

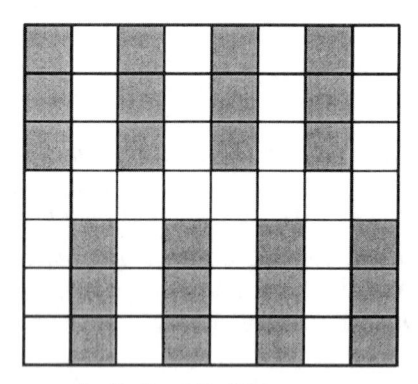

FIG. 3.2. Lena's strategy for finding 3/7 of 56.

FIG. 3.3. Another student's strategy for finding 3/7 of 56.

3. DISCERNMENT AND "WHAT CAN BE LEARNED?"   **73**

strategy for solving a/b of c)? Teacher A introduced a method for computing the fraction of an integer that basically involved dividing the integer by the denominator and multiplying the quotient by the nominator. This method was first applied to one problem, then to another, and finally to a third, that is, the method was the same but the problems differed.

Teacher B offered the students one problem only but invited them to find different ways of solving it. Three different students found three different ways of solving the same problem. Hence, the problem was invariant but the solving strategy varied. This was the opposite of what we observed in the case of teacher A, where the method was invariant and the problem varied. A comparison of the two lessons is illustrated in Table 3.1.

From Table 3.1, it is apparent that there is a systematic difference in the aspects that the two teachers varied and those they kept invariant. Some aspects varied in one lesson, whereas they were invariant in the other and vice versa. In the first case (Teacher A), we find a variation in the algorithmic solution, whereas in the second case (Teacher B), there is a variation in the semantic interpretations of fraction numbers as operator.

Seeing the two lessons in terms of possibilities for discernment (i.e., what might be discerned), the two lessons are also different; different numbers are plugged into the formula in one lesson, and different ways of interpreting and solving the problem, in the other lesson.

Focused Aspects and Dimensions of Variation

For every aspect of the object of learning, there is a corresponding dimension of variation. By that we mean that a particular aspect could be something different. For instance, in the examples just cited, the calculation a/b of c could be done in different ways, and thus the calculation corresponds to a dimension of variation in the solving strategies. One way of solving the problem is a "value" in the dimension of solving strategies, whereas another way of solving is another "value" in the same dimension. When

TABLE 3.1
The Space of Variation Constituted in Lesson A and Lesson B, Respectively

	Teacher A	*Teacher B*
Solving strategy	Invariant	Varied
Parameters of operation	Varied	Invariant
Representation	Varied	Invariant
Students' understanding	Invariant	Varied
Semantic interpretation	Invariant	Varied

studying the lessons from the point of view of how the "enacted object of learning" is constituted, we find that the aspect focused on in each lesson is varied and we describe that in terms of the opening of a dimension of variation of that particular aspect. For instance, in Lesson B, where the focus was on the solving strategy, and different solving strategies were demonstrated, a dimension of that aspect (i.e., methods of solving) was opened. In addition, we saw that the teacher presented different interpretations of the concept and different ways of understanding, and thus that these aspects were also opened as dimensions of variation. In other words, the solving strategies, the interpretation of the concept, and the students' understanding were dimensions of variation that were all opened in Lesson B. In Lesson A, other aspects varied (i.e., the parameters of operation and representation), and therefore other dimensions of variation were opened (see Table 3.1). Thus, the spaces of variation constituted in the lessons were different.

DISCERNING PARTS AND WHOLES

So far in this chapter, we have discussed how different aspects or features of an object of learning are discerned. But the object of learning is always situated in a context, and it has to be discerned from that particular context in order to relate it to other contexts and to other instances and by doing so discern its features. Furthermore, the object of learning is a whole and, as a rule, distinct parts within it can be discerned. These parts can also be described in terms of their features, their relations to each other and to the whole, and in terms of their parts.

In chapter 1, reference was made to Svensson (1976) who stated that the entities, or the phenomenon (we would say the object of learning) we encounter must be delimited (i.e., discerned) by the subject and they can be delimited (or discerned) in different ways. Such differences account partly for the reason why we all see things differently. The example given in chapter 1 was the deer in the forest, but these differences are present in all cases when somebody is learning something. In the examples given in this chapter, we can also see that mathematical problems in the classroom have to be discerned from the context. At very least, the students must be able to distinguish between when the particular problem is discussed and when something else is talked about. Furthermore, if the problem is the whole, there are generally also parts that can be identified, such as separate arithmetic operations, and the meanings that derive from the problem.

Let us look again at the cited example, in which two distinctively different ways of dealing with the operator aspect of the fractional concept were described. According to the methods used in the first example (Lesson A) the students could identify and learn to use an algorithm for the calculation a/b of c, by carrying out the division c/b and thus obtaining $1/b$ of c, and then multiplying by b to obtain a/b. There were four subproblems:

	Answer
1. 2/3 of 90	30
2. 1/5 of 40	8
3. 3/5 of 40	24
4. 3/5 of 60	36

When dealing with this particular kind of problem, the students had to delimit this sequence from the context of the lesson. By doing so, they became potentially capable of relating it to similar kinds of problems in the future. The sequence could then be considered as a part of the lesson, but also as a whole in which the four subproblems could be discerned as parts. Within the subproblems, the three kinds of components—numerator, denominator, and the whole—could be discerned and related to each other within the same subproblem, or to corresponding parts within other subproblems.

As we show in the first example in chapter 4, this process of delimitation also applies to the process of reading a text. When reading texts, the way in which the reader delimits the whole and the parts, and relates them to each other is of vital importance for understanding.

LEARNING ABOUT PROBLEM SOLVING—THE POSTMAN'S ROUTE

The second main data set to be used in this chapter is "the postman's route," which gives a further illustration of the thesis presented in chapter 2. In the Chinese lesson that we describe, the teacher carefully planned the lesson and followed the lesson plan accordingly. We first present a summary of the lesson followed by an analysis.

Summary of the Lesson

This lesson was a demonstration lesson conducted at the National Conference for Open-Ended Questions held in Shanghai in November, 1998 (the data was discussed in Mok, 2000, 2002). Demonstration lessons, in which an expert teacher is invited to teach a class in front of an audience, are a common practice in schools in the People's Republic of China. The classroom was a room much larger than a normal classroom. The front section of the room had the normal classroom setting with a teacher's podium, and the back section was lined with about 50 chairs for the audience. For the demonstration lesson under discussion here, the audience was made up of participants of the National Conference. Despite the demonstration nature of the lesson, it was a real 40-min. primary Grade 4 lesson, conducted during the normal school timetable. There were 28 students and they sat in groups of four. Before the lesson, the teacher gave the audience a one-page lesson plan. It was stated in the plan that the objectives of the lesson were to develop students' problem-solving strategies by solving a postman's problem, and to develop students' creativity and divergent thinking via problem solving. In the lesson plan, it was explicitly stated that the teacher would approach the problem by asking students to design routes for the postman in a real-life context. Following this, the teacher would help students to consider the problem in a mathematical context, by asking them to look for regularities exhibited in the routes that they had come up with, and to think about the possible transformation of the shapes. (The routes became shapes once the direction arrows were taken away.) To begin with, the teacher explained the problem by holding up a sample worksheet (see Fig. 3.4). Here is a translation of the problem statement that was shown on the blackboard and explained by the teacher verbally:

> There are nine dots on the paper. The dot surrounded by a triangle in the left upper corner represents the post office. The postman needs to start at the post office deliver a letter to each of the eight places, and return to the post office. What could be the postman's route?

The lesson consisted of four phases in which the teacher helped the students to tackle the problem according to the lesson plan. The four parts are now illustrated:

Part 1: Students Designing Their Own Routes. The teacher asked the students to work in groups and experiment with as many routes as possible. Each student designed his/her own route on the pieces of paper provided by the teacher, and the designs of all group members were put in a pile. The students were very efficient and only talked with their neighbors occasionally. When they had finished all the papers on their desks, they raised their hands for more. The activity lasted about 10 min.

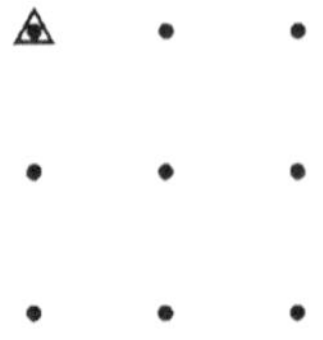

FIG. 3.4. The worksheet.

3. DISCERNMENT AND "WHAT CAN BE LEARNED?" 77

Part 2: Evaluating Their Own Designs Selectively. During this phase, the teacher resumed the attention of the whole class. She posted some of their designs on the blackboard and asked the class to judge whether the designs were correct. One group produced 18 designs and the teacher asked the students to discuss with their group members whether this group's designs were correct (see Fig. 3.5).

After the discussion, the whole class agreed that all of the designs were correct. Then the teacher pointed to a faulty design produced by another group, and asked whether it was correct (see Fig. 3.6).

The students pointed out that the arrows were missing from this design, and that there was no indication of how the postman could return to the post office. Following this, the teacher asked the class to think of ways to determine which design was the best. After a few exchanges of ideas between the class and the teacher, they agreed that the shortest route was the best. Then the teacher guided the class to compare the number of straight and diagonal

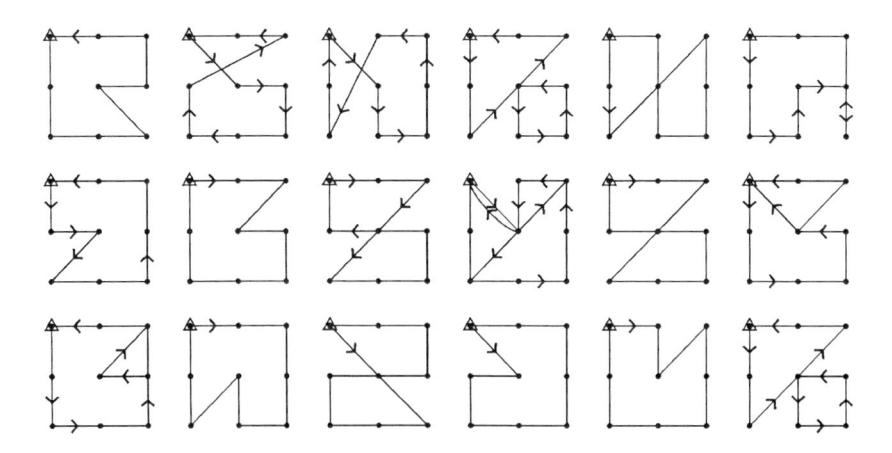

FIG. 3.5. The 18 routes.

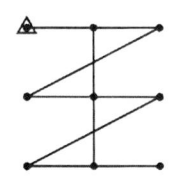

FIG. 3.6. The wrong route.

segments in the designs, and to determine the shortest route based on this information (see Fig. 3.7). The teacher removed the longer routes, leaving seven on the board.

Part 3: Group Interchange in Order to Supplement Additional Best Routes.
After this, the teacher asked the students to supply more of the shortest routes from their own piles of designs. They handed in 5 more, which made a total of 12 on the blackboard. The teacher guided the class to remove the repetitions and to disregard the arrows. Eventually only 8 designs remained on the board (see Fig. 3.8).

Straight segments	Diagonal segments
8	1
8	2
8	2
7	2

FIG. 3.7. The four patterns and the number of line segments.

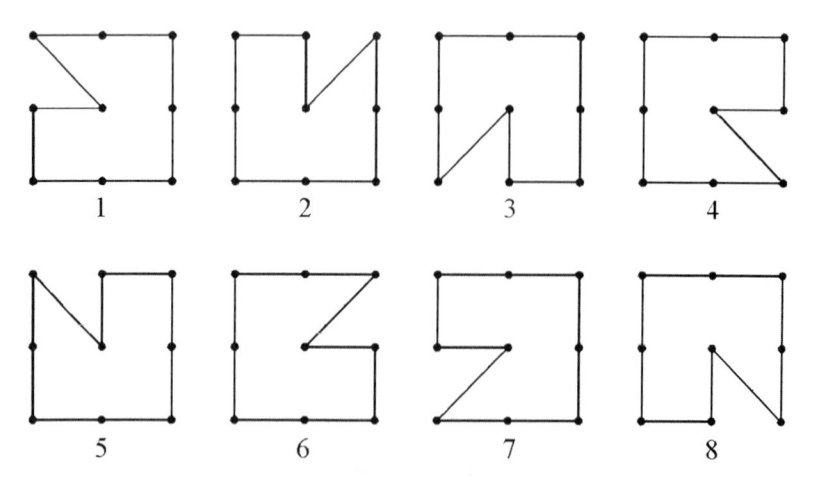

FIG. 3.8. The 8 patterns after neglecting the arrows. Note that (1) has the missing part facing left whereas (2) has the missing part facing up.

3. DISCERNMENT AND "WHAT CAN BE LEARNED?"

Part 4: Converting a Practical Problem Into the Mathematical Problem of Categorizing the Routes According to Their Shapes. Once the arrows were discarded, the designs of the routes became geometric shapes. In this part of the lesson, the teacher asked the students to categorize the shapes according to the way they saw the relationship between them. There were very lively class discussions, and the students gave a lot of suggestions, such as how to rotate the shapes (see Fig. 3.9) or flip them over (see Fig. 3.10).

Consequently, the students had different ideas about the number of categories, for example, infinity, 2, 8, and 16.

Toward the end of the lesson, the teacher invited the class to think about a related problem, which had the additional constraint suggested earlier by a student, that is, what the postman would do if there was an urgent letter.

Analysis of the Lesson: The Possibility of Discernment

Different Solutions to the Same Problem. At the outset, the teacher asked the students to work in groups and experiment with as many possible routes as they could think of. It is significant that the teacher asked for as many routes as possible instead of the best route. This demand for as many solutions as possible created a dimension of variation in the possible routes. When the designs were put on the board, the opportunities for discerning alternative routes became manifold because each student had to consider not only the routes proposed by their group members, but also those suggested by members of other groups.

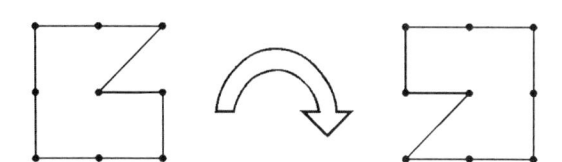

FIG. 3.9. A rotation.

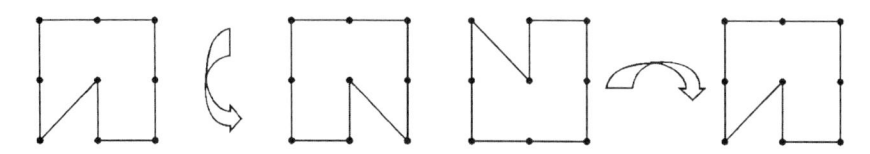

FIG. 3.10. Reflections.

Possible Versus Impossible Routes. In order to help students discern the critical features of a possible route, the teacher deliberately focused the students' attention on a faulty design (i.e., an impossible route), and asked the class whether this design was correct (see Fig. 3.6). In the discussion about whether the route was correct or not, one student pointed out that the arrows were missing, and another student pointed out that the route did not lead back to the post office.

In other words, by juxtaposing possible routes with an impossible route, the teacher was able to help students discern two critical features of a possible route. One is that to constitute a route, there has to be an indication of the direction of the route, and using an arrow to indicate direction is important. The other is that the route needs to reach a particular destination. In this case, the postman needed to be able to go back to the post office after delivering the letters. Discerning these two critical features helped the class to consider the designs that they had come up with and eliminate the impossible routes.

Possible Routes Versus Best Routes. After this, the teacher raised the question of how to decide which design was best. The following is an excerpt from the discussion.

3.3. [Math Lesson/Primary Grade 4]
T: How should we decide which design can be called the best design?
S3: Use the shortest route?
T: "Use the shortest route," good. Any others?
S4: Don't repeat the route.
T: Good, "Don't repeat the route." Any others?
S5: If there is an urgent letter that needs to be delivered first, what should we do?
T: Good, "If there is an urgent letter." Very good. Any others? [No more suggestions.]
T: Let's first put S5's problem aside and assume that there are no urgent letters. All letters are equally important. Then, which is the best design?
S6: The shortest route.

By asking the students to think about what constituted a "best route," the teacher was trying to get the students to revisit the routes that they had designed from a different perspective: that is, what is possible versus what is best. The students' judgment of the best route was at first simply an intuitive judgment with reference to the postman's problem. The criteria for the best route were not formalized. Subsequently, the teacher guided the students to

3. DISCERNMENT AND "WHAT CAN BE LEARNED?" 81

count the number of straight line segments (horizontal, vertical, and diagonal; see Fig. 3.7). At this point, the teacher was in fact guiding the students to scrutinize the routes from a mathematical perspective.

Up to this point in the lesson, the teacher had taken an open problem, presented at a level very close to the students' everyday experience (designing as many paths as possible from the postman's perspective), and deliberately guided the students to twice revisit the designs that they proposed: first to pick the correct routes and then to pick the best route. In this way, the students not only had the chance to see that the problem was open, but also to see that there were many possible solutions. In other words, the problem was the invariant in the lesson, whereas a dimension of variation was created in the methods of solving the problem. Because of the variation created, students were given opportunities to see various aspects of the problem—the many possible solutions to the same problem; the difference between possible and impossible solutions; the difference between possible and best solutions; and that the criteria used may vary between an intuitive choice and a mathematically grounded choice.

Categorization of Shapes: Rotations and Reflections. In the fourth part of the lesson, the teacher asked the class to discern the regularities exhibited in the eight shapes that remained on the board, and to categorize the shapes (see Fig. 3.8). This task generated a very lively whole-class discussion. The following is an excerpt from the discussion:

3.4 [Math Lesson/Primary Grade 4]

T: Now, we are not going to consider direction anymore. Look at these shapes. I would like you to use different methods to categorize them. [Referring to Fig. 3.8.]

S11: There are eight shapes. According to the direction in which the missing part is facing, there are four categories. There are two shapes for each category. Eight altogether.

S12: Move the second shape [referring to shape 6 in Fig. 3.8] on the second row around, then it becomes the third shape [shape 7] on the second row. [The teacher then moved the shape according to the student's instruction.]

T: Very good. She found that after rotating, these two shapes [6 and 7], become the same. Any more suggestions?

S12: Move the third shape [7] on the second row, it then becomes the third shape [3] on the first row.

T: Let me first label these patterns. One, two, ... eight [Students said the numbers aloud and the teacher wrote the numbers under the patterns.]

S13: [inaudible]

T: S13 said that rotating the sixth shape [6] will result in the eighth shape [8]. What next?

S14: [inaudible]

T: S14 said that rotating the eighth shape [8] will again result in the seventh shape [7]. [The teacher wrote "6–8–7" on the board.]

S15: Turn the fifth shape [5], and turn again. It will result in the eighth shape [8]. Turn the third shape [3] upward. No, flipping it over will result in the fifth shape [5]. [Flipping the shape will produce an image by reflection; see Fig. 3.10.]

T: We started by suggesting rotation. Now S15 suggested flipping over the shapes. Are there any more suggestions? [The teacher recorded the flipping in another row on the board; see Fig. 3.11.]

After labeling the shapes 1 to 8, students became very active in putting forward their ideas for rotating them. The teacher put down a record of the rotations (6, 8, 7, and later 5) that the students suggested (see Fig. 3.11). However, rotation was not the only way to move the shapes about. Some students found that they could also obtain matching images by flipping over the shapes vertically or horizontally (i.e., by reflection; see Fig. 3.10). The students suggested altogether 18 rotations and seven reflections.

Let us examine what happened in this excerpt. The first student (S11) suggested that the eight different shapes could be put into four categories according to the direction in which the "missing part" was facing, that is, whether it faced left or right, up or down. This student was looking at the shapes as static figures. After this, another student (S12) suggested that moving the second one on the second row (i.e., 6 in Fig. 3.8) would result in the third one in the second row (i.e., 7). This approach suggested seeing the shapes as dynamic by moving them and looking for a matching image by rotation. In other words, in this example, the seventh shape could be seen as an image of the sixth shape after a clockwise rotation. In a similar way, another

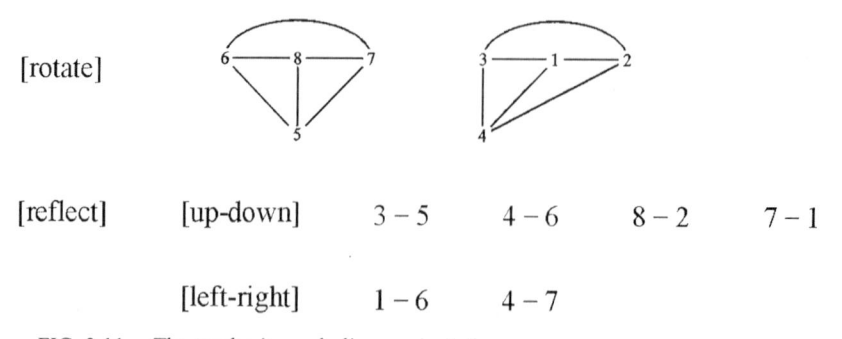

[rotate]

[reflect]   [up-down]   3 – 5   4 – 6   8 – 2   7 – 1

[left-right]   1 – 6   4 – 7

FIG. 3.11. The teacher's symbolic representations.

3. DISCERNMENT AND "WHAT CAN BE LEARNED?" 83

student (S14) saw the eighth and seventh shapes (i.e., 8 and 7) as images of the sixth shape after consecutive rotations. By doing this, the shapes were no longer different, they were simply different orientations of the same shape resulting from rotations and reflections. In other words, the shapes constituted a dimension of variation in the orientation of an invariant shape. The discernment of the equivalence between the shape and its matching image was made possible when the teacher rotated and flipped over the shapes on the board following the students' suggestion (see Fig. 3.9).

It is clear that the students' focus, in this part of the lesson, was on the transformation (rotation and reflection) of the shapes. They imagined the shape turning in their minds and made suggestions to the teacher. With trial and error, it was not difficult for some students to see that there were two possible means of transformation, that is, rotation and reflection, and that the rotational images could be categorized into two types. This categorization became explicit when the teacher asked a new question, near the end of the lesson, that required the students to think about their observations at a higher level of abstraction. The following is an excerpt from the discussion:

3.5 [Math lesson/Primary Grade 4]

T: Let's first look at 1, 2, 3, 4, these four shapes. What do we notice? [Referring to Fig. 3.8.]

S33: [If we] keep rotating [the shape], eventually it will become the first again.

T: How about 5, 6, 7, 8? Does the same rule apply?

Ss: [inaudible]

T: Now, can we tell how many categories there are all together?

S33: Eight.

S34: Infinitely many.

T: "Infinitely many" refers to the designs. But we said at the beginning there are eight best designs. If we go back to the problem of the postman delivering letters, how many categories of best designs are there?

S35: Infinitely many.

S36: Two.

S37: Eight.

S38: 16.

T: Why?

S36: Because there are eight shapes. After changing the directions (of the routes), there will be 16.

T: Good. Then, how did S36's suggestion of "two" come up?

S38: Because all these shapes can be obtained by rotating two different shapes.

T: Good. These are the different ways of categorization. Here, we conclude from the simple problem of the postman. There were 16 best routes. In the earlier part of the lesson, S5 suggested the problem of an urgent letter. Teacher gave you this to think about as a postlesson problem. If we need to send an urgent letter to the third point, how many types of best design are there? Don't forget to tell the teacher your findings. This is the end of the lesson. Bye, class [Class dismissed].

In the above excerpt, the teacher requested the students to reflect on the relationship between shapes, and asked for the number of categories of the shapes. When the students were unable to come up with the correct answer, the teacher brought the class back to the everyday context of the postman. As we can see, this contextual shift enabled some students to come up with the correct answer. It is highly likely that as soon as these shapes were seen as the postman's routes, the critical features of possible routes and best routes that were discussed earlier in the lesson, that is, the indication of direction and shortest distance respectively, came to the fore of the students' awareness. The fact that there were eight shortest routes and that the postman could either go clockwise or counterclockwise, as pointed out by S38, led to the answer of 16 routes. Here we see that the students' answers were once again focused on the postman's routes, but that this time the answers were enriched with an understanding of the mathematical meanings.

Contextual Variation. When we look back at the lesson as a whole, it is not difficult to see that the problem went through a shift of context from real life to mathematical, and vice versa (see Fig. 3.12). The problem was first introduced in a real-life context that was easily accessible to the students. The different solutions were examined in terms of feasibility (whether the routes were correct or not) and the optimum requirement (which one was the best). In both cases, the use of the postman's route as a context for understanding possible routes and best routes was a powerful one. It was easy for students to relate to the possible routes and the best routes from the postman's perspective: that is, he must be able to return to the starting point, the post office, and he should be able to finish his mail delivery as efficiently as

Real-life context:	Mathematical context:	Real-life context:
Many possible routes	Different rotations	16 best routes
Correct/faulty routes	Different reflections	The "urgent letter" problem
The best routes	Categories of routes	

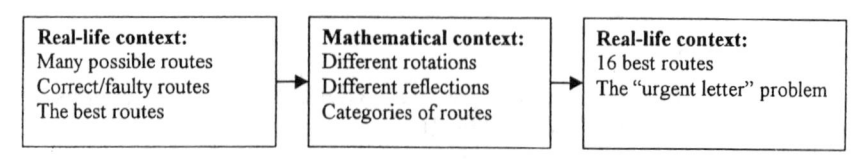

FIG. 3.12. Contextual variation.

possible, that is, no part of the route should be repeated unnecessarily. The teacher shifted into a mathematical context by inviting the students to categorize the routes. The students then examined the different solutions and their relations, using rotation and reflection. What is interesting is the way in which the teacher exploited the contextual shift back to the postman's route when the students had difficulties coming up with the correct answers for categorizing the routes. Even more important, the teacher referred to the postman's problem again at the end of the lesson, and concluded the discussion by affirming that there were 16 best routes. This conclusion was built on the comparison between the many possibilities, different rotations and reflections, and the directions of the routes. At the end of the lesson, after the various stages of exploration, the way in which the students discerned the postman's problem was undoubtedly different from their understanding of this problem at the outset of the lesson. The lesson provided a rich experience of problem solving reinforced by the teacher with careful planning. However, the students also played a crucial role in the construal of the object of learning. For example, when the class was discussing the best route, one student imagined the situation of an urgent letter. This showed that the student's reflections on the solution were very much in a real-life context at this stage. The teacher skillfully kept the students' focus according to her original plan, and put this novel idea aside for that particular moment. However, after examining the solutions of the problem from a mathematical perspective, the idea of "an urgent letter" became a meaningful alternative problem. The problem was the same type of problem as the original one, but with a variation, and as such, it was an opportunity for the students to put what they had just experienced into practice.

This example provides a wonderful illustration of the way in which a teacher can provide students with a rich understanding of the many facets of problem solving even with the use of one single problem. The lesson also supported the teacher's lesson objective "to enhance students' problem-solving ability and strategies" in an efficient and stimulating way.

WHAT COULD BE LEARNED?

We started this chapter by saying that understanding something as something implies discerning features, or aspects, of that which is experienced. Certain learning takes the simultaneous discernment of certain critical aspects of the object of learning. That is, the critical aspects are held in the focal awareness at the same time. However, an aspect can only be discerned if it is experienced as a dimension of variation. From this assumption, we argue that those dimensions of variation that are present in the learning environment are critical for learning what is possible to learn. In other words, if an aspect is presented as a dimension of variation to the learners, it makes it possible for the learners to discern that particular aspect. And if several dimensions of variation are open simultaneously, it makes it possible for the learners to discern all of these aspects simultaneously. So, what is varying, what is invariant, and what is varying at the same time are important for what is possible to learn.

We have analyzed three mathematics lessons from the point of view of the pattern of variation that was constituted during the lesson, and have identified the pattern of variant and invariant aspects in the three lessons respectively. From this we can draw some conclusions about the possibilities to learn that were provided for the learners.

In the first two example lessons, in which the object of learning was fractional numbers as operator, we can see that there was a difference in what it was possible to learn. Teacher A provided the learners with the possibility to learn to solve different problems with the same strategy, whereas Teacher B provided the learners with the possibility to learn to solve the same problem with different strategies. In Teacher A's lesson the changing of the parameters in the operation opened a variation of different examples, whereas in Teacher B's lesson, the parameters were invariant and the strategy varied (Fig. 3.1). In addition, in Teacher B's lesson, the learners had the possibility to discern a semantic aspect of fractional numbers; this did not occur in Teacher A's lesson. On the other hand, the students in Teacher A's lesson were presented with a variation of how a fractional number could be represented, and thus the possibility to discern this particular aspect.

It is obvious that these two lessons were very similar on one level, for instance in the teaching methods and the arrangement of the learning situation. However, on another rather more subtle level (but one that is important from the point of view of the students' potential for learning), they were very different. When comparing two lessons as we have done here, it seems natural to ask, "Which one is the best?" However, there can be no general answer to that question. The answer to any assessment of this kind will always need to take into consideration the capabilities the teacher wanted the students to develop, and thus the intended object of learning.

The lesson on the postman's routes showed how the teacher very thoughtfully, and jointly with her students, constituted a pattern of variation that was very rich in several aspects. The learners, in the same way as those in Teacher B's lesson, were afforded the opportunity to discern that there can be many possible solutions (routes) to the same problem. As well as this, they were provided the opportunity to evaluate (scrutinize) the solutions in different ways, in an everyday context and a mathematical context, and in terms of whether the solutions were feasible (possible or impossible) and optimal (best). They were also required to discern the character of a shape by the variation in the orientation of the same shape after rotation and reflection. That is, within the mathematical context, the same shape can produce many different possible routes by rotation or reflection. Rotation and reflection were two ways by which the students could see ostensibly different shapes as the same. Further, the students were able to see the same problem and its solutions differently, before and after scrutinizing the solutions in a mathematical context.

Although our focus has been on the importance of the object of learning, we do not wish to imply that classroom arrangements are unimportant. As we have seen in two of the examples (Teacher B's lesson and the Chinese demonstration lesson) the students contributed very much to the constitution and the widening of the space of variation. It is reasonable to assume that this variation was a result of the group discussions that took place before the whole-class sessions. In both of these lessons, the students were allowed, and even encouraged, to discuss the problem with their peers. Thus a certain arrangement (group work) facilitated the opening of variation. However, what we want to stress is that it is not a certain arrangement in itself that makes a certain learning possible, but rather that the possibility to learn is provided by what it is possible to discern.

In this chapter we have focused on the possibilities to learn, rather than what the students actually learned. We have also described the enacted object of learning as a potential for student learning seen from the point of view of the researcher. However, we would not argue that what was possible to experience was indeed what the students actually experienced. It is likely that the students learned different things. What we do argue is that it is likely that the students learned certain things in one lesson, and other things in another.

4

Simultaneity and the Enacted Object of Learning

Pakey P. M. Chik
Mun Ling Lo

In the three previous chapters, the important role of variation in opening up possibilities for a particular learning (or the development of certain capabilities) to take place was described and exemplified. We also illustrated that the way in which we experience or understand something depends on which features of it we are aware of and can discern simultaneously. Thus, when different aspects of the same thing are discerned and focused on, different ways of understanding will result. More powerful ways of understanding amount to a simultaneous awareness of those features that are critical to achieving certain aims.

In this chapter, we primarily focus on describing one of the two forms of simultaneity discussed in chapter 1: *synchronic simultaneity*, which refers to experiencing discerned features at the same time, where the discerned features may be held in two different types of relationship. When the discerned features are seen as aspects of something, we refer to relationships of this kind as *aspect–aspect relationships*. For example, when we see a person writing an essay on a computer, we may experience it as someone engaged in an act of essay writing as well as an act of word processing. The other relationship involves seeing the discerned parts of the whole, and the whole that is delimited from a context, at the same time. For example, one may discern the eyes, muzzle, and limbs as different parts of the body of a deer, which is in turn delimited from the woods (Marton & Booth, 1997). The kind of linkages established between an object or a phenomenon and its parts being discerned are referred to as *part–whole relationships*.

Things might or might not be experienced simultaneously, and in teaching, various things may or may not come to the fore simultaneously. In this chapter, we compare lessons that differ in this respect; that is, the intended object of learning is the same, but the enacted object differs, as does what the students learn (i.e., the *lived object of learning*).

Let us, however, start with a study in which the learners were facing the same situation, but the way they discerned and experienced the relations between parts and wholes differed. Säljö (1982) carried out a study to investigate the different ways in which university students in Sweden comprehended the same text. He found that although these students were reading the same text (which was, by the way, about different perspectives of learning), the students saw different meanings in it. Two distinct ways of understanding the text were identified. In the first way, the students saw the text as having a sequential structure, with different perspectives of learning being described, but bearing no relationship to each other. In the second way, the students discerned a main theme (the *forms of learning*) illustrated by a number of subthemes (*different perspectives of learning*). They saw the text as having a hierarchical structure with clear part–part relationships (between the subthemes) and part–whole relationships (between the subthemes and the main theme). In both ways of comprehending the text, all the parts contained in the text were distinguished, but these parts were seen as occupying different structural positions. Säljö (1982) also found that the students who understood the text in the hierarchical way had a more organized and meaningful understanding, and were better able to grasp the main idea of the text than the students who understood the text in the sequential way.

It is not difficult, therefore, to imagine why it is that in any one particular classroom situation, different students will have different levels of understanding even though they all are given the same presentation by the teacher. What students gain from a lesson, and how well they understand that lesson, depends on the way they comprehend the structure of the presentation; this in turn depends on what they focus on and what recedes to the background (or is taken for granted) when they try to understand the lesson. Some students will see no relationship between the different parts of the presentation, whereas others will be able to comprehend the presentation in more powerful ways (especially if they can simultaneously see clear relationships between the parts and the way in which these parts are related to the presentation as a whole). It then follows that students will learn more effectively if the teacher is able to consciously structure the presentation in such a way as to bring out clearly the critical features of the object of learning, as well as their relationships to the object of learning and to each other. In other words, the way the lesson is structured will have an important influence on student learning.

We now provide three sets of classroom data—comprising six pairs of lessons—to illustrate the ways in which teachers can structure their lessons

4. SIMULTANEITY AND THE ENACTED OBJECT OF LEARNING

to enable their students to discern the aspect–aspect (or part–part) and part–whole relationships of various features of the object of learning. In particular, we look at what it is possible to learn regarding specific objects of learning (i.e., enacted objects of learning) and what is actually learned by students (i.e., lived objects of learning).

The first pair of mathematics lessons is drawn from Runesson's (1999) study and is used to illustrate the aspect–aspect relationship. The second and the third pairs of lessons are taken from a 2-year research project undertaken by a research team in Hong Kong,[1] and involve a pair of primary Grade 2 Chinese language lessons and a pair of primary Grade 1 English language lessons, respectively (for detailed information and discussions about other aspects of these two pairs of lessons, see Chik, 2002; Lo & Chik, 2000, and Mok et al., 1999). These three pairs of lessons will be mainly used to illustrate part–whole and aspect–aspect relationships. Each pair of lessons was on the same topic, but taught by two different teachers.

The analysis is based on the audio or video recordings of the lessons and the subsequent transcriptions. In order to explore the impact of the structural differences between the lessons on student learning outcomes, the lesson analyses of the second and third pairs were also compared against the student data, which include the worksheets completed by the students immediately after each lesson.

A PAIR OF MATHEMATICS LESSONS

The two mathematics lessons focused on teaching two different aspects of fractional numbers: the part–whole aspect and the division–quotient aspect, where the former aspect involves adding up parts to a whole (e.g., 12 quarters add up to 3) and the latter involves dividing up a whole into parts (e.g., 12 divided by 4 is equal to 3). The different ways in which these two aspects and their relationship are simultaneously brought to the students' focal awareness are compared.

Description of Lesson A

This lesson consists of three main episodes. In Episode 1, the teacher drew the students' attention to the part–whole aspect of fractional numbers. She used an iconic representation to show six pieces of 1/3 of a pizza and invited the students to represent this with mathematical symbols[2] (i.e., symbolic representation). The following suggestion was arrived at by the students:

$$\frac{6}{3} \text{ or } 2$$

(6 pieces of pizza, each 1/3 of a whole, equal 2 whole pizzas)

In Episode 2, the teacher focused on the division–quotient aspect of fractional numbers (6 divided by 3), and asked the students, "How can this be represented by (mathematical) symbols?" The same representation was arrived at again by the students:

$$\frac{6}{3} = 2 \quad (\text{6 divided by 3 equals 2})$$

The teacher further illustrated this with an example of dividing 6 by 3 (e.g., 6 pieces of pizza are divided among 3 persons):

$$\bullet\ \bullet\ |\ \bullet\ \bullet\ |\ \bullet\ \bullet$$

In Episode 3, the teacher brought the two aspects together by explaining to the class:

> T: ... the result is the same, but it is said differently. Sometimes I will say. "20 divided by 4" and sometimes I will say, "20 quarters" ... the result is 5 anyway. But you should know that although these are actually quite different [concepts], the result is the same.

Description of Lesson B

This lesson can also be divided into three main episodes. In Episode 1, the teacher drew a picture of 12 apples on the blackboard. He said that 3 persons were to share them equally (the division–quotient aspect of fractional numbers was focused on), and asked the class to think in silence how many apples each person would get.

Meanwhile, he drew a new picture—a bowl with a lot of triangles in it (where each triangle was supposed to be 1/3 of an apple)—and asked the class:

> ... If you have to pick up as many pieces of apple from the bowl as you have there (meaning the same as the total of the problem just given), how many pieces of apple do you have to pick up?

Again, the students were instructed to think about the answer in silence.

In this way, the teacher introduced both the division–quotient aspect and the part–whole aspect by using icons (i.e., the pictures of apples) and made the difference between the two aspects visible by asking the students to mentally solve two problems that resulted in the same number (i.e., 4).

In Episode 2, the teacher referred back to the first example (12 apples shared equally by 3 persons) and asked his students to represent it using mathematical symbols. He also asked for the result of the operation. The teacher then wrote the student's suggestion on the blackboard:

4. SIMULTANEITY AND THE ENACTED OBJECT OF LEARNING 93

$$\frac{12}{3} = 4 \text{ (apples)}$$

Next, the teacher referred to the second example (thirds of apples) and asked, "How many thirds of an apple did we need to pick up, and how could that be written with symbols?" The teacher wrote down what the students suggested:

$$\frac{12}{3} \text{ (i.e., } 12 \times 1/3 \text{ apple)}$$

Again, both aspects were focused on simultaneously in this episode.

In Episode 3, the teacher asked the students to consider and compare the two examples. After some questions and comments from the students, the teacher finally concluded:

> ... 12 divided by 3, and 12 thirds, the result is the same. So whether you have 12 apples shared by 3 or you have 12 thirds, you will get the same result.

Again, the teacher linked the two aspects of fractional numbers by concluding that they corresponded to the same number (4).

Thus, throughout this lesson, the teacher had kept the two aspects together.

Aspect–Aspect Relationship Shown in Different Lesson Organizations

Although both lessons were teaching the same content, the part–whole aspect and the division–quotient aspect of fractional numbers, they differed significantly in terms of what aspects were kept in focus, what varied, and whether the aspects were varied at the same time (see Fig. 4.1).

In Lesson A, the two aspects of fractional numbers were brought up one after the other (i.e., first, the part–whole aspect and then the division–quotient aspect). It was only in the last episode that the two aspects were brought together as two aspects of a fractional number. Thus, a conscious effort to set up the condition for the students to discern the aspect–aspect relationship between the two aspects simultaneously was observed in the final

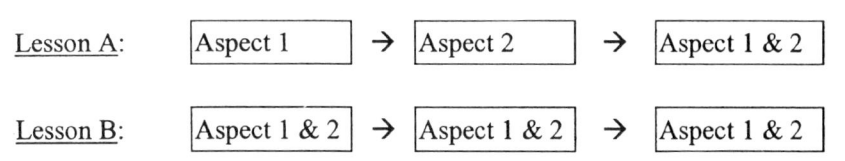

Lesson A: | Aspect 1 | → | Aspect 2 | → | Aspect 1 & 2 |

Lesson B: | Aspect 1 & 2 | → | Aspect 1 & 2 | → | Aspect 1 & 2 |

FIG. 4.1. The focused aspect(s) in different episodes of Lesson A and Lesson B.

episode of Lesson A. In comparison, the teacher of Lesson B focused on both aspects in each of the three episodes. He first asked the class to mentally work out the solutions of two problems, each pointing to one of the aspects of fractional numbers and resulting in the same number (4). Then, he asked the students to represent their solutions in terms of mathematical symbols. He concluded that the same number could be arrived at by methods that reflected the different aspects of fractional numbers. In this way, the relationship between the two aspects permeated the whole lesson and the condition for the experience of the relationship was consciously created all through the lesson. This is an example of the pattern of variation referred to as *fusion* in chapter 1: The two aspects vary together to bring about a simultaneous awareness of both in the learners.

The two lessons illustrate how two aspects of the same direct object of learning (fractional numbers) can be brought into students' focal awareness simultaneously. In the following sections, we try to investigate how students' learning outcomes are affected by the way in which a lesson is structured—from the point of view of the part–whole relationships.

A PAIR OF PRIMARY GRADE 2 CHINESE LANGUAGE LESSONS

Two primary Grade 2 Chinese language lessons taught by two different teachers from the same school were selected for the study. Both lessons were the first of a series of lessons dealing with the teaching of vocabulary in a text. Both classes (2A and 2B) consisted of students with similar abilities. The title of the text was "A polite little guest." The complete text is translated into English and reproduced in Table 4.1.

Description of Lesson 2A

The lesson can be roughly divided into four episodes. In Episode 1, the teacher introduced the main theme of the text as "being polite." This was

TABLE 4.1
The Text Used in Both Lesson 2A and Lesson 2B

Lesson 10: A Polite Little Guest

Father intended to visit a friend with us. He asked, "What must one do to be a polite little guest?" My younger sister said, "When we are eating, we should not turn food over again and again to select food in the dish." My elder sister said, "We should look at the person we are talking to, not look from side to side. When other people are talking, we should not interrupt." I said, "On leaving, we must say goodbye." Father was very pleased after hearing these, he promised to give us the chance to show ourselves to be a polite guest.

4. SIMULTANEITY AND THE ENACTED OBJECT OF LEARNING

done by asking the students to first nominate the classmates that they considered to be polite, to give their reasons, and then to read the text in silence to find out what was meant by being polite.

In Episode 2, the teacher taught the attributes (e.g., forms, pronunciations, and meanings) of seven words[3] that had been pre-identified from the text. Many teaching aids were used to show the meaning of each word (e.g., drawings and real objects). References were also made to show how the meanings of these words contributed to the theme of the text—being polite. With each word they studied, the teacher posted up on the blackboard the corresponding word card.

In Episode 3, the teacher asked the students to find the sentence in the text where each word that they had studied was used, and to read the sentence out loud. The sentences were then posted up. When all the sentences (each involving one or two of the words) were found, the teacher told the students that if they did all of the things that were described in the sentences, they would be polite children. The phrase "polite children" [有禮貌的孩子] was also posted up. The students were then asked to read the text together. In this way, the teacher focused the students' attention on the words as parts of the sentences, which were in turn parts of the text and its theme of "being polite."

In Episode 4, the teacher taught the students how to write some of the characters.[4]

Description of Lesson 2B

There are five main episodes in the lesson. In Episode 1, the teacher gave the students an overall idea of what the text was about by asking a few questions to introduce the content of the text.

In Episode 2, the teacher focused on teaching the forms of a number of characters that she thought her students might find difficult. Individual students were invited to come out and try to write each character on the blackboard. The other students were required to pay attention and to judge whether the character was correctly written or not. If not, the teacher would invite other students to try until the character was correctly written. In some cases, the teacher also posted up a word card highlighting the structure of the character.

In Episode 3, the teacher identified a set of words from the text and taught the meaning of each word. From time to time, the students were invited to give a verbal explanation of a certain word or to act out its meaning.

In Episode 4, the teacher focused on teaching the pronunciation of the words in the text. This was done by asking different groups of students to take turns reading them. Instant feedback was given when the students could not pronounce the words correctly.

In Episode 5, the teacher introduced a matching game. In this game, the teacher showed the students three phrases one by one and asked them, in groups, to match the phrases by finding a word in the text that conveyed the same meaning.

Part–Whole Relationship in the Hierarchical Structure of Lesson 2A

Lesson 2A was structured in a hierarchical way that showed clear part–whole relationships between the word attributes (each as an aspect of a character), the characters (each as part of a word), the words (each as part of a sentence), the sentences (each as part of the text) and the text (as contributing to the understanding of its theme). Figure 4.2 illustrates the part–whole relationships in the hierarchical organization of Lesson A.

For example, the character that has the meaning of "insert" [插] was first learned on its own with a particular form, pronunciation, and meaning. It was then referred to in the context of the word "interrupt" [插嘴], which is made up of two characters, "insert" [插] and "mouth" [嘴]. The characters now took on a different meaning in combination. In this way, their relation was such that they were no longer two separate parts put together, but constituted a whole, in which each was a part. Hence, when the word "interrupt" [插嘴] was focused on, the characters "insert" [插] and "mouth" [嘴], as well as their relation to each other, were brought simultaneously to the stu-

```
Text (A Polite Little Guest [有禮貌的小客人])
  Theme (Being Polite [有禮貌])
    Sentence (when others are talking to each other, we should not
        interrupt [別人談話時，不要隨便插嘴。])
      Word (e.g., interrupt [插嘴])
        Character (e.g., insert [插])
          Attributes (i.e., form, pronunciation,
              decontextualized meaning)
```

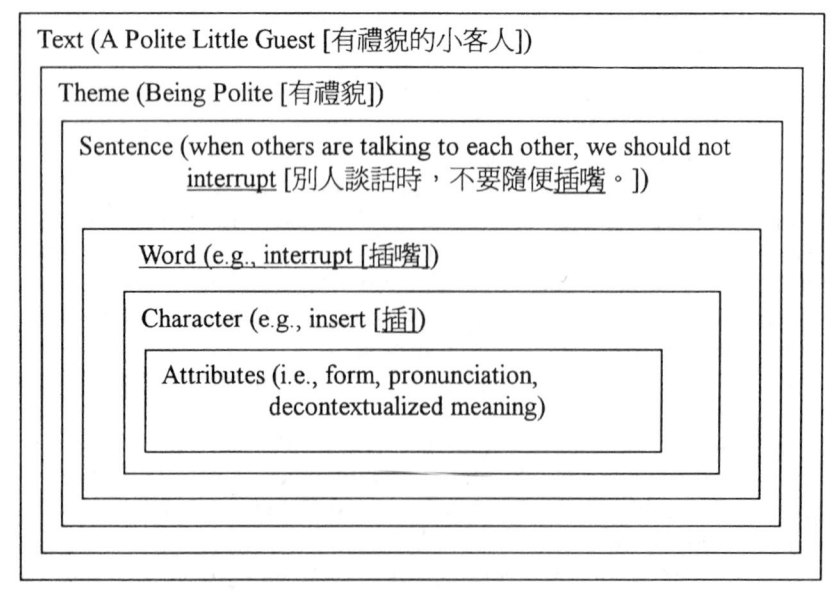

FIG. 4.2. An illustration of the part–whole relationship shown in the hierarchical structure of Lesson 2A.

dents' focal awareness. Next, the word was seen again in a sentence, "When others are talking to each other, we should not *interrupt*" [插嘴]. Here the word, which comprises two characters, becomes part of a sentence on politeness that contributes to the learning of politeness. Thus, the part–whole relationships between the characters and the word, as well as the word and the sentence, become clear. Finally the sentence, which involved the word as a part, was seen in the context of a text. Together with all the other sentences identified from the text, it also contributed to the understanding of the theme of the text. Again, while focusing on the text, the sentence, the word, and the characters were simultaneously focused on to facilitate the discernment of the part–whole relationships as well as the relationships between each part.

In this way, Lesson 2A demonstrated how the parts (e.g., different attributes of a character, and different characters that make up a word) were embedded in the wholes (e.g., a character is embedded in a word; a word is embedded in a sentence). Therefore it provided the students with a simultaneous experience (and hence, discernment) of these part–whole relationships throughout the lesson. The students could refer to the word cards, the sentence strips, and the text throughout the lesson, thus making possible the discernment through synchronic simultaneity.

Part–Whole Relationship in the Sequential Structure of Lesson 2B

The teacher of Lesson 2B spent most of the class time on vocabulary teaching, which she organized under the three attributes of words (form, pronunciation, and meaning) and presented in a sequential manner (see Fig. 4.3).

In this lesson, the different attributes of a character were taught in different episodes, but no attempt was made to relate the different attributes of each character to one another (the aspect–aspect relationships). As a result, some students may have understood the characters as totally discrete entities. Let us take for example, the word "interrupt" [插嘴], which consists of two characters, the first one meaning "insert" [插], and the second meaning "mouth" [嘴]. Instead of teaching the forms of these two characters at the

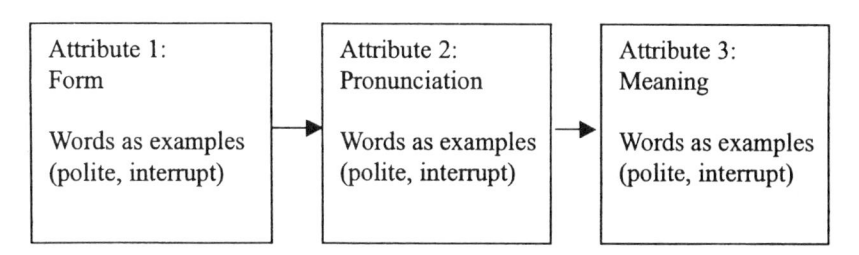

Attribute 1: Form Words as examples (polite, interrupt)	Attribute 2: Pronunciation Words as examples (polite, interrupt)	Attribute 3: Meaning Words as examples (polite, interrupt)

FIG. 4.3. The sequential organization of Lesson 2B.

TABLE 4.2
A Comparison of the Structures of Lessons 2A and 2B

Lesson 2A			Lesson 2B		
Word 1 →	Word 2 →	Word 3 → ...	Form →	Pronunciation →	Meaning
form;	form;	form;	word 1;	word 1;	word 1;
pronunciation;	pronunciation;	pronunciation;	word 2;	word 2;	word 2;
meaning	meaning	meaning	word 3;	word 3;	word 3;
			...	...	...

same time as teaching the way in which they combine to form the word "interrupt" (as the teacher in Lesson 2A did) the teacher of Lesson 2B taught the forms of the first character on its own in Episode 2, and the pronunciation of this character as part of the word "interrupt" in Episode 4. Furthermore in Episode 5, the word "interrupt" was given a definition ("joining in others' conversation" [加入別人的談話]) that was neither situated in the context of being polite, nor related to the text.

Thus, in each of the three consecutive episodes of Lesson 2B, one of the word attributes (form, pronunciation, or meaning) was kept invariant, and thus became superordinate, while the characters/words that varied were used to illustrate the attribute. By contrast, the words were the focus of Lesson 2A, and each word became superordinate while the three attributes (or aspects) varied at the same time, in order to enhance the simultaneous experience of the word attributes. This is another example of the pattern of variation called *fusion*. A major difference between the two classes is whether attributes or words were superordinate, as determined by the different ways in which the lesson was structured (see Table 4.2).

The question we need to ask is, does this difference have an impact on students' learning outcomes?

Describing Learning Outcomes

After each lesson, the students in both classes were requested to complete a worksheet. Thirty worksheets were collected from Class 2A, and 31 from Class 2B. The worksheet contained two parts. In the first part, the students were asked to put down what they thought was the most important thing taught and/or learned in the lesson. The second part required the students to complete a text by filling in blanks with appropriate words that had been taught in the lesson (see Table 4.4 for the text).

4. SIMULTANEITY AND THE ENACTED OBJECT OF LEARNING 99

What Was Taught and Learned From the Students' Perspective? In answering the first part of the question, some students put down more than one response. As shown in Table 4.3, the responses of both classes fell into two main categories. Some students reported that they were taught the theme (e.g., "how to be polite," "being a polite guest") and subthemes of the text (e.g., "When others are talking to each other, we should not interrupt."), and some reported that they were taught vocabulary. However, differences were observed in their pattern of responses.

More students from Class 2A reported the main theme of the text or the subthemes as the most important thing taught. In contrast, a higher proportion of Class 2B considered vocabulary the most important thing taught in the lesson.

When we look at the breakdown of the students' responses, we can see that the answers of the students in Class 2A covered all subthemes of the text, whereas the answers of the students in Class 2B only covered two of the subthemes.

With regard to the learning of vocabulary, the students of Class 2B mostly described what they had learned in more general terms (e.g., "using words to make sentences," "reading words," etc.). By contrast, a higher proportion of the students in Class 2A wrote down specific words that they had learned.

What Were the Learning Outcomes? The result of the second part of the worksheet is shown in Table 4.4. To assess the appropriate use of words, the students' answers were marked correct even if they had made minor mistakes in the written form of the words. With respect to the words "interrupt" and "polite," which had been given special emphasis during teaching in both classes, we can see that Class 2A performed much better in using these words to complete the given text (30 out of 30 correct for Class 2A, and only 9 out of 31 for Class 2B). Regarding the characters ("insert" [插] and "appearance" [貌]) whose forms both teachers had spent time teaching, again the students of Class 2A were better able to write these characters than the students from Class 2B. Only one mistake (on "insert") was made in Class

TABLE 4.3
The Students' Responses Shown in the First Part of the Worksheet*

General Question:	What is the most important thing taught/learned in the lesson?	
Class (*N* = total number of responses)	2A (*N* = 35)	2E (*N* = 39)
1. The main theme and subthemes of the text	18	10
2. Vocabulary	5	22
3. Irrelevant responses	12	7

*Some students put down more than one response.

TABLE 4.4
The Students' Performances as Shown in the Second Part of the Worksheet

Second Part: Complete the following text with appropriate words/phrases you have learned in the lesson.

Our teacher often tells us that when we meet teachers and classmates in school, we have to greet[a] them. In the classroom, when the teacher is talking with other classmates, do not interrupt[b] as one likes; when the teacher talks to you, do not look from side to side.[c] After school, we have to say goodbye to our teachers and classmates. Then we can be counted as good students who are polite.[d]

[English translation]

Class		2A	2E
1. Use of words			
1.1 Appropriate for all blanks		30	9
1.2 One to three blanks missing/inappropriate		—	22
2. Form of characters			
Wrongly written			
Not taught in the lesson:	"Mouth"	8	4
	"Wave"	1	—
	"Watch"	1	—
	"West"	—	1
Taught in the lesson:	"Insert"	1	7
	"Appearance"	—	4

Note. [a]The word "greet" [打招呼] is made up of three Chinese characters, "beat" [打], "wave" [招], and "call" [呼].

[b]The word "interrupt" [插嘴] is made up of two Chinese characters, "insert" [插] and "mouth" [嘴].

[c]The word "look from side to side" [東張西望] is made up of four Chinese characters, "east" [東], "open" [張], "west" [西], and "watch" [望].

[d]The word "polite" [禮貌] is made up of two Chinese characters, "polite" [禮] and "appearance" [貌].

2A, whereas 11 mistakes were noted in Class 2B (7 on "insert"; 4 on "appearance").

Simultaneity and the Possibility for Learning. In order for the students to be able to use the words learned in the lesson to fill in the blanks of a given text, it was not enough for them simply to know how to write the form of the characters that made up that word. The students also had to understand the meaning of the words, and be able to use them in an appropriate context. That is, they had to be able to discern simultaneously the form, the meaning, and the usage of the word. Lesson 2A was structured in such a way as to allow the students to be simultaneously aware of the word attributes (form and meaning) that are critical to the words being used appropriately. Correspondingly, we found that the students in Class 2A were better able to discern these attributes simultaneously than the students of Class 2B.

In Lesson 2B, although the students were also taught the same words, the critical attributes of each word were taught in different episodes, and there was no attempt to help the students link these aspects together. Although the form of the character meaning "insert" was taught in Episode 2, and the meaning of the word "interrupt" (which consists of the two characters "insert" and "mouth") was taught in Episode 3, the students were not made aware simultaneously of these two attributes (form and meaning) of the character "insert," and may have considered them as two different, unrelated entities. In other words, even if only three words were taught in the lesson, if the three different attributes of each word were taught as unrelated entities—instead of presenting them as three attributes of three words—some students may perceive these attributes as nine unrelated entities to be learned. The large number of unrelated entities might cause some students to be confused, whereas others might not be able to cope with so many new things in a short time. This may account for the fact that although the teacher of Lesson 2B spent much time teaching the students how to correctly write the forms of the words "insert" and "appearance," many students still got them wrong. Of course, some students might still be able to experience the attributes simultaneously because of previous experiences. However, the simultaneous experience of different attributes was not brought about by the conscious effort of the teacher, unlike in Lesson 2A, where the teacher consciously structured the learning experiences to facilitate such an experience.

A PAIR OF PRIMARY GRADE 1 ENGLISH LANGUAGE LESSONS

In this section, we further illustrate our point by looking at two double periods of English language lessons taken from two primary Grade 1 classes (Class 1B and Class 1E) that were taught by two different teachers in the same school. Both lessons were one of a series of lessons on "Food in the supermarket." Before this lesson, both classes of students had already learned the names of several items of food and drink. Building on this prior knowledge, the teachers aimed to develop the students' ability to use different language items to describe food and drink (nouns: e.g., crisps, milk; partitives: e.g., a bottle of, a packet of; and adjectives describing size: e.g., large, small), as well as their ability to extract specific information (prices of food and drink) through the use of dialogue ("How much is it?" "It is ____ dollars.").

The two classes were of similar ability and most of the students were quite good at English as far as speaking and listening were concerned.

Description of Lesson 1B

This lesson consisted of four main episodes, each focusing on an object of learning. In Episode 1, the teacher revised the names of eight kinds of food and drink that the students had learned in previous lessons. Pictures and word cards were shown.

In Episode 2, the teacher introduced the phrases "a bottle of" and "a packet of" to describe the attributes of some of the food and drink items shown in Episode 1. She explained to the class that there were some food items that needed a partitive and some that did not. She represented the phrases in pictorial, spoken, and written forms. Also, when she explained the word "packet," which was new to the students, the teacher made reference to the more familiar word "bag" that carried the same meaning as "packet."

In Episode 3, the teacher explained the use of the words "large" and "small" to describe different sizes of the same kind of food/drink for identification purposes—in her words, "so that people know which one you are talking about." Again, pictures and word cards were used. The meaning of the word "large" was also explained in terms of another word, "big," which was more familiar and has a similar meaning to "large."

Finally in Episode 4, the teacher used the context of a supermarket to introduce the dialogue, "How much is it?" "It is ____ dollars," which was then posted on the blackboard. The students practiced the dialogue in two different tasks: guessing the prices of different food and drink items, and role-playing the act of buying in a supermarket. In both tasks, the teacher did the questioning while the students were invited to respond by giving the "it is" statement either on a whole-class or individual basis.

Description of Lesson 1E

This lesson comprised three interrelated episodes. In Episode 1, the teacher introduced the main theme of the lesson, "Buying food in a supermarket." Specifically, the teacher focused on two main aspects, namely the food and drink that could be found in the supermarket, and the dialogue used to ask for the prices of food and drink.

4. SIMULTANEITY AND THE ENACTED OBJECT OF LEARNING

In Episode 2, the teacher began by asking, "What kinds of food and drink can we find in a supermarket?" Then, the teacher used pictures to introduce eight pairs of food and drink items one by one. Each pair consisted of two different-sized versions of the same kind of food/drink (e.g., one large and one small bottle of water). The teacher required the students to name each pair of items (e.g., "a large bottle of water" and "a small bottle of water"). In this way, the words describing size, the partitives, and the names of particular kinds of food and drink were presented to the class simultaneously.

In Episode 3, the teacher told the class, "Well, here are some kinds of food and drink that we can find in a supermarket. If we want to buy them, what should we say?" Then, she posted up the dialogue "How much is it?" "It is _____ dollars," and introduced it as a way of finding out the price of food and drink items in a supermarket. The students then practiced the dialogue by engaging in different tasks, such as guessing the price of certain items of food and/or drink and pretending to buy things in the supermarket.

Part–Whole Relationships in Different Lesson Organizations

Although the lessons both dealt with similar teaching contents, the two teachers used different ways of structuring their lessons, and hence the relationships established simultaneously between the objects of learning were also different. In Lesson 1B, the teacher presented the objects of learning (nouns for describing food and drink; adjectives describing size; partitives used in conjunction with uncountable nouns; and a dialogue pattern) in a sequential way (see Fig. 4.4). For instance, in order to focus on "small," the teacher showed many examples of small items of food and drink. Then, in order to focus on "large," she showed many examples of large items of food and drink. As a result, despite the fact that the same examples of food and drink were used throughout the lesson, only one object of learning was brought to the fore in each episode. This object of learning was then left in the background in the next episode while something else was highlighted.

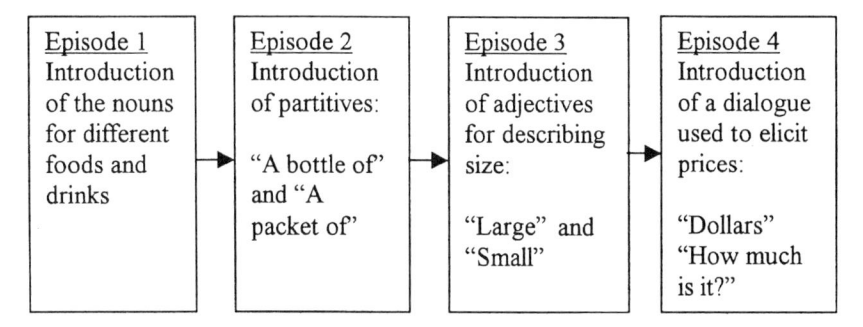

Episode 1 Introduction of the nouns for different foods and drinks	Episode 2 Introduction of partitives: "A bottle of" and "A packet of"	Episode 3 Introduction of adjectives for describing size: "Large" and "Small"	Episode 4 Introduction of a dialogue used to elicit prices: "Dollars" "How much is it?"

FIG. 4.4. The sequential structure of Lesson 1B.

In comparison, the teacher of Lesson 1E focused on each kind of food/drink as an object that had different attributes (name, size, packaging, and price), and set up the learning with the theme of buying in a supermarket. For instance, the food and drink items (which have their own name, size, and packaging) were presented as the things that can be found in a supermarket (whole) and also as the objects being referred to in the buying activity. In this way, the same set of nouns, adjectives, partitives, and dialogue were organized in a manner that related them to each other as attributes of certain food/drink items, as well as to the theme of buying in the supermarket as a whole. Lesson 1E can thus be described as having a hierarchical organization (see Fig. 4.5) that made it possible for the students to experience both the part–whole relationships between things and the aspect–aspect relationships between attributes simultaneously (see also Table 4.5).

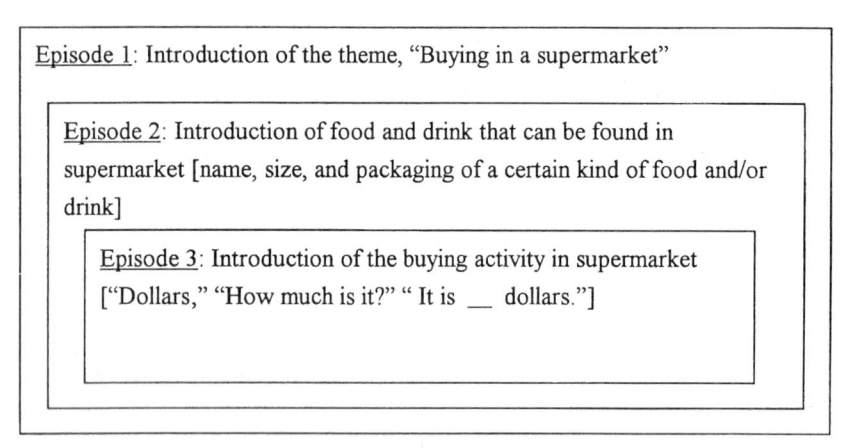

Episode 1: Introduction of the theme, "Buying in a supermarket"

> Episode 2: Introduction of food and drink that can be found in supermarket [name, size, and packaging of a certain kind of food and/or drink]
>
>> Episode 3: Introduction of the buying activity in supermarket ["Dollars," "How much is it?" " It is __ dollars."]

FIG. 4.5. The hierarchical structure of Lesson 1E.

TABLE 4.5
A Comparison of the Structures of Lesson 1B and Lesson 1E

	Lesson 1B			Lesson 1E	
Nouns →	Adjectives describing size →	Partitives	Type of food/ drink 1 →	Type of food/ drink 2 →	Type of food/ drink 3 → ...
food/drink 1; food/drink 2; food/drink 3 ...	food/drink 1; food/drink 2; food/drink 3 ...	food/drink 1; food/drink 2; food/drink 3 ...	noun; adjectives describing size; with or without partitive	noun; adjectives describing size; with or without partitive	noun; adjectives describing size; with or without partitive

4. SIMULTANEITY AND THE ENACTED OBJECT OF LEARNING 105

Because of the different foci and organization of the lessons, the two classes also differed in what came to be superordinate. In Lesson 1B, the nouns, adjectives, and partitives that described food and drink items became superordinate, as each was focused on and illustrated with varied examples of food/drink items, whereas in Lesson 1E, the food/drink became superordinate as the teacher focused on each of the food and drink items and varied the nouns and adjectives used to describe them (see Table 4.5).

In Lesson 1E, however, we find another example of "fusion," that is, different aspects (size, partitives) varying together. What is the impact of this structural difference on student learning?

Describing Learning Outcomes

To investigate the impact of structural difference on student learning, 43 students in Class 1B and 45 students in Class 1E were invited to complete a worksheet immediately after the lesson. The worksheet consisted of two questions. The first question required the students to put down what they perceived as the most important thing taught and/or learned in the lesson. The second question required them to fill in blanks in a dialogue (see Fig. 4.6 where the expected answers are underlined).

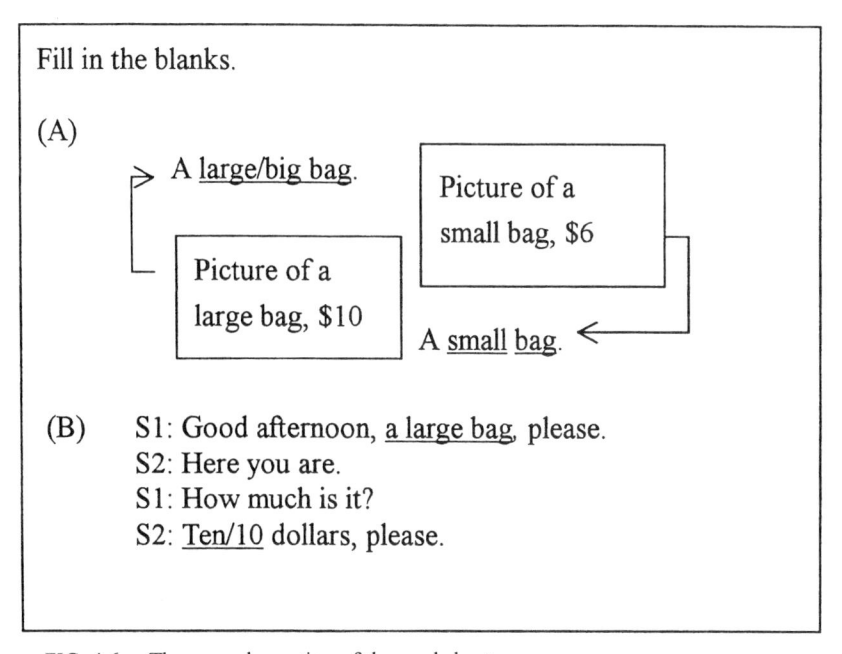

Fill in the blanks.

(A)   A <u>large/big bag</u>.
       Picture of a large bag, $10
       Picture of a small bag, $6
       A <u>small</u> <u>bag</u>.

(B)   S1: Good afternoon, <u>a large bag</u>, please.
       S2: Here you are.
       S1: How much is it?
       S2: <u>Ten/10</u> dollars, please.

FIG. 4.6. The second question of the worksheet.

The Students' Understanding of What They Learned in the Lesson. As shown in Table 4.6, nearly all the students in Class 1B reported that the most important things taught in the lesson were some language items (e.g., names, adjectives describing size, partitives, and the dialogue). Only one student mentioned that they had learned "how to find the prices," a concept that should have been one of the main foci of the lesson.

TABLE 4.6
The Students' Responses to the First General Question of the Written Task

	The first question:	What was the most important thing taught/learned in the lesson?	
	(N = total number of responses; some students gave more than one response)	*Class 1B (N = 50)*	*Class 1E (N = 48)*
	1. Language items	<u>48</u>	<u>40</u>
1.1	Some food and drink items	26	—
1.2	Goods other than 1.1	—	4
1.3	Size	4	8
1.4	Partitives	1	—
1.5	Size and partitives	3	—
1.6	Dollar	10	6
1.7	Prices of different food and drink items	3	—
1.8	Prices of goods other than food and drink	—	4
1.9	The "How much?" dialogue	1	14
1.10	Learning English in general terms (e.g. reading, writing English; some English words)	—	4
	2. Theme	<u>1</u>	<u>8</u>
2.1	How to find the prices	1	—
2.2	Conducting the dialogue or asking the "how much?" question or buying food and drink in the context of supermarket or teaching situation	—	8
	3. Others	<u>1</u>	<u>0</u>
3.1	Irrelevant	1	—
3.2	Missing	—	—

4. SIMULTANEITY AND THE ENACTED OBJECT OF LEARNING

There were relatively fewer responses in Class 1E (40 out of 48) indicating language items as the most important thing taught. One sixth of the students actually quoted some examples from their own personal experience of buying goods at a supermarket; these examples included items mentioned in the lesson (e.g., food or drink) as well as some not mentioned in the lesson (e.g., apples, melons, a teddy bear). None of the students from the other class did so.

Also, regarding those responses that mentioned the theme of buying things in a supermarket, the responses from Class 1E were mostly related to the context of buying in a supermarket, conducting the dialogue, and asking the "How much?" question, whereas, the responses from Class 1B were mainly about eliciting prices, and the context was seldom mentioned.

What Are the Learning Outcomes? The second question required the students to first fill in appropriate words to indicate the different sizes of two bags printed on the worksheet, and then to fill in the missing blanks in a simulated dialogue on buying and selling. In order to be able to fill in the appropriate words in the first section, the students had to be able to differentiate large and small objects and to use the correct vocabulary. In order to fill in the blanks of the dialogue, the students had to be able to recognize the sentences as parts of a dialogue carried out in a buying and selling context before they could choose the most appropriate words to fill in the blanks.

As shown in Table 4.7, nearly all of the students in both classes were able to describe the two bags with appropriate words that indicated their size. This shows that both classes had a good mastery of the words describing size as taught in the lesson. However, a difference was observed in the two classes' performance in answering the second part of the question. Whereas most of the students in Class 1E were able to understand the dialogue as belonging to a buying and selling context, and completed it in a meaningful way, only one third of Class 1B could do so. Many students in Class 1B did not recognize the two sentences as constituting a dialogue, and took them as single sentences unrelated to one another. For instance, some students understood the first incomplete sentence, "Good afternoon. ____, please." in a classroom context, and filled in the words "sit down," even though they made sense of the second sentence, "____ dollars, please." in the buying and selling context, and filled in the word "ten."

Simultaneity and the Possibility for Learning. One possible way to account for these differences in learning is the structural difference observed in the two teachers' ways of handling the objects of learning. The teacher of Lesson 1E organized the direct objects of learning in a hierarchical structure, using "buying in a supermarket" as a theme. Different attributes (name, size, packaging, and price) of each food/drink were focused on at the same time, which afforded the possibility of the simultaneous experience of those attributes. As a result, more of the students in Lesson 1E expressed

TABLE 4.7
The Students' Answers to the Specific Question of the Worksheet

Second part: Fill in the blanks

(A) A <u>large/big</u> bag.

    A <u>small</u> bag.

Class	1B (N = 43)	1E (N = 45)
1 Use of words to indicate size:		
1.1 Appropriate	39	45
1.2 One to three blanks missing / inappropriate (e.g. "a large of bag," "a small of bag")	4	—
2. <u>Wrong</u> spelling of words (large, small, bag)	6	11
(B) S1: Good afternoon, <u>a large/big bag/any goods</u>, please. S2: Here you are. S3: How much is it? S4: <u>Ten</u> dollars, please.		
1. Fill in <u>both</u> blanks appropriately (either using the information from the lesson, i.e. the eight kinds of food and drink items, or that provided in the worksheet, i.e. two bags of different sizes)	15	37
2. Fill in <u>one</u> of the blanks appropriately		
2.1 _____, please.	—	2
2.2 _____ dollars, please.	18[a]	4
3. <u>Inappropriate</u> answers to		
3.1 both 2.1 and 2.2	2[b]	—
3.2 2.1 and leaving 2.2 blank	1[c]	—
3.3 2.2 and leaving 2.1 blank	2[d]	—
4. Did not respond	5	2

Note. [a]Inappropriate answers to 2.1, for example, "sit down," "Miss W," "Have a biscuit," "many in," "you are," "teacher and," "good night," "thank you."
    [b]Inappropriate answers to, for example, 2.1 "you," "teacher and"; 2.2 "here," "it is."
    [c]Inappropriate answers to, for example, 2.1 and leaving 2.2 blank ("many in").
    [d]Inappropriate answers to, for example, 2.2 and leaving 2.1 blank ("it," "it is").

what they had learned in a contextual and organized way. In this lesson, because the food and drink items were superordinate to their attributes, it seems that the students could relate more readily to the fact that the objects of learning were the food and drink items that can be purchased in a supermarket, and that the "How much?" dialogue was used to inquire about price in a supermarket. The students could hence see the relevance of what they learned, because it was familiar to their daily experience. In Lesson 1B, however, because the words and/or adjectives describing the attributes of food and drink were superordinate to the food and drink items, it seems that most of the students not only had difficulties relating these attributes (the language items) and the use of the dialogue to the theme of "buying in a supermarket," but also in relating them to their own daily experiences. Although some students might have been able to recognize the relationship between the two by drawing on their own past experiences, this had been left to chance, instead of being consciously structured by the teacher. In Lesson 1E, on the other hand, the conscious effort of the teacher to structure the lesson using the theme of buying in a supermarket afforded the students the simultaneous experience of context, whole and parts.

Because language items such as partitives were highlighted and kept superordinate in Lesson 1B and not in Lesson 1E, we would expect to see some difference between Lesson 1B and Lesson 1E with respect to the students' understanding of these language items. That is, we should see that some students in Class 1B should be able to identify these items as the most important thing taught in the lesson. This was indeed borne out by the student data: Four students in Class 1B mentioned partitives as being the most important thing being taught, whereas none of the students from Class 1E mentioned partitives (see Table 4.6).

CONCLUSIONS

So far, we have discussed the possible effect of lesson structures on students' learning outcomes. This effect might be understood in terms of whether aspect–aspect and/or part–whole relationships could be experienced simultaneously by the learner. Using the example of the pair of mathematics lessons, we illustrated the different ways in which the teachers created the conditions for the simultaneous experience of the two aspects of fractional numbers. We then gave examples of two Chinese language lessons and two English language lessons to illustrate how the teachers were able to structure their lessons to facilitate the students' simultaneous experience of parts and wholes, and aspects versus aspects.

In the analysis of these two pairs of language lessons, it was also shown that the differences in students' learning outcomes are related to the structural differences in the ways in which the teachers organized the objects of learning, that is, to the differences in the enacted object of learning. The interesting fact is that in the case of these two pairs of lessons, the two teachers used the same teaching material, subscribed to the same intended object of learning, and almost certainly believed that they carried out the same lesson as well. We can presume that both teachers would have said that the enacted object of learning was, of course, the same in both classes.

However, this was not the case—as we have seen. The enacted object of learning differed substantially in both instances. This is because what students learn is not a function of the *intended* object of learning, but of the *enacted* object of learning, and what the students in these two classes learned clearly differed. The teachers were found to have directed students' attention to particular aspects of what was to be learned by structuring the lesson in such a way that the chosen aspects were kept invariant and superordinate to those aspects that varied. But what was invariant and superordinate made a difference to how well the students achieved the expected learning outcomes.

This has significant implications for ways of improving the quality of the teaching–learning cycle. It is likely that students will learn better if teachers can structure their lessons in such a way that students are able to discern and experience simultaneously parts and wholes, and aspects versus aspects.

ENDNOTES

[1] For the background of this research project, see the Epilogue.

[2] It is important to note that according to the notation system used in Sweden, 6/3 has dual meanings: "six thirds" and "six divided by three."

[3] We use "word" here to refer to a meaningful entity in the Chinese language. A meaningful entity can be single-syllabic (consisting of one character) or multi-syllabic (comprising two or more characters).

[4] We use "characters" to refer to the written forms of morphemes in the Chinese language. Some characters are meaningful on their own (single-syllabic entities) and some need to be coupled with other characters so as to make a meaningful entity (multisyllabic entities). Because all the single-syllabic entities referred to in this chapter have their own meanings, and because very often their forms of writing were dealt with in the lesson, we shall refer to these as "characters," and refer to multisyllabic entities as "words" for easy reference.

III

On Language

5

Questions and the Space of Learning

Amy B. M. Tsui
Ference Marton
Ida A. C. Mok
Dorothy F. P. Ng

QUESTIONS

Questions is perhaps the most thoroughly researched area of classroom learning. This is probably because it is the most distinctive feature of classroom discourse. A *lesson* is a speech event where people come together and engage in an activity referred to as "learning." Lessons are organized in such a way that there is at least one person in the classroom who is the "primary knower" (Berry, 1987) and who is responsible for disseminating knowledge to the others.[1] The knowledge gap between the "primary knower"—that is, the teacher—and the "secondary knower"—that is, the students—vests authority in the former in determining the direction that the lesson will take, the activities that will be conducted, the questions that will be asked, and what constitutes appropriate answers to these questions. When a teacher asks a question, the purpose is not to obtain information that the teacher does not have, but to check whether the students have the missing information indicated in the question. When a teacher asks, "What time is it, Johnny?" Johnny knows that he is supposed to tell the teacher the time even though there is a big clock on the wall that everybody can see. If Johnny says, "Well, look at the clock on the wall," or if he puts the question back to the teacher, "What does the clock say?" the class knows that Johnny is heading for trouble.

Students also know that questions are not asked for their own sake, but that they have a pedagogical motivation behind them, even though it may not be clear to the students exactly what that motivation is. Therefore, when a teacher asks a series of questions, the students are supposed to try and answer each one as best they can. They are not supposed to query the purpose of those questions by asking, "What are you trying to get at?" or "What has this question got to do with the preceding question?" at least not in Asian classrooms. Questions serve a number of other purposes in the classroom besides knowledge checking. For example, questions can be used for classroom management purposes such as preventing the students chatting, getting the students to focus on the lesson rather than daydreaming, and so on (see Tsui, 1995). In this chapter, we are not interested in classroom questions per se, but in the way the space of learning is constituted linguistically by the questions asked by the teacher, that is, the responses that can be elicited, and those that are actually elicited, and what the teacher accepts as appropriate.

QUESTIONS AND FOCAL AWARENESS

Questions asked at crucial stages of a lesson can focus students' attention on the critical aspects of the object of learning, create the context that will help students to make sense of the object of learning, and open up the space for exploration of an answer.

The data that we look at in this chapter consists of data sets from science and English classrooms in Hong Kong. Prior to presenting each data set, we provide a brief summary of the classroom contexts and the objects of learning.

Physics Lessons: The Reed Relay

The data set we look at in this section consists of two physics lessons taught by the same teacher, one taught in English, which is a second language for the students (referred to as EMI, English as a medium of instruction), and one in the students' mother tongue, Cantonese (referred to as CMI, Chinese as a medium of instruction). The direct object of learning in both lessons is the same: the function of a reed relay and how it operates. (For a detailed description of the background of these two lessons, see Ng, Tsui, & Marton, 2001.) A brief explanation of the direct object of learning is in order here.

The function of a reed relay is to enable a weak electric current in an electric circuit to start a much stronger current in another electric circuit by connecting the two with a reed switch (see Fig. 5.1 for a picture of a reed relay).

When a weak electric current in one circuit passes through the reed relay, a magnetic field is produced and the coil becomes an electromagnet, causing the two ends of the reed switch to touch one another. Once the two ends of the reed switch touch one another, the circuit that carries a very large electric current is closed and the electric current will pass through and operate

5. QUESTIONS AND THE SPACE OF LEARNING 115

Reed relay

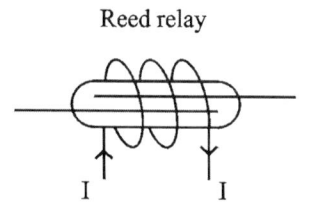

FIG. 5.1. A reed relay.

the device that is connected to it (see Fig. 5.2b and Fig. 5.3b). In the example lessons, the teacher used a device called a light-emitting diode (LED)—which requires only a weak current to operate (see Fig. 5.2a)—and a motor—which requires a very large current to operate (see Fig. 5.3b)—to illustrate how the use of a reed relay enables a weak current to activate a very large current, and cause the motor to rotate.

The structures of the two lessons are almost identical. In both lessons, the teacher first explained the structure of a reed relay by showing that it consists of a reed switch with coils wrapped round it (see Fig. 5.1). She then explained the configuration of a simple circuit connected to an LED (see Fig. 5.2a), and the configuration of a complicated circuit also connected to an LED (see Fig. 5.2b).

The teacher asked the students to conduct two experiments. In the first experiment, students were asked to connect two circuits. One circuit was controlled by a push button switch and connected to an LED, and was re-

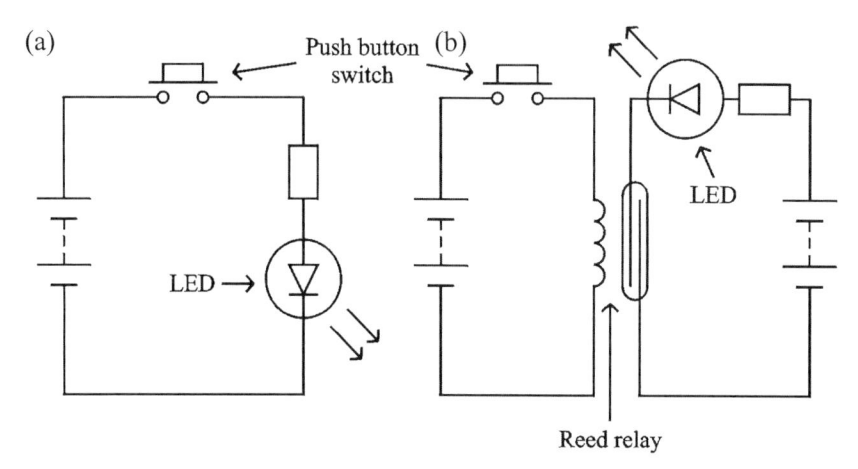

FIG. 5.2. (a) A simple circuit. (b) A complicated circuit with a reed relay.

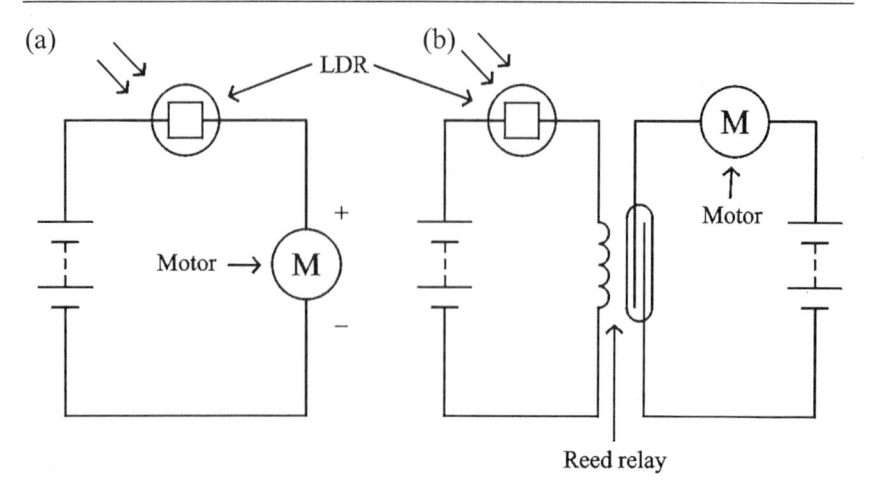

FIG. 5.3. (a) A simple circuit. (b) A complicated circuit with reed relay.

ferred to as the *simple circuit* (see Fig. 5.2a). The other circuit was also controlled by a push button, and had a reed relay connected to it as well as an LED. This circuit was referred to as the *complicated circuit* (see Fig. 5.2b). The teacher asked the students to press the push button switch for both circuits. In both circuits, the LED glowed when the circuits were closed by pressing the push button switch, which allowed an electric current to pass through. In the second experiment, the teacher asked the students to replace the LED with a motor, and the push button switch with an LDR (light-diode resistor)[2] for both the simple and the complicated circuits (see Fig. 5.3a and Fig. 5.3b). An LDR is a light sensitive device that stops an electric current from passing through. When light shines on an LDR, its resistance drops and electricity can pass through. The teacher asked the students to shine a torch on the LDR and watch what happened. The students found that the motor in the simple circuit (without the reed relay) did not move, whereas the motor in the complicated circuit (with the reed relay) did. This is because the electric current that passed through the simple circuit was not big enough to cause the motor to rotate. By contrast, in the complicated circuit, the current became much larger after passing through the reed relay, and hence allowed the motor to rotate.

After the students had performed the two experiments, the teacher went over what they had experienced with the whole class. She asked them to tell her what happened to the LED when they pressed the push button switch and they reported that the LED in both circuits glowed. On hearing the students' reports, the teacher posed the following question:

5. QUESTIONS AND THE SPACE OF LEARNING 117

5.1 [Physics Lesson/CMI][3]

T: It seems that if this is the case, we do not need to use the reed relay. Why use the complicated circuit when the simple circuit can do the job? Do you agree?

The teacher problematized the students' observation by putting a hypothetical statement to them: "If this is the case, we do not need to use the reed relay." Here, "this is the case" refers to the fact that the LED glowed in both circuits, suggesting that there was no difference between the two circuits. However, the teacher signaled that this hypothesis may or may not be confirmed, by prefacing the statement with "it seems that." This prepared the ground for the following question: "Why use the complicated circuit when the simple circuit can do the job?" The presupposition of this question is that the simple circuit can do the job in the same way as the complicated circuit. What is questioned is the reason for using the complicated circuit. The questioned element focused the students' attention on the complicated circuit, and the reason for using it. The juxtaposition of the fact that the simple and complicated circuits could both light up the LED created the need for an explanation (see Ogborn, Kress, Martins, & McGillicuddy, 1996) and opened up the space for exploring the function of a reed relay. The question created the context for making sense of the outcome of the second experiment. To put it another way, the question created the need to look for the answer in the second experiment.

As already described, in the second experiment, the teacher asked the students to replace the push button switch with an LDR and the LED with a motor in both circuits. She asked them to shine a torch on the LDR and see whether the motor moved in each of the circuits (see Fig. 3a and Fig. 3b).

After the experiment, the teacher went over what the students had experienced. She asked the students what had happened to the motor in the complicated circuit. The students reported that the motor rotated. She then continued as follows:

5.2 [Physics Lesson / CMI]

T: Yes, how about this side? [The teacher points at the simple circuit] This side is even simpler. Now, here we go. Strong light shines on the LDR, electric resistance value decreases. We expect that there's an electric current, a stronger electric current, passing through the circuit and the motor should rotate, right? But it is very unhappy. It does not respond. We need to explain this.

This time, the teacher drew the students' attention to the simple circuit by asking, "How about this side?" She problematized the experience by pointing out that the failure of the motor to respond, even though a stronger electric current passed through the circuit, was contrary to what they expected. Again she created a need for an explanation.

Let us pause here and look at why the teacher did not focus on the reason for the motor rotating in the complicated circuit, but instead focused the students' attention on the reason for the motor in the simple circuit not rotating, even though the electric resistance value decreased and the electric current became stronger. Why did the teacher do that?

In the first experiment, the LED worked in both circuits. If the teacher had drawn the students' attention to the complicated circuit, the students would have not been able to discern the difference between the two circuits because in the complicated circuit both devices (the LED and the motor) worked. By juxtaposing a circuit in which the motor worked (a complicated circuit) with another circuit in which it did not work (a simple circuit), the teacher brought into the students' focal awareness different responses of the same device, and opened up the space for exploring the answer in the different configurations of the two circuits.

Subsequently, the teacher put an ammeter in each circuit to measure the strength of its electric current. The readings showed that the electric current in the simple circuit was much smaller than that in the complicated circuit. The teacher then guided the students through each circuit and helped them to formulate the reason why the motor did not rotate in the simple circuit; that is, that although the electric current became stronger when the resistance value decreased, it was not strong enough to cause the motor to rotate.

The teacher did not stop here, however. She then went back to the simple circuit with the LED in Fig. 2a and posed the following question:

5.3 [Physics Lesson/CMI/T8]

T: Why is it that this circuit [the simple circuit connected to an LED] worked? Why was it [LED] so well-behaved? Why did it [LED] light up?

By asking these questions, the teacher was juxtaposing the simple circuit connected to an LED with the simple circuit connected to a motor. In other words, she now held the circuit constant, and varied the device, the motor, and the LED. The questions she asked brought into the students' focal awareness the different responses of the two devices, and opened up the space for exploring the reasons. A correct understanding of the reasons was achieved when one student explained that the circuit with the LED lit up because the electric current needed by the LED was smaller than the current needed by the motor. This is the corollary of why the motor did not rotate.

Let us recapitulate the way in which the teacher structured the learning experience.

5. QUESTIONS AND THE SPACE OF LEARNING

First of all, in the first experiment, the teacher varied the configurations of the two circuits so that there was one without a reed relay (i.e., a simple circuit [C1]), and one with a reed relay (i.e., a complicated circuit [C2]), whereas the device that the students operated was invariant (the LED [D1]). In both cases, the LED lit up.

In the second experiment, the teacher changed the device from the LED (D1) in the first experiment to the motor (D2) for both circuits. This time, it was also the device that was invariant (the motor [D2]), and the circuit that varied (the one with a reed relay [C1] and the one without a reed relay [C2]). What the teacher did is represented diagrammatically in Fig. 5.4a.

However, in the second experiment, the variation that the teacher wanted the students to experience was not the variation between the two circuits, but the variation between what they experienced in the previous configuration (the first experiment) and the present configuration (the second experiment), which was due to the use of different devices: D1 in the first experiment and D2 in the second experiment. The teacher's exhortation for an explanation in the second excerpt (5.2) and the question in the third excerpt (5.3) focused precisely on the different responses of the LED (D1) and the motor (D2). In other words, the teacher was now constructing the students' total experience (of the two experiments) as a whole. She held the circuit configurations constant (in both experiments, a simple and a complicated circuit were involved), and what varied were the devices (in the first experiment an LED was involved, whereas in the second experiment a motor was involved). The structure of the potential learning experience can be represented by Fig. 5.4b, where the bolded parts represent the aspects that were held constant in the first and second experiments, and the underlined parts represent the aspects that varied.

This structure of variation brought the responses of the devices into the students' focal awareness in relation to two contexts: why the motor rotated in the complicated circuit but did not in the simple circuit, and why the LED worked in the simple circuit but the motor did not. If, in the second experiment, the teacher had replaced the LED with a motor only in the compli-

First Experiment	C1 → D1	C2 → D1
Second Experiment	C1 -x-> D2	C2 → D2
C1 = simple circuit	D1 = LED (light-emitting diode)	
C2 = complicated circuit	D2 = motor	
→ caused device to operate		
-x-> failed to cause device to operate		

FIG. 5.4a. Structuring learning.

First Experiment	Second Experiment
C1 → D1	C1 -x-> D2
C2 → D1	C2 → D2

FIG. 5.4b. Structuring of learning; first experiment versus second experiment.

cated circuit (as shown in Fig. 5.4c) both devices would have worked and the students' attention would not have been so sharply focused on what it is that a circuit with the reed relay can do that one without cannot.

Conversely, if the teacher had started off by using the motor as the device for both circuits in the first experiment, then all the students would have seen was that the motor worked only in the circuit with the reed relay. They would not have been able to see that the electric current in the simple circuit was a weak current which could operate an LED, but not strong enough to operate the motor. Consequently, the main characteristic of the reed relay (that it uses a small current to switch on a strong current) would not have been so effectively highlighted.

What is even more interesting is the way the teacher made the students see the interrelationship between the first experiment and the second experiment: that the LED needs only a small current to operate (which is why it worked in the simple circuit), whereas the motor needs a large current (which is why it did not work). In order to make the motor work, a reed relay is needed because it can use a small current to start a very large current. The teacher's explanation can be represented on following page (see Fig. 5.4d).

The way that the teacher structured the learning experience by posing questions at critical points in the lesson brought into students' focal awareness critical aspects of the experiment and opened up the space for exploring the answers to the questions. This was crucial in bringing about the simultaneous awareness of the three phenomena (i.e., the small current required to operate the LED, the very large current needed to operate the motor, as well as the way in which they are related), which was necessary for the students to understand the function of the reed relay.

So far, we have illustrated how questions can be a powerful means for bringing critical aspects of the object of learning into students' focal awareness, and opening up the space for further enquiry. We have also seen how

First Experiment	Second Experiment
C1 → D1	C1 → D1
C2 → D1	**C2 → D1**

FIG. 5.4c. Alternative structuring of learning.

$$C1 < C2$$
$$D1 < D2$$
$$C1 \rightarrow D1$$
$$C1 \not\rightarrow D2$$
$$C2 \rightarrow D2$$

FIG. 5.4d. Teacher's explanation.

the teacher skillfully structured the learning experience by posing questions at critical junctures in the lesson.

In the following section, we see how different questions asked by the teacher can bring different aspects of a phenomenon into students' focal awareness.

English Lessons: "Old MacDonald's Farm"

The data that is discussed in this section consist of two primary Grade 1 English lessons (Class 1D and Class 1E) taught by two teachers who used very similar materials and whose lesson objectives were the same. The topic of the lessons was "Old MacDonald's Farm," an English song about farm animals that is familiar to children of many different nationalities. One of the objectives of the lesson was to teach the determiner "some" to signify inexact quantity. In the song, the word "some" appears many times in the lyrics, and for this reason, the teachers used the song as a vehicle for teaching this determiner to the children. Both teachers used computer-generated images to revise farm animal vocabulary and subsequently to teach "some." (For a detailed description of the background of these two lessons, see Mok, Runesson, Tsui, Wong, Chik, & Pow, 2002.)

Teaching "Some." Both teachers began by revising the vocabulary for farm animals by asking the question, "What can you see?" In each case, the picture of a single animal was presented on the computer, and the responses solicited were "I can see a [name of animal]." The focus at this stage of the lesson was the names of the animals, rather than the number. The important difference between the two lessons lies in the subsequent episodes where both teachers dealt with the teaching of "some."

After the vocabulary revision, the teacher in 1D asked the students to guess the number of different kinds of animals on a farm. She followed this by showing the students different kinds of farm animals and asking how many animals there were in each picture. The following is an excerpt of what took place in the lesson immediately after the vocabulary revision. To make it easier for the reader to follow the subsequent discussion of the data, the parts that will be discussed are underlined.

5.4 [English Lesson/Old MacDonald's Farm/Primary Grade 1/1D][4]

119	T:	... Do you know <u>how many</u> cows or hens? Or <u>how many</u> horses,
120		<u>how many</u> hens, <u>how many</u> pigs are (there) in a farm? Do you
121		know? Do you know?
122	Ss:	No.
123	T:	OK, let's see what's in the farm. All right, OK, which one do you
124		want to see first?
125	Ss:	Cow.
126	T:	OK, you want to see cows. Right. <u>Guess how many cows are there</u>
127		<u>in the farm</u>?
128	S:	[shouting from his seat] Four.
129	T:	<u>How many</u> cows?
130	S:	[shouting from his seat] Four.
131	T:	Yes, Leo.
132	S:	Four.
133	T:	What do you think, Louise?
134	S:	Three.
135	T:	What do you think, Ho Seng?
136	S:	Six.
137	T:	What do you think Elaine?
138	S:	Five.
139	T:	OK, Elaine. <u>Do you want to find out</u>? OK, come here. <u>Let's find</u>
140		<u>out how many</u>. OK, cows. [Speaking to Elaine] Press the button
141		please. [Elaine comes up to the front and clicks the mouse. An
142		image of a cow appears on the screen.] All right, OK. Let's see
143		how many cows in the farm. What can you see here? [Teacher
144		points at the screen.] <u>What can you see here</u>?
145	Ss:	I can see a cow.
146	T:	Good. <u>Now let's find out how many cows there are</u>? [Teacher
147		clicks the mouse and four more cows appear on the screen.] <u>How</u>
148		<u>many cows are there</u>?

5. QUESTIONS AND THE SPACE OF LEARNING   **123**

149	Ss:	Five.
150	T:	Four?
151	Ss:	Five.
152	T:	10?
153		Five.
154	T:	I can see … ?
155	Ss:	… five cows.
156	T:	Right. Or you may say … ?
157	Ss:	I can see five cows.
158	Ss:	I can see a cow.
159	T:	What?
160	Ss:	I can see …
161	T:	Some
162	Ss:	Some cows.
163	T:	Some cows. Yes. There are some cows here. <u>Is it only one</u>?
164		[Pointing at the screen.]
165	Ss:	No.
166	T:	<u>There are four cows</u>. You may say, I can see some cows. OK,
167		whole class.
168	Ss:	I can see some cows.
169	T:	All right, let's continue.… [Teacher clicks the mouse several times
170		and six different types of animals appear on the screen] OK, <u>do
171		you want to find out how many</u> [pointing to the picture of a
172		duck] <u>ducks there [are] in the farm</u>? …

In this excerpt, the teacher started with the question, "Do you know <u>how many</u> cows or hens? Or <u>how many</u> horses, <u>how many</u> hens, <u>how many</u> pigs are [there] in a farm?" The questioned element is the number of animals, and it was repeated four times. As we have pointed out previously, it is the questioned element that focuses the students' attention. The focus on the number of animals was reinforced when the teacher asked the students to guess "how many" cows there were on the farm (see lines 126–127). As we can see from the students' responses, they did indeed focus on the number, and proffered "four," "three," "six," and "five" as answers. After this, the teacher asked the students to find out the answer for themselves by inviting one of them to come up to the computer at the front of the class. The student clicked the mouse and <u>one</u> cow appeared. The teacher asked the student what she could see, and the student said that she could see <u>a</u> cow. This was followed by the teacher showing four more cows on the screen and once again posing the question, "How many cows are there?" By doing this, the teacher was contrasting "one" with "more than one." Moreover, by repeatedly asking the students "how many cows" there were, the teacher was contrasting "one" with "other numbers," that is, with a value of more than one, hence opening up a dimension of variation in <u>number</u>. In other words, what was brought into the students' focal awareness was exact numbers, whereas the objective of the lesson was to teach "some," which is an inexact number rather than an exact number.

The focus on exact number was reinforced by the teacher subsequently getting four students to guess the exact number of cows (lines 131, 133, 135, and 137). When the cows were shown on the screen, the teacher offered different numbers to tease the students and deliberately suspended the evaluative feedback on the exact number that the students provided. It was not until line 156 that the teacher tried to elicit the determiner "some" from the students by using the blank-filling question: "Or you may say ... ?" The students' responses to this blank-filling question were telling. Some students said, "There are five cows," and some said, "I can see a cow." Both answers provided exact numbers, which suggests that exact number was still very much in their focal awareness. The determiner "some" was supplied by the teacher and the students were made to repeat it after her. But it is doubtful if the students fully understood what "some" meant. When the teacher moved on to the next episode (line 170), where she showed the picture of a duck, she again asked the students whether they wanted to find <u>how many</u> ducks there were on the farm.

The focus on exact number was also reinforced by the way in which the teacher introduced the determiner "some." In both cases, the word "some" was introduced at the very end of the episode, by presenting it as an alternative statement to an exact number, for example, "There are four cows. You may say, I can see some cows," "There are seven ducks, or you may tell me, I can see some ducks." In both cases the exact number preceded the inexact number signified by "some."

Let us compare the just cited discourse with the following excerpt that shows what took place in the lesson of Class 1E after the teacher had finished vocabulary revision.

5.5   [English Lesson/Old McDonald's Farm/Primary Grade 1/1E]

70   T: [Teacher clicks the mouse] A dog. [Teacher clicks the mouse
71   again] another dog [Teacher clicks the mouse again] another dog.
72   Wow, <u>what can you see</u>? Alice?

5. QUESTIONS AND THE SPACE OF LEARNING 125

73	S:	I can see three dogs.
74	T:	Very good, three dogs. There are three dogs. Thank you. And you
75		can say that, in other words, we can say that ...
76	Ss:	We can see dogs.
77	T:	<u>Remember the word "some"</u>?
78	Ss:	Yes.
79	T:	Thank you, very well. I can see some dogs. <u>Do you remember the
80		word "some"?</u>
81	Ss:	Yes.
82	T:	Yes, all right. Now, another one. [Teacher clicks the mouse] Another
83		pig. OK. <u>Now, so we have a pig</u>, we'll see OK. Come and press the
84		button. [A student comes out.]
85	T:	Is he finished? Is there another pig there? Press the button. Wow,
86		another pig? <u>What can you see then</u>?
87	S:	<u>I can see some pigs.</u>
88	T:	Very good!

To begin with, the teacher in 1E showed the picture of a single animal, a dog, just as the teacher in 1D had done. However, before she showed the picture, the teacher asked, "What can you see?" rather than "How many dogs can you see?" The questioned element is "what" and not "how many." Asking "What can you see?" did not focus the students' attention on the exact number. It was open to the students to give exact or inexact numbers as answers. When the teacher asked the students to offer an alternative for seeing three dogs, the students said, "We can see dogs." In other words, conceptually, the students were aware that one alternative was to leave out specifying the exact number, and to simply use the plural form to indicate that there was more than one dog. At this point, the teacher provided the linguistic support to the students by reminding them that the word "some" had been introduced before. In the subsequent episodes, the teacher showed three different kinds of farm animals: pigs, ducks and cats. In each episode, she varied one with more than one, and posed the same question, "What can you see?" The students had no problems responding with, "I can see some pigs [some ducks, some cats]." In other words, the questioned element, "what," opened up a dimension of variation in inexact number, that is, one versus some.

After successfully soliciting the determiner "some" from the students, the teacher went on to pose the question, "How many [animals] are there?" in the third episode. Let us consider the following excerpt:

5.6 [English Lesson/Old MacDonald's Farm/Primary Grade 1/1E]

103	S:	I can see <u>some</u> cats.
104	T:	Very good. OK. Wait a minute. <u>How many</u> cats are there?
105		How many cats are there?
106	S:	<u>Four</u> cats.
107	T:	Is he correct?
108	S:	Yes.
109	T:	Very good. Thank you. OK, how about this picture? Alright.
110		[Teacher clicks the mouse.] Ho Ming, would you come out
111		and press it for me to see what picture comes out? [Ho Ming
112		clicks the mouse.]
113	T:	What is it?
114	Ss:	Ducks, ducks.
115	T:	Very good. Thanks. [Teacher asks Ho Ming to click the
116		mouse.] Any more ducks? [Student clicks the mouse and
117		some ducks appear.]
118	T:	Any more? [Student clicks the mouse again and some more
119		ducks appear.] Any more? [Student clicks the mouse
120		again.] No more. OK, <u>what can you see</u> now? Hold the mike
121		and tell your classmates, OK?
122	S:	I can see <u>some</u> duck.
123	T:	Ducks.
124	S:	Ducks.
125	T:	Ducks.
126	S:	Ducks.
127	T:	OK. Very good. <u>How many</u> ducks are there? How many
128		ducks are there?
129	S:	[same student] <u>Five</u> ducks.
130	T:	Five ducks. Thank you very much. Five ducks. Yes, you can
131		see some ducks, you can see some pigs, you can see some
132		cats, and you can see some ...
133	Ss:	Dogs.
134	T:	Dogs. OK....

Let us consider the sequence of questioning from the perspective of the logical relationship between inexact and exact numbers. The determiner "some" signifies a range of numbers or quantities and is inclusive of exact numbers such as 3, 4, 5, 10, and so on. The teacher in Class 1E first posed the question, "What can you see?" followed by "How many?" This is a logical sequence—when requesting information, one often goes from general to specific—and the exact number is seen in relation to the inexact number. By contrast, the teacher in Class 1D started with, "How many cows can you see?" which is already very specific, and therefore renders the use of the determiner "some" to describe an inexact number superfluous. Thus the production of "some" becomes contrived.

What both teachers tried to teach was how to express inexact numbers that are more than one. However, the different questions that the teachers asked, and the way they sequenced the questions, focused the students' attention on different ways of expressing numbers that are more than one (that is, exact number and inexact number), and opened up different dimensions of variation. The enacted object of learning in one case was an inexact number, whereas in the other case, it was an exact number, which was not an intended object of learning.

In postlesson interviews conducted with half of the students from each class, a task was given to solicit the use of "some" to describe a selection of pictures. The results showed that students in Class 1E performed better than students in Class 1D.

QUESTION TYPES, QUESTION SEQUENCES, AND THE SPACE OF LEARNING

Question Types

Many studies have focused on the cognitive aspect of questions, and various taxonomies of question types have been proposed, for example, the system of classifying questions according to whether they require higher or lower order thinking skills. Our concern in this chapter is not to examine question types per se. We are interested in those questions that have been referred to as "open" and "closed" questions, and the opportunities for learning that are afforded by these questions. In particular, we are interested in the ways in which teachers modify and sequence their questions in order to elicit responses from students, and hence how teachers shape their students' learning experiences.

In classroom research literature, distinctions have been made between closed and open questions. However, there are different criteria for identifying these questions. In education research literature, a *closed question* has been understood as having only one right answer, whereas an *open question* is one that has a number of right answers. In this volume, we use *closed questions* to mean questions where there is only one acceptable answer, and *open questions* to mean questions where there is a range of possible answers, or a range of possible ways of *presenting* the answer. For example, "Why does this motor work?" is an open question, whereas "What is the name given to this magnet?" is a closed question. When the teacher asks an open question, the space of learning is widened because the question challenges the students to consider a number of possibilities, and to formulate an answer that makes sense not only to themselves but also to the rest of the class. The formulation of an answer is a process in which the students clarify their thinking and their understanding of the object of learning. On the other hand, closed questions narrow down the possible answers to only one choice, or a limited number of choices, and hence allow little room for learners to explore answers.

In classrooms, it is very common for teachers to decompose a complex open question into a series of simpler questions in order to help students to arrive at an appropriate answer. This is referred to as "piloting" by Lundgren (1977). Studies of classroom questions have identified different sequences of questions used by teachers, and analyzed them as to whether they were successful or not in terms of helping students to answer the question. For example, among the sequences of questions that Brown and Edmondson (1984) identified were these two sequences, which they referred to as "funneling" (p. 114): an open question followed by specific questions; and an open question followed by a narrowing down of this question to recall facts and simple deductions. "Funneling" is most commonly found when the teacher has failed to elicit a response from students with the initial open question.

In classrooms where a language other than the mother tongue is used as a medium of teaching and learning (e.g., in English as a second language classrooms), we typically find modification of wh-questions (i.e., from *why* questions to *what* questions), and changes in question format (e.g., from wh-questions to yes–no questions). This is primarily because responding to why-questions is linguistically more demanding than responding to what-questions (which often require answers consisting of only one or two words or a phrase). And responding to yes–no questions (or alternative questions) is least demanding because it generally involves the production of either a "yes" or a "no" answer (or in some cases, making a choice among the alternatives provided). "Blank-filling" questions (where the teacher provides part of the sentence and blanks out the key word(s) for the students to fill in) are also typically found because they lessen the linguistic burden of the students (see Tsui, 1995).

Let us return to the physics lesson on the reed relay and consider the following extract:

5. QUESTIONS AND THE SPACE OF LEARNING   129

5.7 [Physics Lesson/Reed Relay/EMI/S2/T8]

1	T:	... Oh then surely, now girls, can you explain to me, <u>why doesn't
2		this motor work</u>?
3	Ss:	[silent]
4	T:	Why doesn't this motor work? <u>Just because motor must use ___</u>?
5	Ss:	[silent]
6	T:	<u>The current that is ___</u>? <u>Large or small</u>?
7	S:	Large.
8	T:	Large.

We can see that the teacher asked an open question and no response was forthcoming. Then the teacher provided some linguistic scaffolding in the form of filling in the blanks. When this failed to elicit a response, she provided more linguistic help and again invited the students to fill in the blank. When a response was not immediately forthcoming, she provided a choice for them. This kind of sequence restricts what counts as an acceptable answer; the answer not only has to be appropriate in terms of the content, but also has to fit into the linguistic structure provided. In order to answer the teacher's question, the students had to shift their focus of attention from the substantive part (i.e., the reason why the motor did not work), to an answer that would fit the syntax given by the teacher. When the teacher provided two choices to the students, the cognitive demand was minimal. This kind of funneling effect reduces the space in which the students can explore various possible answers for themselves, and formulate the appropriate answer. It also has the detrimental effect of encouraging students to guess what the teacher has in mind, and to try to produce an answer that will meet the teacher's approval. The following is another excerpt from the physics lesson on the reed relay taught through English (EMI).

5.8 [Physics Lesson/Reed Relay/EMI/S2/T8]

		The teacher asked the students to compare the electric current required to operate a motor and the electric current required for an LED to light up.
17	T:	... <u>Why does the LED work here</u>? [Nominate]
18	S:	[silent]
19	T:	The LED works, but it [Teacher points at the motor] does not
20		rotate. It's [a] similar construction. [Nominate] Tell me, <u>how
21		much current is needed to operate a motor</u>?
22	S:	[silent]

23	T:	How much current is needed? <u>It should be very ___</u>?
24	S:	200mA.
25	T:	Ah, nearly 200mA, very good, very large current. But can you
26		tell me <u>how much current is needed to operate a LED</u>?
27	S:	<u>Very small current.</u>
28	T:	Yes, very small current is enough all right. Then can you explain
29		to me, why does this LED light?
30	S:	[silent]

In this excerpt, the teacher posed an open question in line 17: "Why does the LED work?" When the student had difficulties responding to the question, the teacher modified the question into a more specific one about the amount of electric current required to operate a motor, "How much current is needed to operate a motor?" (lines 20–21). She then narrowed down the question further by turning it into a blank-filling question in line 23, "It should be very ____?" which provided the students with the linguistic structure of the first part of the answer, and only required them to fill in the key word(s). As pointed out before, this kind of funneling often happens in classrooms where the students' language ability is weak because it lessens the linguistic burden on the students to formulate the response.

The use of this type of questioning sequence focuses the students' attention on how they can finish the sentence in a way that will fit into the syntax of the partial sentence provided, and, very often, in a way that will also correspond with the answer the teacher has in mind. In the just cited excerpt, the teacher's subsequent question "How much current is needed?" focused the students' attention on the size of the current. The linguistic scaffolding that the teacher provided required the students to put in an adjective rather than an exact figure (see line 23). The student, however, attended to the "how much" question and provided the exact size of the current. Although this answer was accepted by the teacher, she rephrased it as "very large current." We can assume that the students then realized that the teacher was looking for a general description of the size rather than the exact size of the current, if we look at the subsequent exchange. When the teacher asked, "How much current is needed to operate an LED?" (line 26), a student this time replied, "a very small current" instead of giving the exact size of the current (see line 27).

From this discussion, we can see that the types of questions asked by the teacher can either open up the space of learning by encouraging students to explore possible answers and to formulate their own answers, or reduce the space of learning by confining students to only a restricted number of possibilities and even by encouraging them to engage in guesswork.

Question Sequence and Focal Awareness

So far, we have seen that questions play a very important role in constituting the space of learning in the classroom. They structure the learning experience and they focus the students' attention on different aspects of the object of learning, whether wittingly, or unwittingly, on the part of the teacher. In discussing the data from the English lesson on Old MacDonald's Farm, we have seen that different sequences of questions can focus the learners' attention on quite different things. We also mentioned that teachers often decompose a complex question into simpler questions, and we focused on the ways in which such sequences could reduce the space of learning. In this section, we draw the reader's attention to the fact that such sequences sometimes lead to a shift in focus, with the result that the intended object of learning is lost.

Let us take for example the following two parallel excerpts from the EMI and the CMI physics lessons, where the teachers explained exactly the same phenomenon: why the motor does not rotate in the simple circuit.

5.9 [Physics Lesson/Reed relay/EMI/S2/T8]
1	T:	... Oh then surely, now girls, can you explain to me, <u>why doesn't</u>
2		<u>this motor work</u>?
3	Ss:	[silent]
4	T:	Why doesn't this motor work? Just because motor must use __?
5	Ss:	[silent]
6	T:	The current that is __? Large or small?
7	S:	Large.
8	T:	Large.
		....
17	T:	... <u>Why does the LED work here</u>? [Nominate]
18	S:	[silent]
19	T:	The LED works, but it [Teacher points at the motor] does not
20		rotate. It's [a] similar construction. [Nominate] Tell me, <u>how</u>
21		<u>much current is needed to operate a motor</u>?
22	Ss:	[silent]
23	T:	<u>How much current is needed</u>? It should be very __?
24	S:	200mA.
25	T:	Ah, nearly 200mA, very good, very large current. But can you
26		tell me <u>how much current is needed to operate a LED</u>?
27	S:	Very small current.
28	T:	Yes, very small current is enough. All right. Then can you
29		explain to me, <u>why does this LED light [up]</u>?

30	Ss:	[silent]
31	T:	It [referring to the motor] does not rotate, just because there's
32		no large current. The LED works just because ___?
33	S:	Because the LED—
34	T:	Use—
35	S:	Use small current and the motor use very large current.
36	T:	All right, yes, your answer is so impressive. Would you please
37		repeat it once. It's correct, repeat it once.
38	S:	The LED use[s] small current while the motor use[s] very large
39		current.
40	T:	Yes, very good, the LED use[s] [a] small current while the motor
41		use[s] very large current. All right, OK.

Here the teacher asked two open questions: "Why doesn't this motor work?" and "Why does the LED light [up]?" These questions opened up a number of possible answers, as pointed out before. However, because the teacher used blank-filling questions to help the students to provide an answer to the open questions, the students' focus of awareness shifted from the reasons why the motor did not rotate, and why the LED lit up, to the amount of current needed by the motor and the LED. For example, in lines 20 and 23, the teacher repeated the question, "How much current is needed [to operate a motor]?" In line 26, she asked the same question about the LED. Although the students were able to tell the teacher that the LED needed a very small current, when the teacher posed the question about why the LED did not light up in line 29, there was no response from the class until she gave them some help. In other words, the students' attention was focused on the size of the current but they were unable to relate the size of the current to the reason why the motor did not rotate whereas the LED did light up.

Let us compare the aforementioned example with the following excerpt taken from the CMI classroom.

5.10 [Physics Lesson/Reed relay/CMI/S2/T8]

1	T:	We find that even though we shone a strong light on the LDR,
2		yes, its electric resistance value decreased. But in fact the electric
3		current that will pass through is ___ and the electric current needed
4		to by the motor is ___. Do you know what I would like you to
5		answer? [Nominate] You try, you try to explain why nothing
6		happens here. Now I shine a strong light on the LDR, right? Its

5. QUESTIONS AND THE SPACE OF LEARNING 133

```
7              resistance is ___?
8    S:        Small.
9    T:        Yes, small. So there will naturally be an electric current coming
10             in. Can you guess what the difference is between this electric
11             current and the electric current it actually needs?
12   S:        The resistor's electric current is smaller than the motor's.
13   T:        This means the motor needs an electric current that is ___?
14   S:        Large.
15   T:        Not only large, but very large. Yes, and so ... thank you, you
16             have answered correctly. And so, even though we shine a strong
17             light on the LDR, its resistance value drops, and the so-called
18             larger electric current flows through the circuit. The motor needs
19             a very large electric current to rotate, and so this is the difference
20             between this circuit and the other circuit.
```

In this excerpt, the teacher also asked the students to explain "why nothing happens here," meaning why the motor did not rotate (lines 5 and 6). She also provided linguistic scaffolding to help the students to provide the answer, by asking them what kind of current would pass through and what kind of current was needed (lines 3, 4, and 7). However, after the students had filled in the blanks, she posed an open question once again (lines 10 and 11). All the time, the teacher focused the students' attention on the difference between the current needed and the current that actually passed through the circuit. The modifications of the open question and the sequencing of the closed questions did not shift the students' focal awareness away from the original open question.

Finally, compare the following parallel excerpts from the EMI and the CMI physics lessons where again the same phenomenon was being dealt with; that is, what happened when the light shines on the LDR.

5.11 [Physics Lesson/Reed Relay/CMI/S2/T8]

```
1    T:        OK. [Teacher points to the complicated circuit] We love
2              shining a strong light on the LDR. Now, here it comes, strong
3              light shines on the LDR. [Teacher shines the torch on the LDR]
4              I'll ask you questions step by step. For the circuit on the left side,
5              this circuit, the largest effect is the electric resistance value,
6              right? Strong light shines on the LDR, I've told you before, and
```

7		the electric resistance value drops. OK, <u>what effect will it have</u>
8		<u>on the electric current on this side of the circuit</u>? [nominate]
9	S:	<u>Electric resistance drops</u>.
10	T:	<u>Electric resistance drops, the electric current ___ ?</u>
11	S:	<u>Increases</u>.
12	T:	Yes, the electric current increases, the electric current becomes
13		larger, right? When an electric current flows through the circuit,
14		this coil is no longer simply a coil, it becomes an electromagnet.
15		<u>Electromagnets can produce ___ ?</u>
16	S:	Magnetic fields.
17	T:	Yes, they produce magnetic fields. When it produces an
18		electromagnetic field, it has a series of effects on this side [of the
19		circuit]. <u>Then what</u>? [nominate], you try and continue. [Pointing
20		to the complicated circuit]
21	Ss:	[silent]
22	T:	Now, <u>the coil has a magnetic field, and the reed switch ___ ? The</u>
23		<u>reed switch ___ ?</u>
24	Ss:	[silent]
25	T:	The reed switch, the two ends do not touch each other originally,
26		but now <u>what happens to these two ends</u>?
27	S:	Touch each other.
28	T:	Yes, the two ends touch each other. <u>If the two ends touch each</u>
29		<u>other, how do we describe this switch</u>?
30	Ss:	[silent]
31	T:	The two ends touch each other, how do I describe this switch?
32	S:	Closed.
33	T:	Closed, very good. Yes, thank you. Now, if this switch closes,
34		then the electric current can pass through this circuit. <u>This motor</u>
35		<u>___ ?</u>
36	S:	Rotates.
37	T:	Rotates. Is that OK?

Here the teacher asked four "open" questions (see lines 7, 8, 19, 26, 28, and 29) and four "closed" questions (lines 10, 15, 22, 23, 34, and 35). If we

5. QUESTIONS AND THE SPACE OF LEARNING

examine the content of these questions, we can see that most of them focused on process. For example, what effect the drop in resistance had on the electric current (lines 7 and 8), what happened when the electromagnet produced a magnetic field (line 19), what happened to the two ends of the reed switch (line 26), and what happened to the motor when the electric current passed through the circuit (lines 34 and 35). In other words, the understanding of the processes involved was co-constructed by the teacher and the students. Table 5.1 is an analysis of the contributions made by the students in co-constructing the process with the teacher.

Let us now compare excerpt 5.11 with excerpt 5.12, in which the teacher was explaining the same process.

5.12 [Physics Lesson/Reed Relay/EMI/S2/T8]

1	T:	Why doesn't this motor rotate? [inaudible] The motor is
2		healthy, is healthy, but it doesn't work, why? Surely it
3		should work. Now once again, we discuss it. Now as light
4		shines on the LDR. [Teacher shines the torch on to the
5		LDR in the symbolic representation of the simple circuit on
6		the board.] What happen[s] to its resistor, resistance, what
7		happen[s] to it, [when] light shines on the LDR?
8	S:	Low.
9	T:	Thank you, it reduce[s], it becomes smaller so there should
10		be a larger current flow[ing] through the circuit and the
11		motor should ____ ?
12	Ss:	[silent]

TABLE 5.1
Co-Construction of Processes by Teacher and Students in CMI Physics Lesson

Teacher	Students
Light shines on LDR, resistance	Drops
Electric current	Increases
Electricity flows through current, coil becomes electromagnet	
Electromagnet produces	Magnetic field
Two ends of reed switch	Touch each other (closed)
Motor	Rotates

13	T:	Should work, but it does not rotate this time. How about this
14		circuit? [Teacher goes to the complicated circuit] Now once
15		again light shines on the LDR, its resistance decrease[s]. So,
16		current flows through this circuit. <u>Now it's not only a coil</u>
17		<u>but a ___ ?</u>
18	Ss:	[silent]
19	T:	Now this question again. [nominate] <u>Now this time it is not</u>
20		<u>merely a coil but a ___ ?</u>
21	Ss:	[silent]
22	T:	Artificial magnet, all right. <u>Do you still remember [the]</u>
23		<u>name</u>?
24	S:	Electromagnet.
25	T:	Once again.
26	S:	Electromagnet.
27	T:	Electromagnet, thank you, it became an electromagnet, and
28		it produced a magnetic field. So the switch here will close
29		and a current [will] pass through this circuit, so the motor
30		rotate[s]. There is a sequence of process[es] [that] occur here and
31		it make[s] the motor rotate.

Here the teacher asked an open question (lines 6 and 7): "What happens to it [resistance] when light shine[s] on the LDR?" This question, in a similar way to the question posed in excerpt 5.11, asked for a description of the process. When the teacher failed to elicit a response from the students, she posed three blank-filling questions, one of which is a repetition (lines 10, 11, 16, 17, 19, and 20), whereas the others were closed questions (lines 22 and 23). However, in the course of modifying the open question into blank-filling questions, the blank-filling questions became focused on the devices and the labels (an artificial magnet and an electromagnet), and the description of the process was lost. On the basis of our observation that questions focus students' awareness on the aspect of the phenomenon that was questioned, we can reasonably conclude that the consequence of asking questions about the devices, rather than the processes, would result in the devices being brought to the fore of the students' awareness and the processes receding to the background. And yet, it is the processes and not the devices that are critical to the understanding of the operation of the reed relay.

CONCLUSION

In chapter 1, Marton, Runesson, and Tsui demonstrated the central role played by language in constituting the space of learning, and discussed at length the importance of language as a means of encapsulating experience, making distinctions, and modifying one another's understanding of the world. They also observed the function of language in representing and shaping the structure of awareness of participants in a discourse. In this chapter, we have focused specifically on the structure of questions and how they impinge on the structure of awareness of participants in a discourse. Throughout the lesson on the reed relay, we demonstrated how a teacher was able to help her students discern the critical features of a reed relay at critical points in the lesson, by asking questions that focused their attention on aspects that varied. Throughout the English lesson, we demonstrated how the different questions asked by the teacher could result in students focusing on very different aspects of the object of learning. We also showed that the way in which the teacher sequenced the questions could result in a shift of the learners' focal awareness from the critical aspects of the object of learning to aspects that are not critical. In other words, the teacher's awareness of how questions can shape the space of learning (i.e., the enacted object of learning) is essential if our effort in bringing about powerful learning in the classroom is to result in the convergence between the intended, the enacted, and the lived object of learning.

ENDNOTES

[1] The term *dissemination* is used in a neutral sense; it does not imply a transmissive view of teaching.

[2] For an explanation of the LDR, see chapter 1, endnote 4.

[3] In this chapter, data from the lesson taught in Cantonese will be coded as CMI, and data from the lesson taught in English will be coded as EMI. The data from the CMI lesson is translated semantically, keeping as much as possible to verbatim translation.

[4] All students' names are fictitious.

6

The Semantic Enrichment of the Space of Learning

Amy B. M. Tsui

THE SEMANTIC DIMENSION OF THE SPACE OF LEARNING

In chapter 1, Marton, Runesson, and Tsui proposed that *learning* is the process of developing a certain way of seeing, and pointed out that different ways of seeing allow for different ways of acting. They also pointed out that in order to help learners to develop a capability for seeing things in a powerful way, we need to focus on what is being learned and help learners discern critical features of the object of learning. In other words, investigations of learning involve studying how learners experience the object of learning, and investigations of classroom learning involve analyses of the opportunities to experience the object of learning that are afforded to learners. In this sense, the space of learning is an *experiential space*. An experiential space is not an instantiation, but rather a potential for understanding, seeing, and acting in the world (see Halliday & Matthiessen, 1999). It is in relation to this potential that learners can make sense of a particular object of learning. As such, the experiential space is elastic. The teacher can either widen this space by affording learners opportunities to explore the object of learning in a variety of ways, or narrow this space by depriving them of such opportunities.

In the preceding chapters, we have seen that the way in which the object of learning is experienced by learners depends on which aspects of the object of learning are being focused on and discerned as critical. In this chapter, it is proposed that experiencing an object of learning—in the sense of discerning its critical aspects and experiencing the patterns of variation—

necessarily involves assigning a meaning (or meanings) to it. For example, for a young learner who lives in a country where high-rise buildings do not exist, a "house" means a place where people live, as opposed to places where animals live, such as "stables." A house is therefore a choice in the semantic system of accommodation for different kinds of living things. However, to a young learner who lives in a city where there are high-rises as well as houses, a house means something different. In this instance, "house" is a choice in the semantic system of accommodation for people, where houses and apartments are choices. A house means not an apartment; that is, it is a two- or three-story building, rather than a single unit within a multi-story building comprising many units.

The meanings that learners assign to the object of learning depend on a host of things. The teacher can affect these meanings through examples and analogies, through the stories that he tells, and the contexts that he brings in. The meanings will also depend on the personal experiences that the learners bring to bear on the object of learning. Together, all of these meanings constitute the semantic dimension of the space of learning, of which language plays a central role.

In this chapter, examples from a variety of classrooms are cited to illustrate what is meant by the semantic dimension of the space of learning, and the ways in which the learners' experience of the object of learning is enriched semantically are discussed. The central role played by language in the constitution of the semantic dimension of the space of learning is illustrated by comparing classrooms where rich linguistic resources were available, with those where the linguistic resources were limited.

CONTEXTUAL VARIATION AND THE SEMANTIC ENRICHMENT OF THE SPACE OF LEARNING

It is common practice among teachers, no matter what subject matter they are dealing with, to shift from the classroom context to contexts outside the classroom (ranging from contemporary contexts to historical contexts) in the course of their explanations. However, few teachers ask why they are doing this, and what effect this kind of contextual variation has on learning. In this chapter, it is proposed that contextual variation is a very important and commonly used practice that helps learners to make sense of and to relate to the object of learning.

Mathematics Lesson: The Postman's Route

Let us take, for example, the mathematics lesson on the postman's route discussed in chapter 3. To help the students to see the relationships between patterns (as seen through rotation and reflection), the teacher started by asking the students to come up with as many patterns as possi-

6. SEMANTIC ENRICHMENT OF THE SPACE OF LEARNING   **141**

ble, by connecting the dots that stood for delivery points. In order to facilitate task completion, the teacher provided the context of a postman having to deliver letters to eight different places and then return to the post office. When the students had completed the task, the teacher asked the students to figure out what was wrong with one particular design that he [the teacher] identified, and then to decide what constituted the best route. The students had no difficulty pointing out that the design in question failed to show the direction of the route, and failed to show how the postman could get back to the post office. They also had no difficulty deciding that the best route was the shortest route. The tasks were not difficult for the students because the context of a postman delivering mail was very familiar, and it was easy for them to identify the routes in relation to what a postman's job involved. Once the eight best routes were identified, the teacher switched from the everyday context to a mathematical context, so that the designs took on a different meaning. They were no longer routes but patterns. The concept of routes necessarily involved having a direction and being able to return to the starting point, which made it very easy for the students to think of the criterion for the best route. If the teacher had started the lesson by presenting the patterns in a mathematical context, the students would have had to think in symbolic and abstract terms and the task would have been more difficult.

What is interesting is that when the students failed to see the relationship between the eight patterns and hence were unable to categorize them, the teacher switched back to the context of the postman's route, which immediately made the task easier. The students were then able to see that the eight routes were related in two different ways: rotation and reflection. In other words, the students were able to draw on their everyday knowledge to make sense of what the patterns meant.

English as a Second Language (ESL) Lessons: Weather and Seasons

In a study of primary ESL teaching, Chan (2002) studied the primary Grade 4 lessons taught by two teachers, in which the direct object of learning was weather, clothing, and seasons. In the first part of an 80-minute lesson, both teachers used pictures to elicit the vocabulary for weather and clothing. Having established that there was shared knowledge of different weather conditions and the corresponding types of clothing, both teachers introduced "seasons" and asked students to deduce the season from the clothing that they showed them. In so doing, both teachers were trying to help their students see that weather and clothing were related in meaningful ways. We could say that the teachers were trying to establish a semantic field with two semantic domains: weather and clothing. Subsequently, both teachers introduced a further semantic domain of "seasons," hence widening the semantic field so that the three semantic domains (seasons, weather, and clothing) were understood not only on their own, but also in relation to each other.

In the latter part of each lesson, the teachers used a story as the context for recycling the vocabulary items introduced, and for reinforcing the students' understanding of weather and seasons. The stories that the two teachers told, however, were very different.

Teacher A told a story about a poor little girl, Mary, who was driven out of the house by her stepmother in the winter when it was cold and snowing. The stepmother said that she would not let Mary back in unless she brought back some beautiful flowers. Mary walked up the hill and fell asleep with exhaustion. Four brothers, the four seasons, came to her rescue. Brother Spring waved a magic wand and the weather became warm and rainy. Mary was then able to get flowers for her stepmother. But when Mary brought the flowers home, her stepmother would not let her in and told her to get some apples. This time Brother Summer came to her rescue, and the weather became hot and sunny so that Mary could pick some apples. The story continued and all four brothers came to her rescue in turn, each time the greedy stepmother made unreasonable demands for something that could not be found in that particular season.

Let us consider the semantic dimension of the space of learning that was opened up with this story. Prior to telling the story, the teacher had already established the relation between two semantic domains (seasons and weather) by showing how one is related to the other. The story provided the context not only for making sense of the relationship between weather and seasons, but also for introducing another semantic domain related to weather and season, that is, plants and fruits. While plants and fruits were part of the students' existing knowledge, it was the teacher who brought the relationship of this domain with seasons and weather into the students' focal awareness. What is interesting is the way the teacher varied the relationships between seasons, weather, and plants and fruits. She started with a negative relationship between them by getting the students to see *what could not be found* in a particular season, and she helped the students to make sense of this negative relationship through the character of the stepmother, who made impossible demands on little Mary. Later, a positive relationship between these domains was established when each of the four brothers came to Mary's rescue by changing the season and the weather so that the plant or the fruit demanded by the stepmother could be found.

As the lesson progressed, there was a gradual widening of the semantic field from weather and clothing, to include seasons, plants, and fruits. The following excerpt is an example of how the teacher related one semantic domain with another.

6.1 [English Lesson/P4/Weather and Season]
T: Mary's mother says, "No. I don't want you. Go away." Her mother says, "Okay, you ask me to let you come back, but unless you get me some beautiful flowers (I won't)." Can you get some beautiful flowers in winter?
Ss: No.
T: Outside it is ____ .
Ss: Cold and snowy.
T: Can Mary get some flowers?
Ss: [loudly] No!

The readiness with which the students responded to the teacher when she asked if Mary could get flowers in the winter when it was cold and snowy showed that they were able to make sense of the story and see the relation between the semantic domains.

Teacher B also told a story after introducing all the vocabulary items for weather, clothing, and seasons. The story was about a little boy, Billy, and what he did on each of the seven days of a week and what the weather was like. For example, on Monday, when it was raining, Billy watched television; on Tuesday, when it was sunny, Billy played basketball; and so forth. The students were asked to learn the days of the week, and to say what Billy did and what the weather was like. The way in which the teacher tried to relate the three semantic domains was largely arbitrary. Although certain activities were logically related to the weather conditions (e.g., "swimming" and "sunny weather"), there were others that were not (e.g., "watching television" and "rainy weather"). Activities and days of the week are of themselves not logically related either. When the three semantic domains were taken together, they did not form a semantic field. The story therefore did not serve as a meaningful context to which the students could easily relate, nor did it help the students to make sense of each of the semantic domains in relation to the other two. In other words, the students' understanding of the relationship between the three domains was not enriched semantically by the story. If anything, the story confused the students' understanding because of the arbitrary relationship that the teacher had tried to establish.

Science Lesson: Neutralization

To further illustrate what can be achieved by contextual variation, let us take a look at an example of a secondary Grade 2 level science lesson (Hoare, 2003). The object of learning in the lesson was "neutralization." The teacher first introduced the concepts of *acidity*, *alkalinity*, and the use of the *pH value scale* to measure the strength of acids and alkalis. She also asked the students to find out the acidity and alkalinity of some acids and alkalis by using pH paper. After this, she asked the students to test the pH value of several household substances, such as lemon juice, vinegar, toothpaste, baking soda, bleaching agent, and a canned soft drink. The following is an excerpt from the classroom.

6.2 [Science lesson/S/Neutralization/EMI]

T: … Okay, now, in our daily life we have, um, we come into contact with many things, right? For example, toothpaste, lemon juice, etc.. Do you know what is the pH value of this? Is this a strong acid? Is it a weak acid? Is it a strong alkali or weak alkali? We don't know. So in the following I want you to do [the] experiment on page ____ .

S: 167, 167.

T: 167, is that right? And then we have to test the pH value of lemon juice, bleaching agent, baking soda, detergent, glass cleaner, toothpaste, 7-Up™, but don't drink it [students laugh], milk of magnesia, sea water …

S: I['ll] drink it.

T: Don't drink it.

S: Why?

T: I [will] have to call the ambulance. So, you do the same. Use the pH paper. How many of them?

S: Those 7-Up, change [them] to Coca-Cola™ ah [Meaning replace 7-Up with Coca-Cola]

T: Yes.

S: Ten …

S: Those 7-Up change [them] to Coca-Cola.

T: Yes, you know that there is Coca-Cola there.

S: [inaudible]

T: Yes, sorry, ah, maybe 7-Up was difficult to buy.

S: Ah I don't … I can go to the 7-11™ to buy it.

T: Okay, after this lesson. Okay we change [them] to Coca-Cola. But don't drink it. Remember.
[Students conducted the experiment and recorded the pH values of the substances.]

T: Now okay look here. Lemon juice is of pH …

S: Three.

T: So we call it ____ .

Ss: Strongly acidic, strongly, strongly acidic.

T: How do we describe it?

Ss: [silent]
T: Yes, it is a strong acid, so it is strongly acidic ....

Prior to this experiment, although the students were familiar with the household substances listed by the teacher, these substances meant nothing more than things that they found in supermarkets and kitchens. In other words, the meanings of these substances were interpreted in the semantic domain of the supermarket or the kitchen, and the level at which the students were operating when they thought about these objects was the level of everyday knowledge. However, when the teacher asked the students to do an experiment on household substances (i.e., when the students were engaged in finding out their pH values and using technical language, such as "acid," "alkali," and "strongly acidic" or "weakly acidic" to describe these substances), the household substances were reconstrued, not in the semantic domain of everyday items, but in the domain of chemicals. At this point, the level at which the students were operating changed from the level of everyday knowledge to the level of scientific (or technical) knowledge. What is interesting in the just mentioned excerpt is that we can see the students and teachers operating at both knowledge levels and in both semantic domains. In other words, we may say that the semantic dimension is enriched in the sense that there is an additional layer of meaning.

Having established the concepts of alkalinity and acidity, the teacher introduced the concept of *neutralization* by asking the students to mix an acid (hydrochloric acid) with an alkali (sodium hydroxide) until they obtained a pH value of seven, a point at which the solution becomes neither acidic nor alkaline. The teacher explained that neutralization is a process by which an acid is added to an alkali until the resulting solution is salt and water. After the students had done the experiment, the teacher tried to help them to make sense of neutralization by shifting from the science laboratory context to an everyday context. She used a number of examples to explain the applications of neutralization. One example was that of using toothpaste to brush our teeth. She explained that the acid produced after eating food causes our teeth to decay, and that toothpaste neutralizes the acid. Another example was the use of milk of magnesia to neutralize excessive acid produced by food in the stomach, and thus alleviate stomachache. Yet another example was the use of ointment containing alkali to neutralize the acid produced by mosquito bites. In this section of the lesson, we see the reverse process of contextualization happening. Previously, neutralization was merely a laboratory process in which chemicals were mixed together. Here, neutralization was presented as a process that takes place frequently in our everyday lives. Acids and alkalis were no longer understood only as chemicals in science laboratories but as chemicals that could be found in many different substances outside the laboratories. Once again, there were two levels of knowledge operating, and also two semantic domains in which neutralization was understood: a scientific process domain, and a daily life process domain. The following excerpt shows that as soon as the teacher explained the toothpaste as an example of neutralization, the students were able to make sense of neutralization in another daily life context—the use of magnesia to neutralize acids in the stomach.

6.3 [Science lesson/Neutralization/S2/EMI]

T: Ah, toothpaste is alkaline, and it neutralizes the acid in our mouth after we have taken some food .... And neutralization takes place there so that we can have healthy teeth. Okay. Second, I know some, many, people would like to have many—a full lunch .... When you have taken a lot of food, and sometimes you find that this part is not okay. Stomach ____ ?

S: Stomachache.

T: You have stomachache. Okay.... When you have taken a lot of food, your stomach will give out acid to make the food into small pieces so that you can take in the food, okay? ... So at that time when your stomach gives out a lot of acid, you find that it is painful .... So what should you do at that time? Some people would like to take some tablets. Okay this is one of the tablets. We call it milk of magnesia .... Has anybody taken this before? When you have stomachache, you can take one ...
... Why do we have to take one?

S: Neutralize.

T: Yes, ... the reason is that it neutralizes the acid from our stomach so that you become peaceful ....

As in the previous excerpt (6.2), we may say that by varying the context, the semantic dimension was enriched and the teacher was able to help students assign an additional layer of meaning to the object of learning.

COLLABORATIVE ENRICHMENT OF THE SEMANTIC DIMENSION BY LEARNERS

So far, the examples examined were classroom examples where the teacher enriched the semantic dimension by bringing in stories or contexts outside the classroom and the laboratory to help learners to make sense of the object of learning. In this section, we look at examples in which the learners brought in their own experience to assign meanings to the object of learning and see how the space of learning was enriched semantically by the collaborative construction of meaning among the learners.

Chinese Lesson: The Sloth

The data presented here come from a primary Grade 3 Chinese language lesson, "The Sloth," the background of which has already been introduced in chapter 2. We shall now see how the learners assigned meanings to a video that they watched together, how they collaboratively constructed a written representation of the video, and how the space of learning was enriched.

In the lesson on the sloth, the object of learning was to write a description of the appearance of a young sloth, and a story about its search for a new home after it lost its mother and had eaten all the leaves on the tree where it lived. The teacher provided a framework for describing an animal that was based on the description of a panda that they had studied in the previous lesson. The teacher used the word "appearance" as a hyponym for body or trunk, head (brain), four limbs and color (of the fur or skin). Then he pointed out to the class that it was also necessary to describe what the animal was like when it was in motion. For example, the movement of a panda is very clumsy. He also pointed out that it was necessary to describe the sloth's eating habits and character. After providing the framework, he showed a video of the story of a sloth. One striking feature of this lesson is the way in which the teacher repeatedly showed the video, at first with narration and later without narration, each time showing a different segment of the tape with a different focus. This repetition not only reiterated the content, but also opened up the space for students to explore the ways in which they could make sense of the features of the sloth. Students were then asked to work in groups and produce a written text to describe what they had seen.

In the following discussion, we examine some of the texts produced by the students, and the discussion data that led to the production of these texts. We see how the students assigned meanings to the video, and how their construal of what they had seen enriched the semantic aspect of the space of learning.

Sloth's Head and Body. The following is a written description produced by Group 2:[1]

> It is a sloth, its head is like a *big chicken egg*, its body is like a *big ostrich egg*, very long, and the three claws on its forelimbs are particularly long. Its color is black, white, gray, brown. Very short tail. To look for food and a home, the sloth slowly climbed down the tree, and swam freestyle. It crawled to the shore. As soon as it reached the shore, it glanced to the east and the west. Very soon, it found a tree. It finally found a new home.

Let us focus for the moment on the students' description of the head and body of the sloth. Although most groups simply made use of the teacher's suggestion that the sloth's head was like a monkey's head, this group felt that using another animal to describe the sloth was not adequate, and that they ought to use something else for comparison. The following excerpt shows how the students explored the description of the sloth's head.

6.4 [Chinese lesson/P3/The Sloth/Group Discussion/Group 2]

296	S:	What's it [the head] like?
297	S:	Like a monkey's head.
298	S:	<u>This is not saying anything</u>.
299	S:	They are both animals.
300	S:	Its head …
301	S:	<u>Is like a chicken egg.</u>
302	S:	<u>Is like an oval chicken egg.</u>
303	S:	Just like a chicken egg is okay.
304	S:	No need to say that it is oval as well.
305	S:	Just [putting down] chicken egg is okay?
306	S:	Like a chicken egg is okay.
307	S:	<u>Chicken eggs are always oval.</u>
308	S:	<u>It's got to be bigger than an egg. It's not that small.</u>
309	S:	That's right, chicken eggs are very small.
310	S:	That's right.
311	S:	What's it like again?
312	S:	Like a big chicken egg.
313	S:	A big chicken egg is not that big.
314	S:	That's okay. You describe the head …
315	S:	<u>A big goose egg.</u>
316	S:	A big goose egg is fine.
317	S:	A big chicken egg is fine.
318	S:	How do I write the word "egg"?
319		[The students helped each other write the word "egg"]
320	S:	Let's see, what's a big ostrich egg like. Let's say a big ostrich
321		egg, is that okay?
322	S:	Okay, ostrich egg.
323	S:	Ostrich eggs are very big?
324	S:	Okay, let's describe the body.
325	S:	[reminding the student who is writing] Big ostrich egg.
326	S:	Ostrich egg.

6. SEMANTIC ENRICHMENT OF THE SPACE OF LEARNING 149

From this discussion (6.4), we can see that two critical features were being explored by the students: namely, shape and size. Of particular interest is the initial comparison of the sloth's head with the monkey's head by one student (line 297), the rejection of this comparison by another student (line 298), and the justification of the rejection by a third (line 299). What was happening in that section of discourse? Why did the second student say, "This is not saying anything," meaning that comparing the sloth's head with a monkey's head was not informative at all? For the first student, what came to the fore of his awareness was the comparison of the sloth with other animals. The dimension of variation was "heads of animals" (which was also what the teacher had previously illustrated). However, for the second and third students, what came to the fore of their awareness was not to compare the sloth with other animals, as can be seen from line 299. Their subsequent discourse shows that it was the *shape* that was in their focal awareness, and thus they accepted the analogy of a chicken egg that made the shape immediately apparent. "Oval" was a shape that was considered by the group to be a critical feature of the shape of the sloth's head. The students were trying to decide which was the best analogy to use to describe the sloth's head and its body. The debate about whether it was necessary to specify oval when using a chicken egg as an analogy is interesting both at the conceptual level and the linguistic level. Conceptually, oval can be a feature that is quite independent of an object. For example, a table can be oval, round, or square. Specifying the shape of an object presupposes that there are shapes other than that which is specified. From the discussion, it is clear that for some students, oval was considered to be an inherent feature of a chicken egg, which rendered the use of the adjective "oval" to describe the egg redundant. This is a fairly sophisticated level of understanding that the students were able to reach through collaborative talk. Linguistically, "chicken egg" was used to describe the shape, and "chicken egg" took on a meaning that was synonymous with oval.

The other feature is size, but here we see the opposite happening. Although there are chicken eggs that are big and those that are small, the variation implied by describing the sloth's body as a "big chicken egg" (as opposed to "chicken egg" for its head) was considered inadequate because even big chicken eggs were thought to be too small. Instead, the students proposed the *kind* of egg as a dimension of variation. Thus they proposed goose egg and ostrich egg as a variation in size, and finally decided on ostrich egg. Here we can see three terms in the students' semantic system of size: chicken eggs, which are small; goose eggs, which are bigger than chicken eggs; and ostrich eggs, which are biggest of all three. In the final draft that the students produced, they added the adjective "big" in front of ostrich egg to describe the size of the body. By doing this, the students have added one more term to their semantic system of size to make finer distinctions in size.

The collaborative construal of the appearance of the sloth is evident in the way the students questioned each other's contribution and then came to a consensus on the most appropriate description.

Sloth's Eyes. Let us now consider the description produced by another group, Group 4. When describing the appearance of the sloth, one student in Group 4 said that the sloth's eyes were black. However, the other group members immediately pointed out that everybody knew eyes were black, implying that this piece of information was superfluous. However, another student pointed out that the eyes of a rabbit were special, and another student chipped in and said that rabbits' eyes were red. In this discussion, we can see that initially for the students, all eyes were black and therefore there was only one term in the system of meaning of color of eyes. However, as soon as the color of rabbits' eyes was brought in, the meaning of the color of eyes changed. Black was no longer *a given*, but *a choice* in the system of color—which at that particular point in the discourse consisted of black and not black, that is, red. In other words, we could say that the color of the eyes was an aspect that was not discerned initially (at least by some of the students). It was taken for granted. However, when an alternative eye color was explicitly brought up, a dimension of variation in color was opened up. Discerning that the color of the sloth's eyes is black implies a dimension of variation with at least two possible values: black and not black. Describing the eyes of the sloth as black meant that color was in the focal awareness of one of the students. It was by varying the color of a sloth's eyes (and a rabbit's eyes) that students were able to discern that having black eyes was a critical feature of the sloth's appearance.

Sloth's Body. Although most groups described the body of the sloth as "roundish," plump, or like a big ostrich egg (as Group 2 did), Group 5 described the sloth's body as very thin. The following excerpt shows the meaning that Group 5 attached to this description.

6.5 [Chinese Lesson/P3/The Sloth/Group Discussion/Group 5]
S: Now, it's body [shape] ...
S: It's body [shape], it's body is quite big, huh?
S: Thin!
S: Thinnish! ... Looks like he is undernourished.
S: No!
S: Thin! He is very thin!
S: His body shape ...
S: In fact, it was his fur that covered it up.

6. SEMANTIC ENRICHMENT OF THE SPACE OF LEARNING 151

S: Oh no!
S: The fur covered it up
S: His body shape ...
S: Yeah!
S: In fact he is very plump!
S: He is very thin.
S: Yeah, think about this. Plump because of the fur, his fur covered up his body.
S: Because his fur is long
...

This debate went on for quite a while and finally the students agreed to put down "thin." What happened here was that this group's construal of the sloth's appearance was made in the context of the narration that said that the sloth's mother had died, that it was alone, and that the leaves on the tree where it lived had all been eaten up. For this reason one of the students said that the sloth was "undernourished." In order to reconcile the discrepancy between what they saw on the video and their understanding of what his appearance should be, they came up with an interesting explanation: that the sloth looked plump only because of its fur. This suggests that the meanings that are assigned by the students to the phenomenon under discussion may lead to a different construal of the object of learning.

Sloth's Diet. Let us take a look at an excerpt from the discussion in Group 4 on the sloth's diet. The video narration only provided the information that the sloth ate leaves from one particular tree:

> It [the sloth] looks around and tries to find a tree where it would like to live. The tree should be of the same species as the one that it lived on before because when a sloth gets used to the taste of the leaves of a certain kind of tree, it will not change what it eats.

6.6 [Chinese Lesson/The Sloth/P3/Group Discussion/Group 4]
S: It eats ... it only eats leaves.
S: It does not eat anything else, it only eats leaves.
S: Eats leaves.
S: Eats leaves, if ... if ...
S: Like a big bear, it's *pin sihk*^{2} (Cantonese) [偏食] ("a fussy eater"). Like the panda, it's *pin sihk*.
S: Hey ... there's more
S: It's a *pin sihk* animal.
S: It does not eat meat and ...

S:	It does not eat meat and does not eat fish. Does it eat fish?
Ss:	No!
S:	No, it also says ...
S:	When it gets used to the taste of one kind of leaf, it will not eat ...
S:	That's why [I said] it's *pin sihk*.

In the original narration, the narrator explained that the sloth had to find a tree of the same species because of its preference for a certain type of leaves. The students in Group 4, however, assigned further meaning to the sloth's preference for leaves. They used a single expression, *pin sihk* (Cantonese) [偏食], an adjectival phrase for describing someone who is a fussy eater, to describe the eating habits of the sloth. The students were bringing in their own experience of being told by their parents that they should eat everything and not be fussy about their food (a common exhortation made by parents to their children). The phrase *pin sihk* is at a higher level of abstraction and generalization than the description given in the video. Moreover, the students were also able to relate the sloth's eating habits to the eating habits of the panda, something that they had learned about in the previous lesson. The phrase *pin sihk* proposed by the students has the following semantic features: does not eat meat or fish, and eats only one kind of leaves. There are at least two animal members belonging to this category: pandas and sloths.

The question is, how were the students able to collaboratively construct such a rich text, both spoken and written? How is it that the same video could be construed in such a semantically rich manner? How did the teacher bring this about?

It seems that there were two things that the teacher did that were quite crucial. The first has to do with the way he varied the showing of the video with and without the narration.

Variation: Video With and Without Narration. When the teacher showed the video for the first time, the narration was given. But when he showed segments of the video, he took away the narration. The purpose of making the video soundless was, as the teacher told the students, that if he played the narration as well, then there would be nothing for the students to talk about. In other words, the narration in the first viewing gave the students an idea of what the story was about. In a way, one could say that the narration provided the context in which the appearance and the movement of the sloth could be interpreted. This is most evident in the description made by one group of students who described the sloth's eyes as looking like two teardrops. This construal was obviously made in light of the fact that the sloth had lost its mother and had to struggle for survival.

6. SEMANTIC ENRICHMENT OF THE SPACE OF LEARNING **153**

For the second viewing, the narration was removed in order to allow the students to interpret what they saw in their own ways. By doing this, the teacher opened up the space of learning. The students were free to bring in their own experience and previous learning to make sense of what they saw on the video without being constrained by what was said in the narration.

In other words, what the teacher varied was the narration and what he kept constant was the visual images. By so doing, the students became very much aware of the lack of narration, and the fact that they had to write the narration themselves. In order to fulfill the task, they needed to focus their attention on the visual images, especially the appearance and the movement of the sloth.

Let us imagine that the teacher asked the students to do the same task, but retained the narration when showing the video the second time. What would have happened? As the students had been given the task of writing a narration of the story, it is likely that the structure of their awareness would have changed. What would have come to the fore of their awareness, or what would have been figural, would be the narration; what the narrator actually said. The actual appearance and the movement of the sloth would have receded to the ground. What the teacher would very likely have achieved is that the students would have tried to regurgitate the narration rather than coming up with their own descriptions.

Variation: Teacher-Led Discussion and Student-Led Discussion. Researchers have pointed out that working in groups is naturally conducive to making use of variation (see Wistedt & Martinsson's work, 1994, on inexact decimal representation of the fraction "one third," cited in Marton & Booth, 1997). However, this does not mean that group work will necessarily lead to successful learning. Whether successful learning is achieved or not depends on whether the teacher has exploited the conduciveness to variation in the group work. Citing the work of Lybeck (1981) on group work (in which the teacher confronted the students with variations in the concept of *density* proposed by other students, and put the variations under scrutiny), Marton (1986) observed that the teacher "functioned as the architect of the pedagogical milieu, the midwife of experience and the sculptor of thought" (cited in Marton & Booth, 1997, p. 69).

In the lesson on the sloth, the teacher focused the students' attention on the critical features of the sloth, such as its appearance (which is static), and its movements (which are dynamic). This teacher-led discussion provided the scaffolding for the subsequent student-led discussion in groups. The teacher also emphasized the collaborative nature of group work, and told the students that it was important for them to pay attention to the contributions of other group members, to think about these contributions, and to try to improve on them. These are the instructions he gave to the students after he had put the structural components of the description of the sloth on the board.

6.7 [Chinese Lesson/P3/The Sloth]
T: After watching the video, each group will discuss among themselves.... You have to collaborate. Don't just write it all by yourself. You must work together and contribute your opinion. You have to see whether what another member has said is right or not, and whether it is good or not. After a member has offered a [descriptive] sentence, you can add your opinion. Like, "It would be better to write it this way ...," "It would be better to say it that way ...," or "No, I disagree, I saw it [the sloth] making this kind of movement." and you can give your own account [of what you saw]. If everybody agrees, then you write it down.

By providing the students with a detailed explanation of what was expected of them when they engaged in group work, the teacher was opening up the space for variation in discerning the critical features of the sloth. The data from the group discussions show that each group was able to bring their own experience to bear on the description, and different dimensions of variation were opened up.

Although the initial discussion was teacher-led, the learning space was jointly constituted by the teacher and the students in the sense that the students offered descriptions of the critical features of appearance, such as the head, the body, the color, and the four limbs of the sloth, as well as its movements.

The teacher also provided scaffolding for the group discussions by reminding students which aspects they should be focusing on in the course of the discussion. For example, he reminded the students that they should have finished discussing the appearance and should be moving on to the description of movement. As the students were discussing the movements, he reminded them of the various movements they should be describing, such as swimming, crawling up the river bank, climbing up the tree, and so on.

Table 6.1 summarizes the contributions made by the students in the teacher-led discussion and the student-led discussion in four groups out of six. The features in the student-led discussions that were not found in teacher-led discussions are in italics.

When the groups had finished drafting their descriptions, the teacher asked each group to present their descriptions as the narration as he played the video again. Here the teacher was further widening the space of variation by getting students to listen to the descriptions written by other groups. The different descriptions showed that different aspects of the sloth were in the focal awareness of each group.

TABLE 6.1
Description of the Sloth in Teacher-Led and Student-Led Discussions

Teacher-Led Discussion		Student-Led Discussion				
T	Ss	Group 1	Group 2		Group 4	Group 5
Movement	Slow, slowly climbing up a tree.					
Appearance	Furry	Mouth (beak) —very flat, like a duck, very short	Very short tail		Nose: black, body: black, eyes: black (as opposed to red), mouth: flat, protruding, blunt	Face: white, eyebrows: brown, eyes: triangular, like monkey's eyes, body: like a human being, very small, only half a year old, like the thigh of a baby, like a big winter melon
Color	Brown, white		Grayish, whitish, brownish and whitish, black, brown			
Head: like monkey's head	Head very round, very small, neck is very long, limbs are very long		Looks like a monkey's head, chicken egg, big goose egg, big duck egg, big ostrich egg		Head is like a monkey's, head can turn 360 degrees	Round, oval

(continued on next page)

155

TABLE 6.1 (continued)

Teacher-Led Discussion		Student-Led Discussion				
T	Ss	Group 1	Group 2	Group 4	Group 5
Four limbs, fingers, paws	Paws, claws, three sharp claws		*Very long, especially the claws of the forelimbs,* three claws	Hands and legs are very long, *nails are very pointed (sharp),* four limbs are very long and small, claws are *very long and razor sharp*	
Movement: crawling	Very slow, slowly climbs up a tree looking around		Very slow, slowly climbs down the tree, *exhausted,* looking around as soon as it reached the bank, climbed up the tree, it finally found a new home		
Swimming			*Free style*	*Puppy style, frog style (breast stroke), free style*	
Diet				*Only eats leaves, like the panda, it is pin sihk (fussy eater), does not eat meat or fish*	*Eats only leaves, any kind of leaves that it likes.*

Note. The features in the student-led discussions that were not found in teacher-led discussions are given in italics.

LINGUISTIC RESOURCES AND SEMANTIC ENRICHMENT

In this section, we look at the way in which the same object of learning was construed semantically in very different ways in two classrooms because of the different linguistic resources available to the teacher and the learners, that is, one of the classes was taught through the medium of Chinese, which was the mother tongue for all students (CMI), and the other through the medium of English, which was a second language for all students (EMI).

The history lessons used as examples in this section further illustrate what we mean by the *semantic dimension* of the learning space. (For the background of these lessons, see Tsui, Aldred, Marton, Kan, & Runesson, 2001.) The extracts are from two secondary Grade 2 (S2) (i.e., Grade 8) classrooms in which the same topic was taught, and illustrate the difference in the semantic space opened up because of the different linguistic resources available to the students.

History Lessons: The Market in Early Rural Communities

In these two history lessons, the object of learning was the concept of *market* in early rural communities in Hong Kong. The critical features that distinguish this market (which perhaps translates more accurately as "fair") from the market in modern societies, are the different functions. In its historical context, the market was a place where people would come both to buy produce and to sell their own produce, or sometimes even to exchange goods. The market was also a place for social interaction, and was located in a particular place that was accessible to many villagers and clans. However, due to poor transportation markets were not held every day but at regular intervals.

The following is an excerpt from the EMI lesson in which the teacher tried to elicit from the students the critical features of the market in its historical context.

6.8 [History Lesson/S2/EMI]

1	T:	Do you think the market at that time is the same as you['ve] got now?
2	Ss:	No.
3	T:	How [was it] different?
4	Ss:	[silent]
5	T:	Huh?
6	Ss:	[silent]
7	T:	How [was it] different? Can you imagine? In the past, market [writing
8		the word "market" on the board]. You['ve] got a market, there, isn't it?

9		Is it a market there? [Points to the market next to the school.] Have you
10		been there?
11	S:	Yes.
12	T:	Yes. But in the past we call[ed] it *heui*. (Cantonese) [墟][Writes the
13		Chinese character *heui* (Cantonese) [墟] on the blackboard.] *Chan*
14		*heui*. (Cantonese) [趁墟] And then at that time people going to
15		market, we call[ed] it *chan heui*.
16	Ss:	[laughter]
17	T:	[writes the words *chan heui* (Cantonese) [趁墟]on the blackboard]
18		And then what does it mean? At that time the people—you find out that
19		for the market ...?
20	S:	[silent]
21	T:	The market opens every day? Is it? There? [Pointing at the market outside
22		the window]
23	Ss:	Yes.
24	T:	But at that time the market [did] <u>not open every day</u>. They will fix some
25		day, for example, for each month, [on the] fifteen[th] and thirt[ieth], they
26		will have [the] market. And then people go there, and then to sell ... what
27		they produce. For example, you look at him, he go[es] there to sell his pigs
28		and cocks, and at the same time by making money he can buy something
29		that he did not produce by himself. Understand? So it is different from
30		your market, isn't it? And at the same time, at that time the market has a
31		function. First of all, it is selling and at same time you buy something. And
32		also you find out that, in the second paragraph, what did he say?
33		[referring to the diary of Tang Tai Man.]
34	Ss:	[silent]
35	T:	What did he say?
36	Ss:	[silent]
37	T:	What did he say?
38	Ss:	[silent]
39	T:	Huh? [Nominate], what did he say in the second paragraph?
		....
45	S:	[reading from the second paragraph of the diary of Tang Tai Man]

6. SEMANTIC ENRICHMENT OF THE SPACE OF LEARNING 159

46		"Today I also met my friends coming from another village, we
47		chat[ted]."
48	T:	Okay, okay, so what did, what did he do in the second paragraph?
49	S:	[silent]
50	T:	What is happening to him?
51	S:	He met his friends.
52	T:	He met his friends. Okay, sit down. You found out that then, for the
53		market at that time, it also provides a chance for them to meet their
54		friends.... You found out that at that time [there was] no transport, you
55		can only ____?
56	S:	Walk.
57	T:	Walk. Then sometimes it is difficult for you to find your friends, is it? So
58		the market provide[d] a place for them to meet their friends.... You think
59		about now, is it very easy for you to see your friends?
60	T:	... So you find out that here this is the function of the market [referring to
61		the handout] ...

Here the teacher was trying to bring out the differences between the market in the past and the market in the present, and its functions in early rural communities in Hong Kong. She started with an open question of how the market in the old days was different from the market nowadays (see line 3, "How [was it] different?"). When she failed to get an answer, she narrowed down the question to specific features. First, she tried to draw on the students' mother tongue resources by invoking the expression *chan heui* (Cantonese) [趁墟], an expression that all students were familiar with as evidenced by the laughter. She asked them to extrapolate one of the features of the market from the meaning of this expression. (The word *chan* (Cantonese) [趁] means to take the opportunity, and the word *heui* (Cantonese) [墟] was used by the teacher as an equivalent of the market in the past. Therefore, *chan heui* implies that the market was not open every day, and that when it was, people took the opportunity to get what they wanted from the market.) This technique did not meet with much success because unpacking a Chinese expression in English was far too difficult for the students. Failing to get a response, the teacher simply pointed out that unlike the market next to their school, markets in the old days were not open every day.

After dealing with the first critical feature, the teacher went on in the same turn to provide the second critical feature of the market: Unlike today, people went to the market not only to sell their produce or to buy something they needed, but to do both at once. From lines 32 to 58, the teacher tried to elicit a third critical feature of the market from the students, by asking them to look at the second paragraph of the diary that she had been referring to earlier. One of the students, after struggling with the teacher's instructions, simply read out the second paragraph instead of inferring from the text what the third critical feature was, as the teacher had wanted. Although the student was able to provide an appropriate answer after several prompts from the teacher (see line 51), the connection between what appeared in the text and the third critical feature of the market (i.e., that the market provided a place for people to meet their friends) had to be made by the teacher. The connection between the function of the market for social interaction and poor transportation was also made by the teacher.

We can see in the just cited excerpt that the teacher tried to focus the students' attention on the critical features of the market in old rural communities by varying the contexts of past and present. However, because of the students' limited linguistic resources in English, the teacher had problems engaging the students in making sense of the contexts in which these features were to be understood.

Let us compare this lesson with an excerpt below from a CMI lesson, where the same concepts were being explicated.

6.9 [History Lesson/S2/CMI]

[The teacher asks the students to identify on the map places that contain the word *heui* (Cantonese) [墟] [standing for "market."] Then he continues to ask the students the functions of a "market."]

1	T:	Next I want to ask you, what are the functions of a *heui*?
2	S:	[cheekily] No use.
3	T:	What? What are the functions of *heui*. Has anybody heard the
4		saying "Three, what, make a *heui*?"
5	Ss:	Three women!
6	T:	What does that mean? Now we are not discriminating against fe-
7		male students. We are not saying that female students are talkative. So
8		what is the function [of a *heui*]? In fact, how can three people make
9		a *heui*? What is the characteristic of a *heui*?
10	S:	Very noisy.
11	T:	Very noisy. Maybe we should not use [the word] noisy.
12	S:	Busy.
13	T:	Busy! A lot of fun. Other than this? What else?
14	S:	Lots of things for sale.
15	T:	What function does the market have?

16	S:	<u>Transactions</u>.
17		Conducting transactions, that's right. What kinds of things for us to
18	T:	buy? In earlier societies?
19	S:	Jewelry.
20	T:	Jewelry. Anything else?
21		…
22	T:	That is, the market has the function of [conducting] transactions.
23		Where is it?
24	S:	"<u>Open air nightclub</u>"[3]
25	T:	"Open air nightclub." That's right. Usually it is on a piece of flat
26		land. Whereabouts? Is it near the village? Inside the village? No.
27		Usually … can you imagine?
28	S:	Near the villages.
29	T:	Hmm, any other suggestions?
30	S:	Where there are lots of people.
31	T:	Where there are lots of people. Any other suggestions?
32	S:	Where lots of people can get to it.
33	T:	Where lots of people can get to it. Is it a place only where people
34		with the surname "Tang" can go?
35	S:	No.
36	T:	The place is a piece of flat land where usually other villagers can get
37		to as well. That is where the market was located. Also, in the old
38		days, there were no buses, no subway, so it wasn't so convenient.
39		So would there be a market every day? Would people go to
40		the market every day?
41	S:	No.
42	T:	That seldom happened. Usually there was a fixed time, usually
43		several times a month, or once a week. Besides being a place
44		for conducting transactions, what other function did it have?
45		Just now we said that three women make a market, very busy,
46		[people] chatting to each other. What function [of the market]
47		can you deduce from this? Ah, "You come from the nearby
48		village, how is so and so?"
49	S:	<u>Social interaction activities</u>.
50	T:	What kind of function did it have?

51	S:	Social interaction activities.
52	T:	That's right. You are correct. It actually had a kind of interactive
53		function, the interaction between villages, among people from
54		different clans.

We can see from this excerpt that in the CMI classroom, the learning space in which the features of the market was understood was jointly constituted by the teacher and the students. It was also semantically much richer than that constituted in the EMI classroom.

Firstly, by alluding to the Chinese colloquial expression, "Three women make a market," the teacher was immediately able to get the students to associate the expression with "very noisy" and "busy" (lines 10 and 12). When he asked the students where the market would normally be located, they used the analogy "open-air nightclub" (line 24). (The "open air nightclub" was a large, well-known, open-air night market in Hong Kong, that besides having a variety of things for sale, also had entertainment shows, fortune-telling, and hawker stalls. People went there not just to buy and sell things, but also to have a good time.) The teacher picked up on the student's analogy (line 25) and further developed the topic by involving students in exploring the locations of markets. Again drawing on students' knowledge of the expression, "three women make a market," the teacher solicited from the students that another critical feature of the market was its function for social interaction (line 49).

Here we can see that the rich linguistic resources of the mother tongue enabled the teacher and the students to collaboratively construe a rich picture of the market with a number of semantic features: for example, noisy, busy, joyous; with lots of activities going on; buying and selling; people from different villages and clans meeting up and making friends; people performing and watching entertainment shows. Going to the market (*chan heui*) was a social event that took place at regular intervals rather than every day because of the lack of transportation. We can also see that the students' understanding of the market was much more sophisticated due to the use of their mother tongue. For example, the concept of *social interaction* is much more sophisticated than just "meeting friends" and "entertainment," and the concept of *transaction* is much more sophisticated than "buying and selling."

The following table summarizes the semantic features of the market in the two lessons (see Table 6.2).

CONCLUSION

In this chapter, we have looked at another very important aspect of the learning space, that is, the way in which the object of learning (in the sense of the lived object of learning) is construed by the learners when they are

TABLE 6.2
Features of the Market in CMI and EMI Lessons

EMI Lesson	CMI Lesson
Functions of market	*Functions of market*
• Selling as well as buying	• Transactions (food and other things)
• Meeting friends (because of poor transportation)	• Social interaction between villages and clans.
	Imagery
	"Three women make a market" (to deduce functions)—noisy, busy, a lot of activities, joyous social interaction.
	Analogy
	"Open air nightclub"—buying and selling, food, entertainment shows, having a good time.
	Location
	Accessible to people from different clans and villages.
Opening	*Opening*
Not open daily (no reasons given)	Not open daily; poor transportation, not enough goods and produce for sale.

able to bring in their own experiences, their own culture, their former learning, folklore, and so forth. We referred to this aspect of the learning space as the semantic dimension of the space of learning, and proposed that this semantic dimension is elastic, that is, that it can be enriched or impoverished. We illustrated how the teacher enriched the semantic dimension of the space of learning by helping learners to perceive the interrelationship of aspects of the phenomenon that were hitherto perceived as unrelated. By introducing new semantic domains or different levels of knowledge in which the phenomenon can be construed, the teacher enriched the learning space semantically. We have also illustrated how the learners themselves enriched the learning space semantically by bringing their own experiences to bear on the object of learning, and how they can thus collaboratively construct and assign new meanings to the object of learning. The way in which the semantic dimension of the learning space is enriched and thus helps learners experience the object of learning in a certain way in each lesson is an instantiation that will eventually lead to the enlarging of the semantic potential in which the object of learning is being construed. Finally, by comparing the differences in semantic richness of construal of the object of learning—in classes where learners have the necessary linguistic resources (mother tongue medium), and classes in which they do not (second language medium)—we have illustrated the way in which language plays a central role in the semantic enrichment of the space of learning.

ENDNOTES

[1] The written texts produced by the students were in Modern Standard Chinese. The translations of the texts presented here are semantic translations but the syntactic structures of the texts have been retained as far as possible.

[2] In this volume, characters and words spoken in Cantonese are transcribed in the Yale system, which is used by some Cantonese-learning materials produced by the Yale University, and by The University of Hong Kong in its Cantonese–English, English–Cantonese dictionaries. (Note that diacritics that are used to indicate Cantonese tones have been left out. These diacritics are very difficult, if at all possible, to produce using Word, and some research reports using the Yale system simply do not include the diacritics.)

[3] "Open air nightclub" is the name given to a large, well-known, open-air night market in Hong Kong. It does not exist anymore in its original form.

7

The Shared Space of Learning

Amy B. M. Tsui

Marton and Booth (1997) expounded the qualitatively different ways in which learning can be experienced: The learner may focus largely on the *situation* in which the phenomenon is embedded, or on the *phenomenon* as it is revealed in the situation (see p. 83). They observed that the aspects of the phenomenon and the relationships between them that are discerned and held in awareness simultaneously determine the way the phenomenon is experienced by the individual. Therefore the same phenomenon may be experienced in qualitatively different ways by individuals because the aspects and the relationships that they discern may be different, and what is held in awareness simultaneously may also be different. When this happens, the lived object of learning will be different from the enacted object of learning. To bring about successful learning, it is necessary that the teacher and the learner share a large common ground in relation to the object of learning. The task before the teacher, therefore, is threefold. First, the teacher should ensure that the conditions are there for the learner to be able to discern and simultaneously hold in awareness the critical aspects of the object of learning, and the relationships between these aspects. Secondly, the teacher should be aware of the learner's experience of the object of learning (see also Alexandersson, 1994), and be vigilant of signals from learners indicating a lack of common ground. Thirdly, the teacher should try to widen the shared common ground. These three tasks cannot be achieved independently of each other; they are intertwined.

What does all this mean to the practitioner, and how is this threefold task realized in classroom discourse? Before we proceed to address this question, we need to have some understanding of what is involved when two or more people are engaged in a discourse of some sort.

DISCOURSE AND COMMON GROUND

When two or more people engage in a discourse of some sort, they bring with them a set of assumptions that they believe are shared between them. There are certain assumptions that pertain to communication in general. For example, that these people speak the same language, that they are aware of and observe similar conventions regarding discourse rules, that neither of them have speech and/or hearing impairments, and so on. These assumptions pertain to the channel of communication and not to a specific utterance under discussion. There are also assumptions that are more specific to the communicative situation. For example, when we talk to a colleague, we assume that they have shared knowledge about people and events in the workplace that are relevant to the day-to-day operation, the lines of responsibility, and so on. However, exactly how much knowledge we share is not known until we actually enter into a discourse. Let us take the following piece of conversation—which is fabricated but which typically occurs—between two colleagues, A and B, for example:

7.1

1 A: So the meeting's been changed to Friday?
2 B: What meeting?
3 A: The departmental meeting.
4 B: Oh, I thought it was canceled.
5 A: Apparently not.
6 B: I don't know. Ask Rebecca. She would know.
7 A: OK. Thanks.

When A asked B whether the meeting had been changed to Friday (line 1), A had certain assumptions. A assumed that, first, B knew what meeting A was referring to; second, B knew that the date of the meeting had been changed; third, it was likely that B would be able to provide the answer. However, A could not be absolutely sure that these assumptions were shared until B responded. B's response (line 2) indicated that A's assumption was not shared, and that B did not know which specific meeting A was referring to. Bruner (1987) pointed out that reference typically "plays upon the shared presuppositions and the shared contexts of speakers" (p. 87). A's reference to the meeting involved mapping A's subjective sphere onto B's. Upon hearing B's question, "What meeting?" (line 2), A realized that this first assumption was in fact not shared by B. A then immediately clarified the referent, that is, "the meeting," by explicitly identifying it as "the departmental meeting" (line 3). B's response to A's clarification (line 4) showed that A's second assumption that the meeting had been changed was not shared, and A's subsequent response showed that B's assumption that it had been canceled was not shared either (line 5). Finally, B's response showed that A's first assumption (that B might know the answer) was not shared (line 6). B directed A to another colleague, Rebecca. B's assumption was that A knew who Rebecca was, and that there was a reason for directing the question to Rebecca. This assumption was indeed shared, and A thanked B for the redirection (line 7).

At the end of the exchange, the common ground between A and B had widened. There was more shared knowledge between them now than before. Any kind of discourse is a process of widening the common ground between participants, and this is one of the major motivations for people to talk to each other. *Discourse* is therefore a process in which meanings are negotiated and disambiguated, as well as a process in which common grounds are established and widened (see Tsui, 1994).

CLASSROOM DISCOURSE AND ESTABLISHING COMMON GROUND

In classroom discourse, there are also certain shared assumptions between the teacher and the students. For example, there are shared assumptions that students should follow the teacher's instruction, that they should answer questions when called on to do so, and so on. These pertain to the general classroom protocols that differ from culture to culture; culture in the sense of ethnic culture as well as social class culture. For example, in many Asian classrooms, the protocol requires that students stand up when they answer the teacher's questions because the teacher is a figure of authority. In classrooms where middle-class culture predominates, working-class children are seriously disadvantaged because they do not share the same assumptions as middle-class children. Classroom socialization and acculturation are important aspects of classroom learning, but in this volume, we are not particularly concerned with the shared common ground in this respect. We are more concerned with the aspects of common ground that are pertinent to the object of learning.

There are also assumptions that the teacher and the learners hold that are specific to the object of learning. It is not uncommon for the teacher to be working on certain assumptions that are not shared by the students, or vice versa. When this happens, the ability of the teacher to negotiate and widen the common ground between himself and the students is critical to effective learning.

Let us take as an example some data from a primary Grade 4 (P4) English lesson on "The Weekly Plan." (For the background of this lesson and other aspects of this lesson, see Lo & Ko, 2002.). Let us call this class, Class A. The intended object of learning in this lesson is the use of the simple present tense to indicate habitual action. The teacher, Teacher A, presented a diary of Mickey Mouse that shows that he does different activities on different days of the week. He also does some of the activities for more than one day. After getting the students to focus on "How often does he do (activity)?," the teacher wanted to focus on the tense used.

7.2 [English Lesson/P4A/Weekly Plan]

30	T:	... he goes to the library only one, one time, OK? One time,
31		OK? So we say once a week. But why [do] we add "-es" at
32		the end of the word "go?" [Teacher pointing at the "-es"
33		ending on the board.] Can you tell me? [Ss put up their
34		hands.] Yes?
35	S8:	Because he, she, it.
36	T:	Yes, he, she, it, but what is linked to the tense? The verb ...
37		the form of the verb? Samuel?
38	S9:	Present tense.
39	T:	Present tense. What kind of present tense? Simple—
40	Ss:	Simple present tense.
41	T:	Why [do we use] "simple present tense?" Why? Why do
42		you think it is about simple present tense? Because it is
43		about __?
44	S10:	[sitting in her seat] He do after school.
45	T:	[pointing at S10] Yes?
46	S10:	Because it is about ... he do after school.
47	T:	Yeah, it is about the things, OK, he, Mickey Mouse, he
48		Mickey Mouse, do [does] the things after school. We are
49		telling people about his habit. OK?

From the student's response in line 35 in the aforementioned excerpt, we can see that what came to the fore of this student's awareness on hearing the question, "Why [do] we add '-es' at the end of the word 'go'?" is "subject–verb agreement." It is a perfectly appropriate response to the teacher's question. However, it was not what the teacher was looking for. This is evidenced by the teacher accepting the answer but continuing with the disjunctive "but," which is typical of disagreement. The answer that the teacher was looking for was "simple present tense" (see line 40). In fact it is both the third person singular and the simple present tense that necessitate the inflection of the verb "go." If the subject were the first or second person, there would have been no need for the inflection even if the verb were in the simple present tense. As the discourse unfolds, we can see that the teacher was enacting a script in which

7. THE SHARED SPACE OF LEARNING

the teacher's focal awareness was very much on the use of the simple present tense in describing habitual action (see line 49), and not subject–verb agreement. The latter, however, was very much in the student's focal awareness when they answered the question. The teacher, being unaware of how the students were experiencing the object of learning, dismissed valuable contributions from the students as irrelevant.

Let us consider another example taken from the physics lesson on the reed relay reported in chapters 1 and 5, and see the difference that was made by a teacher who shared a large common ground with the students. In the lesson on the reed relay, after the students conducted the second experiment (in which the teacher asked the students to connect a motor to both the simple circuit [without a reed relay] and the complicated circuit [with a reed relay]), the teacher explained the different outcomes observed in the simple circuits in the two experiments.[1] First, she explained why the motor did not rotate in the simple circuit without a reed relay. Then she went on to explain why the LED lit up in this circuit.

Let us examine the following extract:

7.3 [Physics Lesson/S2/CMI]
```
 1  T:  ... Why is it that it [the LED] works in this circuit? [pointing at
 2      the simple circuit with the LED] Why was it so well-behaved?
 3      Why did it [LED] light up? [nominate]
 4  S:  Because the resistance that the LDR needs, no, the current that it
 5      needs is smaller than [that needed] by the motor.
 6  T:  Say that once again, you are right, I understand you.
 7  S:  LDR needs
 8  T:  Which is the LDR? This one?
 9  S:  Because the electric that LED needs compared ...
10  T:  Electric what?
11  S:  Electric current is smaller compared with the motor.
12  T:  That's right. So if I press it [the push button switch] here, there
13      will be enough current to make this LED glow. OK? Now, we
14      found that if we don't use the reed relay [in the circuit with a
15      motor], then there are problems because some circuits must use a
16      reed relay to operate. Let me give you an example ...
```

In this excerpt, the teacher asked an open "why-question" that required the students to explain why the simple circuit connected with an LED worked (see Fig. 2a in chap. 5). The student was trying to construe the experience gained from the experiments and present it to the teacher. She was trying to relate the reason for the device lighting up with the size of the current that was needed by the two devices (the motor and the LED). In line 4, we can see the student struggling with this because although she was aware of the fact that the size of the electric current needed by the motor was bigger than that needed by the device that lit up (LED), she had erroneously labeled the LED as LDR, and had misrepresented electric current as resistance (see lines 4 and 7). It is clear that the student had some problems in construing what she had experienced in the experiment through a meaningful linguistic representation. The teacher, instead of dismissing the student's contribution as wrong, understood that the student was formulating her thoughts as she went along. She assured the student that she understood what she was trying to say and encouraged her to represent her construal of the experience once again. As soon as the teacher pointed at the diagrams on the board, where the labels for the devices were given, the student realized that what she had thought was an LDR was in fact an LED, and she corrected herself. The teacher further helped the student to represent her construal in more precise terms by getting her to revise "electric" to "electric current." In contrast to the previous classroom excerpt, (7.2), the common ground shared by the teacher and the students was much larger. As a result, the student was able to construe her experience in a meaningful way and to make a valuable contribution to the discussion.

STRUCTURE OF AWARENESS AND THE SHARED SPACE OF LEARNING

To further elucidate the notion of the shared space of learning, let us consider the notion of structure of awareness that was discussed in chapter 1. We argued that *awareness* is the totality of experience, and that characteristically only a limited number of things come to the fore of our awareness and the rest recedes to the ground. Marton and Booth (1997) referred to this structure as figure–ground. However, what comes to the fore of one's awareness varies. When the teacher and the learners, for various reasons, are working on different assumptions, their structure of awareness may be different. What is figural to the teacher may be ground to the learners, and vice versa; equally, what is figural to some learners may be ground to others. When this mismatch occurs, we say that the space of learning is not shared, or only partly shared.

Let us compare data from Class A (the English lesson on "The Weekly Plan" cited before) and another primary Grade 4 lesson on the same topic, with exactly the same intended object of learning. Let us call the latter, Class B. In Class A, the teacher put up on the board the diary of Mickey Mouse that says what he does from Sunday to Saturday. Above the schedule is the question, "What does he do after school?" (see Table 7.1)

7. THE SHARED SPACE OF LEARNING 171

TABLE 7.1
English Lesson/Weekly Plan/Primary Grade 4/Class A
White Board Description

Mickey Mouse's Picture	*What Does He Do After School?*
Sunday	Library
Monday	Piano Lesson
Tuesday	Basketball
Wednesday	Swimming
Thursday	Basketball
Friday	Swimming
Saturday	Basketball

The following is an excerpt from Class A, from the point in the lesson when the teacher directed the students' attention to Mickey Mouse's diary on the board.

7.4 [English lesson/P4/Weekly Plan/Class A]

12	T:	... So let us look at his [Mickey Mouse's] diary, OK? What does
13		he do after school? OK. [Teacher points at the diary on the
14		board.] This is the thing that he does after school. OK, what
15		does he do after school? [Teacher puts a strip of paper with
16		question "What does he do after school?" on the board.] Can
17		you tell me, "What does he do after school?" Anybody?
18		[Students raise their hands]. Yes.
19	S2:	He goes to the library on Sunday.
20	T:	Yes, he goes to the library on ____ ?
21	S:	Sunday
22	T:	Sunday. Yes, after school, OK? He says he goes to the library
23		after school. "After school." OK, how about ... What else? How
24		about others?
25		[Students raise their hands. The teacher looks at one of the
26		students signaling to her to answer the question.]
27	S3:	He has a piano lesson on Monday.
28	T:	Yes. We say—we don't say "on Monday" first, OK? The

29		question is "What does he do after school?" So he says that he
30		has a piano lesson after ____ ? School.
31	Ss+T:	School
32	T:	OK. Do you understand?
33	Ss:	Yes.
34	T:	Yes, OK. How about the other things? What does he do after
35		school? What else? [Students raise their hands.]
36	S4:	He play basketball after school.
37	T:	Yeah, he says he plays basketball after …
38	Ss+T:	School.
39	T:	"Plays," [stressing the "s" sound] OK? Remember "plays,"
40		OK? What else? One more thing. Samuel?
41	S5:	He … he plays basketball on … after …?
42	Ss+T:	School.

Here we see that when the students were asked to describe Mickey Mouse's diary, they provided the activity and the day of the week (see lines 19 and 27). However, what the teacher wanted to elicit from the students was what Mickey Mouse does after school (see the teacher's correction of the students' answers in lines 22 to 23, and lines 28 to 30). It was only after the teacher made it clear to the students that they should not say the day of the week (line 28), that the students produced what the teacher considered to be the correct answer (line 36).

What was happening in this piece of discourse? How much common ground was shared between the teacher and the students? When the students produced the "correct" response, in what way was the common ground widened? Was this common ground pertinent to the object of learning of the lesson?

To understand the mismatch between the students' answers and what the teacher wanted to solicit from them, we need to see the items on the white board as an integral part of the situation in which the phenomena of habitual action and frequency are embedded. On the white board were the following items: Mickey Mouse's picture, the diary stating what Mickey Mouse did each day of the week, and the question "What does he do after school?" Together they constitute a piece of text that says that Mickey Mouse does some activities that vary according to the day of the week. The question "What does he do after school?" provides the context for interpreting the activities as outside school hours. The aspects of Mickey's diary that were discerned by the students, and were focal in their awareness, were the aspects that varied: activities and days of the week (as can be seen from S2's and S3's responses in line 19 and line 27 respectively). The fact that Mickey Mouse conducted these activities after school was very much kept in the ground of the student's awareness. This is not surprising because the time when these activities were conducted, that is, after school, was invariant; it was the same every day (except for Sunday).

The students' responses, "He goes to the library on Sunday" (line 19), and, "He has a piano lesson on Monday" (line 27), were perfectly appropriate answers to the teacher's question (line 17) because Mickey Mouse does different things on different days of the week. However, the responses were considered incorrect by the teacher, and both were amended by replacing the day of the week with "after school." Ironically, the student's answer in line 19 was more appropriate than the teacher's correction, "He goes to the library after school" (line 23), which was in fact wrong because there is no school on Sunday.

The aspects that the teacher wanted the students to keep in their focal awareness were "the activities" and "after school," and not "the days of the week." This is because the teacher wanted to pave the way for teaching the use of the simple present tense to describe habitual action and indicate frequency. The day of the week on which the activities were carried out was therefore unimportant. This can be seen in the subsequent discourse when the teacher tried to get the students to use the phrases "once a week," "twice a week," "three times a week," and so on, in answer to the question "How often?" Subsequently, the students did omit the days of the week and simply said "after school" (see 7.4, line 36, line 41, and line 42). However, it is highly likely that the students produced the response simply because this was what the teacher wanted, not because it was a better or a more appropriate answer. The common ground that was widened between the student and the teacher therefore was "what the teacher wanted," as opposed to what constituted an appropriate response.

The description of habitual action requires students to be simultaneously aware of both the use of the present tense and the inflection of the verb for third-person singular. The students' awareness of subject–verb agreement, as indicated in their responses, was an excellent basis for the teacher to bring in tense as a dimension of variation, which would have helped the students to discern the use of the present tense to denote habitual action, as opposed to, say, the use of the past tense to denote past action. However, this possibility for learning was not exploited by the teacher because she failed to see how the student's answer related to the object of learning.

Let us compare the just mentioned example with what happened in Class B. The teacher started the lesson by revising the vocabulary for describing activities by showing the students pictures. After this, she put on the white board a picture of Cindy, a picture of Timmy, and a weekly plan below Cindy's picture (see Table 7.2).

TABLE 7.2
English Lesson/Weekly Plan/Primary Grade 4/Class B

	Cindy		Timmy
	Weekly Plan		
Days of the week	Things to do		
Sunday	Play table tennis		
Monday	Go to the library		
	Have a piano lesson		
Tuesday	Have a dancing lesson		
Wednesday	Go to the library		
Thursday	Have a computer lesson		
Friday	Play table tennis		
Saturday	Have a computer lesson		

The items on the white board also constitute a piece of text. This text says that Cindy does some activities each day of the week. The presence of Timmy means that there are two people involved in this piece of text. The variants in this piece of text are *the day of the week* and *the activity*. The weekly plan belongs to Cindy. Timmy does not have a weekly plan. The teacher had set up a dialogue between Cindy and Timmy whereby Timmy asks, "What do you do on (day of the week) '+ s'?" and Cindy answers, "I (verb + activity) on (day of the week) '+ s'." For example:

Timmy: What do you do on Wednesdays?
Cindy: I go to the library on Wednesdays.

Both variants, day of the week and activity, were focused on simultaneously by the students and the teacher, and both were evaluated by the teacher when she went through Cindy's weekly plan with the students. What was invariant was the question from Timmy, and the linguistic structure of the answers from Cindy that provided the scaffolding for the students. The teacher also drew the students' attention to the plural form of the days of the week to signify recurrence, which is an important feature of habitual action.

After the teacher had gone through all the days of the week and the corresponding activities, the teacher asked the students to summarize Cindy's schedule for Timmy and solicited from the students descriptions of frequency, such as "you go to the library twice a week," "you play table tennis three times a week," and so on. As these structures were solicited, the frequency of occurrence came to the fore of the students' awareness, and the day of the week receded into the ground. What the students held in their awareness simultaneously were the activity and the frequency. This is evidenced by the fact that when the students were asked to come up with their own weekly plans and to conduct a dialogue asking each other about their weekly plans and how often they conducted the activities, they did not have problems.

In Class B, the conditions obtained for discerning the critical aspects of habitual action, which were namely the activity itself and the frequency of occurrence or recurrence. The way that the teacher set up the situation in which the habitual action was embedded enabled the students to experience the object in the way that the teacher intended. The structure of awareness of the teacher and of the students converged, unlike in Class A, where the teacher's and the students' foci of awareness differed. We could say that in Class B there was a wider shared space of learning than in Class A, and that the learning outcome—as evidenced by the students' oral performance of the task—showed that the teacher in Class B was more effective than the teacher in Class A in designing the learning experience, as far as the teaching of habitual action was concerned.

NEGOTIATION OF MEANING AND THE SHARED SPACE OF LEARNING

In the 7.1 conversation example given at the very beginning of this chapter, we saw that participants A and B were involved in a process of negotiating the referent for "the meeting" and widening the common ground that was shared between them. In the classroom excerpts (7.2) and (7.3), we saw that when certain assumptions were not shared between the teacher and the students, valuable contributions from students could be dismissed or not valued. Because of the unequal power relationship between the students and the teacher, students were often unable to engage in the kind of negotiation of meaning that is prevalent when the power relationship is symmetrical, such as what we saw in the conversation between colleagues (7.1). It is therefore important for the teacher to be vigilant of assumptions that are not shared with learners, as well as to be sensitive to signals of the lack of common ground, and to be able to respond to such signals by engaging in a negotiation of meaning with the learners.

Let us take, for example, an excerpt from the lesson on the sloth, which was discussed in chapter 6. In this lesson, the teacher was revising what the class had covered in the previous lesson, that is, the description of a panda, and what details need to be covered when the students write a description of an animal.

7.5 [Chinese Lesson/P3/The Sloth]

1	T:	[Holding up a textbook showing the chapter on the
2		panda] OK, today, we will do some writing. Our
3		writing will follow the chapter on the panda.... I want
4		you to tell me, when we write about an animal, <u>what
5		do we need to include in the contents</u>? ... Put up your
6		hands. <u>What do we need to write about first</u>?
7		[A student raises his hand.]
8	S1:	Body.
9	T:	"Body" is what?
10	S1:	Huh? [Meaning he does not understand the question]
11	T:	Body.
12	Ss:	Body [Students say this in English, from their seats.]
13	T:	Body. What else? [Writes "body" on the board.]
14	S2:	The brain. [meaning "head"]
15	T:	Yes, the head. What else? [Writes "head" on the
16		board]
17	S3:	Four limbs.
18	T:	Yes, four limbs .... any more? Yes.
19	S4:	The skin, the color of the fur.
20	T:	Color. Yes. [Writes "color" on the board]
21	S5:	<u>Appearance.</u>
22	T:	<u>Appearance. In fact, the word "appearance," where
23		should we put it</u>? [Referring to location on the board]*
24	Ss:	In front.
25	T:	In front of four limbs?
26	S5:	In front of four limbs.
27	T:	<u>In front</u>? <u>In fact, I think</u> ... [pauses]
28	Ss:	The head.
29	S6:	After the head.

7. THE SHARED SPACE OF LEARNING 177

30	T:	In fact I think if you add all of them together [meaning
31		all the parts written on the board], the word that we
32		should use is ...?
33	S7:	Appearance.
34	T:	It's "outward appearance," appearance. [Writes the
35		Chinese characters for "outward appearance" [外貌] on
36		the board before body]. Outward appearance. When we
37		describe animals, we should start by writing about their
38		appearance first, and when you write about their
39		appearance, you will include these things [pointing to
40		the rest of the words on the board]

*See the teacher's white board writing in Table 7.3.

This part of the lesson dealt with the structure of a descriptive text about an animal. The teacher had in mind three important component parts, its appearance (which is static), its movements and eating habits (which are dynamic), and its character. In this excerpt, the teacher was dealing with the description of appearance. He asked the students what they would write about first (see line 6), and one student suggested "body" (line 8). When the teacher asked, "Body is what?" (line 9), he was apparently trying to get the students to subsume "body" under the superordinate "appearance" (see lines 30 to 32, and line 34). However, when the students indicated that they could not make sense of his question, he abandoned this line of questioning and invited students to give further specific components (line 13). In line 21, when finally one of the students suggested "appearance" (*yeuhng maauh* in Cantonese [樣貌]), the teacher asked the students where he should put the word (or the characters) on the board. Again, the teacher was taking "appearance" as a superordinate, and was trying to guide the students to see that this term subsumed all the physical features that they had proposed so far (see lines 34 to 40). However, the stu-

TABLE 7.3
Teacher's Writing on the White Board

Color of Fur	Four Limbs	Appearance (Students' Suggestion)	Head	Body	Appearance (Teacher's Suggestion)
顏色	四肢	樣貌	腦袋	身體	樣貌

Note. The teacher wrote in Chinese. Chinese writing is often read from left to right, as here.

dents apparently understood "appearance" as meaning just the facial appearance of the animal. This is evidenced by the fact that they suggested that the description of appearance should come before the description of the four limbs in the text, and after the description of the head. Finally, the teacher made explicit the relationship between "appearance" and the specific features (see lines 30 to 32, and lines 30 to 40).

The fact that there are certain grounds that are common, but that there are also others that are not shared between the teacher and the students is not unusual in classroom discourse. There could be a number of reasons why this happens, but frequently such divergent perceptions are caused by linguistic means, for example, by the questions the teacher asks, by the pragmatic and semantic presuppositions carried by the words used, by the way the teacher responds to the students' questions or responses, and so on. In this particular excerpt, there were several causes for the unshared ground. Firstly, the initial questions asked by the teacher, "What do you need to include in the content? ..." "What do you need to write about first?" (line 5 and line 6) were open to a number of interpretations. It would have been appropriate for students to provide either a list of specific features or the superordinate first. It is clear from the data that the relationship between appearance, or "outward appearance" to be precise, and the other features was very much in the teacher's focal awareness, whereas it was the specific features that were very much in the students' focal awareness. Secondly, the unshared ground was also caused by the semantic ambiguity of the word "appearance" in Chinese (*yeuhng maauh* in Cantonese) [樣貌] can mean facial appearance or the entire outward appearance. The teacher was using the word in the sense of "outward appearance," whereas the students were using it in the sense of "facial appearance."

We can see, however, that the teacher was able to respond very quickly to signals of assumptions not being shared by the students by abandoning the initial line of questioning and allowing the students to list the specific features. The teacher was also able to negotiate the meaning of the word "appearance," with the students by asking them where the word should be placed on the board, and guiding them to see the word "appearance" as a superordinate (lines 30 to 32). In this way, the teacher widened the common ground shared between himself and the students, so that eventually they were able to agree on a descriptive structure that formed the scaffolding for the rest of the lesson. In the subsequent discussion among the students in small groups, it was clear that the students had a good understanding of "appearance" as a superordinate that subsumes specific physical features.

COLLABORATIVE CONSTRUCTION OF MEANING AND THE SHARED SPACE OF LEARNING

In elucidating the notion of the shared space of learning, we proposed that there is another sense in which the space of learning is a shared space; that

7. THE SHARED SPACE OF LEARNING

is, when the space of learning is jointly constituted by the teacher and the learners through the collaborative construction of meaning.

The joint construction of meaning between children and adults is well documented. Halliday's work on child language development provides ample examples of how a child, through interaction with an adult, is able to construe experience into meaning. Typically, the child's response to the environment is interpreted by the adult as indicating communicative intentions, and responded to accordingly. In the course of responding to the child, the adult contributes to the co-construction of the meaning in the discourse (see, e.g., Halliday, 1973, 1975, 1993). Wells (1986) provided the following example of co-construction of meaning between a parent and a 2-year-old child.

7.6 [Wells, 1986, p. 46]

Mark (2;3) is standing by a central heating radiator and can feel the heat coming from it. He initiates the conversation by sharing this interesting information with his mother.

Mark: 'Ot, Mummy?
Mother: Hot? [checking] Yes, that's the radiator.
Mark: Been- burn?
Mother: Burn? [checking]
Mark: Yeh
Mother: Yes, you know it'll burn don't you?

In this piece of data, as Wells (1999) observed, the child responded to the central heating radiator by making a comment. His mother checked that she had correctly interpreted the child's utterance, and told him that the radiator was the source of the heat. The mother's correct interpretation of the child's utterance enabled him to extend the exchange and bring in the word "burn," which was in turn extended by the mother as "Yes, you know it will burn, don't you?" Subsequently in the discourse (not shown here), the child was able to take over the meanings that were initially co-constructed and apply them to a novel situation where he saw a bonfire in the garden and was able to say that it was hot and that it would burn as well.

Let us consider how this happens in classroom learning. In the history lesson that we discussed in chapter 6, the concept of *clan* was taught in the context of early rural communities in Hong Kong. In this context, a clan is a community of people with the same surname who live together in one area, and are also somewhat related by blood. The following is an excerpt from a Chinese medium classroom (CMI), where Chinese was the students' mother tongue, in which the teacher explored with the students why clans were formed and for what purpose.

7.7 [History Lesson/S2/CMI]

1 T: ... So, people with the same surname stay together.... <u>Why do they</u>
2   <u>stay together? Why do they stay together? Why</u>?
3 S: <u>Convenient</u>.
4 T: <u>It's convenient. Would it be better for them to go their separate ways</u>?
5   <u>Would it be better for you to go your own way? Who says it's</u>
6   <u>convenient</u>? ... <u>What are the advantages of living together</u>?
7 S: <u>They can help each other</u>.
8 T: Help each other. Yes, that's right. Very good.... <u>What kind of things</u>
9   <u>do they need to help each other with</u>? I want to ask all of you.
10 S: <u>Farming</u>.
11 T: Yes, farming, they need help from each other. You work on this part
12   [of the land] and I work on another part [of the land]. We help each
13   other. <u>What else, apart from farming</u>?
14 S: Hunting.
15 T: Hunting, OK. But we know that it was an agricultural society already,
16   so there was not much hunting.
17 S: Raising animals.
18 T: Raising animals, that is, raising cattle and sheep. Yes. What else?
19   What else?
20 S: Not to be bullied by others.
21 T: Not to be bullied. <u>Actually this is very important. To protect each other,</u>
22   <u>mutual protection</u>, apart from farming together, living together.
23   Some students said looking for food together. There is also the function
24   of protecting each other. Why did they have to protect each
25   other? So that they would not be bullied, because they came to Hong
26   Kong from a faraway place and they did not know the place, right?
27   They did not know whether they would be disliked by other clans.
28   What if they were attacked by them? That's why they needed mutual
29   protection. They had to be armed. In addition, <u>there were blood ties as</u>
30   <u>well</u>. Just now I told you that they had the same surname ... <u>Another</u>
31   <u>function was to preserve the traditional life style</u>.

In this excerpt, the teacher posed a number of open questions. Each time a student responded, the teacher took on the response and opened it up for inquiry. For example, in line 2, the teacher asked why people with the same

7. THE SHARED SPACE OF LEARNING

surname stayed together and one student responded that it was for convenience (line 3). The teacher took on the response and asked why it was convenient. When no response was forthcoming, the teacher rephrased the word "convenient" as "the advantages of living together" (line 6), and asked the students to list the advantages. As we can see, this immediately elicited the response "help each other" (line 7) from another student. At the end of a sequence of interaction around the topic, a semantic network relating to the formation of clans was collaboratively constructed by the students and the teacher: that is, mutual help (farming); mutual protection (so as not to be bullied by others; line 20 and line 21); blood ties (because they all had the same surname and therefore had the same ancestor; line 29 and line 30); and preservation of the traditional lifestyle (line 31).

The collaborative construction of the semantic network during the interactive process is illustrated in Fig. 7.1.

Figure 7.1 shows the way in which the teacher and the students co-constructed the space of learning by engaging in a negotiation of meaning. For example, the word "convenient" suggested by the student was too vague, and so the teacher clarified and elaborated the meaning of "convenient" by rephrasing it as "the advantages of staying together." The teacher's interpretation of the student's intended meaning helped to move the discussion for-

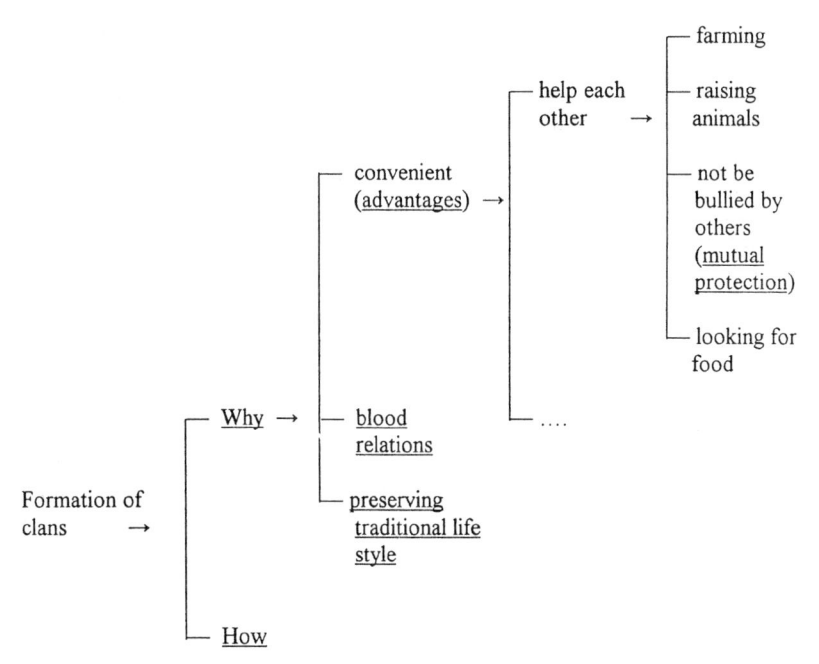

FIG. 7.1. Collaborative construction of a semantic network of formation of clan. Note: Words underlined are contributions from the teacher and other contributions are from students.

ward, as can be seen from the immediately forthcoming response from another student. Had the teacher misinterpreted the student's meaning, the subsequent contributions from the students would probably not have been forthcoming or they would have been different (see Wells, 1999). By asking the students what the advantages of staying together were, the teacher opened up a dimension of variation for exploring the benefits that people gained by staying together. When the students proffered "help each other" as an instance in the dimension of advantages, the teacher took on the response and opened up a further dimension of variation for exploring the different ways in which members of a clan needed to help each other. The students suggested "farming," "hunting," "raising animals," and "not to be bullied by others," as instances along this dimension. The teacher highlighted the importance of not being bullied and rephrased it at a higher level of abstraction by using the phrase "mutual protection." Finally, the teacher contributed two more reasons for the formation of clans: blood ties and preserving traditional life style. The interaction between the teacher and the students was a process in which questions posed by the teacher opened up dimensions of variation that afforded opportunities for students to explore the reasons for people to stay together. These opportunities were taken up by the students, and their contributions were in turn used by the teacher to open up further dimensions for exploration. The space of learning opened up was therefore a collaborative effort between the teacher and the learners. In this sense, the space of learning was a shared space.

Embodied in the notion of the joint constitution of the space of learning is also the collaborative construction of meaning among learners. This is particularly evident when learners are engaged in group work. For example, in chapter 6, we saw how learners brought their own knowledge of the world, and their previous experience, to bear on the object of learning as they collaboratively constructed texts on the story of the sloth.

LINGUISTIC RESOURCES AND THE SHARED SPACE OF LEARNING

As we have already pointed out, attempts made by the teacher to widen the shared space of learning may not always be successful. The cause of this mismatch could be linguistic, or it could be due to the fact that the structure of the learning experience brought about different foci of awareness. In classrooms where the medium of instruction is not the students' mother tongue (i.e., a language in which the students are less competent), the failure to widen the shared space of learning may be caused by a lack of linguistic resources (particularly on the part of the students, although sometimes it can also be on the part of the teacher).

Let us look at the following excerpt from an English medium lesson (EMI; English was not the students' mother tongue) on the same history

7. THE SHARED SPACE OF LEARNING 183

topic as the CMI lesson just cited (and in chap. 6), on the early rural community. In this lesson, the teacher asked the students to compare the diaries that they had written before the lesson, with those written by a father, Tang Tai Man, and his son, Tang Siu Man, in the days of the rural communities (these were given as handouts). The teacher's intention was to bring out the different lifestyles of people today and people in the past.

7.8 [History Lesson/S2/EMI]

The teacher asked the students to write a diary prior to this lesson and then asked them to compare their diaries with the two diaries on the handout by Tang Tai Man and his son, Tang Siu Man.

1	T:	... OK, look at the one of Tang Siu Man, Tang Siu Man. Is it
2		different from yours?
3	Ss:	Yes.
4	T:	How different? Can you tell me how different? Stephanie,
5		give me one difference.
6	S:	[speaking very softly] I have not the chicken.
7		...
8	T:	Yes, then what else? Why [does] the boy have chickens,
9		ducks, and pigs? What did he do?
10	S:	[silent]
11	T:	What did he do? How come he has the chickens, ducks, and
12		pigs? What did he do in his daily life?
13	S:	[silent]
14	T:	Understand my question?
15	S:	[speaking very softly, inaudible]
16	T:	What is his work, Stephanie? Angela, can you help? ...

In line 4, the teacher took on Stephanie's response that her diary was different from Tang's, and tried to open it up for inquiry by asking her how they were different. Stephanie tried to explain that she did not rear chickens. The teacher took on Stephanie's response and again tried to open it up for further inquiry by asking her why Tang Siu Man had chickens, ducks, and pigs. The teacher was hoping that Stephanie would point out the differences between life in early rural communities and life in modern urban societies. However, Stephanie was tongue-tied, even after prompting from the teacher twice (line 10 and line 11). Finally, the teacher had to ask another student to help out.

Throughout the whole lesson, there were a number of instances in which no response was forthcoming, even after the teacher had repeated or rephrased the question. In other words, the teacher had considerable difficulties trying to co-construct the space of learning with the students due to the students' lack of linguistic resources.

A quantitative analysis was conducted on the two history lessons (one EMI and one CMI) that were discussed in this chapter and in chapter 6 and two other history lessons (again, one EMI and one CMI) teaching the same topic to see how often the teachers were able to make use of the students' answers to open up the space for further inquiry, and facilitate the collaborative construction of meaning between teacher and students. The findings are presented in Table 7.4.

We can see from Table 7.1 that in the two EMI lessons, over half of the students' responses were simply accepted or repeated by the teachers without further elaboration or comment. The situation is almost the mirror image of the two CMI (i.e., mother tongue) lessons. It is not difficult to see that in CMI classrooms, the teachers and the students were engaged in making sense of the object of learning collaboratively. By contrast, in EMI (nonmother tongue) classrooms, the interaction was very much unidirectional and the learners played a much more passive role.

CONCLUSION

In chapter 1, we proposed the notion of the space of learning being characterized by classroom interaction in the light of a specific object of learning. And we pointed out that the space of learning is constituted by the possibilities for learning brought about by what is taking place in the classroom in relation to the object of learning. The possibilities for learning (i.e., what we have referred to as the enacted object of learning) cannot be brought about by the teacher alone, or by the learners themselves; they must be

TABLE 7.4
Teachers' Responses to Students' Answers in EMI and CMI Classrooms

Teachers' Responses to Students' Answers to All Teacher Questions	EMI 1	EMI 2	CMI 1	CMI 2
Rejection	0	1 (1%)	1 (1%)	1 (3%)
Accepting/repeating student's answer	50 (69.5%)	42 (59%)	16 (17%)	12 (34%)
Extending student's answer	16 (22.5%)	14 (20%)	69 (73%)	22 (63%)
No comment/new question	6 (8%)	14 (20%)	9 (9%)	0
Total number of responses	72 (100%)	71 (100%)	95 (100%)	35 (100%)

7. THE SHARED SPACE OF LEARNING 185

jointly constituted by both the teacher and the learners. In light of this, we proposed, in this chapter, that the space of learning is a shared space.

The joint constitution of the shared space of learning has very much to do with the structure of awareness of the participants in a discourse. If what comes to the fore of their awareness is different, participants talk at cross purposes. In a classroom situation, the learners' structure of awareness is often shaped by the way in which the teacher organizes the learning experience, and the way in which he presents the materials. Using data from two primary Grade 4 lessons on "the weekly plan," we illustrated the way in which the learners' structure of awareness was shaped by the materials that the teacher put on the board, and the way in which more effective learning was brought about when the teacher's structure of awareness accorded with that of the students.

The space of learning is a shared space in the sense that the interaction between the teacher and the learners is felicitous only when both parties share some common ground on which further interaction can be based. We have looked at examples of casual conversation and classroom data to see what happens when there is little or no common ground shared between participants. In the case of the conversation between two colleagues (7.1), the interlocutors had to work very hard to widen the common ground in order to advance the conversation. In the case of the English lesson on the weekly plan in primary Grade 4A, an appropriate contribution by a student was dismissed by the teacher because the latter failed to see the rationale behind the student's answer, and hence an excellent opportunity for learning was lost. By contrast, the classroom data from the reed relay experiment (7.3) and the lesson on the sloth (7.5) showed how possibilities for learning were opened up when the teacher was aware of the common ground shared between himself or herself and the learners. In these two examples, we also saw how the shared space of learning was widened by the negotiation of meaning between the teacher and the learners in the lesson on the sloth, and by the teacher helping the learner to clarify his or her thinking and linguistic representation in the lesson on the reed relay.

The space of learning is a shared space also in the sense that the possibilities for learning are jointly constituted by the teacher and the learner. In the Chinese medium history lesson, we saw how the teacher opened up possibilities for learning by asking questions on the basis of the students' responses (7.6), and how, as a consequence of the teacher's questioning, a semantic network of "clan" was collaboratively constructed by the teacher and the students.

The proposal that the space of learning is a shared space jointly constituted by the teacher and the learners is an important one from the perspective of the way we describe teaching and learning in relation to one another. Investigations of teaching and learning must take into consideration not only the possibilities for learning being opened up by the teacher, but also which possibilities are actually made use of by the learners.

ENDNOTE

[1]The simple circuit without the reed relay carries a very small current and is therefore able to light up the LED, which only requires a very small current to light up. The complicated circuit with the reed relay can carry a very large current once the reed switch is closed and can therefore cause the motor to rotate.

IV

On Improving Learning

8

Toward a Pedagogy of Learning

Mun Ling Lo
Ference Marton
Ming Fai Pang
Wing Yan Pong

The research reported in this volume stems from a set of studies based on one methodological idea. In each study, we compared the teaching in two or more classes where the intended object of learning was the same, and in this way observed the differences in the way in which the object of learning was dealt with. We then examined these differences from the point of view of the learning that was made possible for the students during each lesson. We have argued—and hopefully shown—that such differences can be described in terms of those aspects of the object of learning that the teacher varied, and those aspects that the teacher kept invariant; moreover, that the dimensions of the aspects that vary form the *space of learning*. It is this space of learning that either constrains learning or makes learning possible. When looking at the learning outcomes, we found empirically what might seem self-evident: that is, that it is more likely that students learn when it is possible for them to learn, than when it is not.

In all the classes that we have used as examples, the lessons were allowed to run their own course without any input from (or intervention by) the researchers, who simply described what they observed. However, if we really know what is critical in order for learning to take place, should we not try to make use of our insights to help shape the lessons for better learning? It is exactly such studies that we are going to report in this final chapter. We suggest that these studies show how the theory of variation works in practice.

Our point of departure is that teaching is—or should be—a rational activity. In planning a lesson or a unit, the teacher must take into account the characteristics of the students (e.g., age, general ability) as well as the physical conditions of the classroom (e.g., class size, equipment available). However, all these concerns must be translated into actions that can help achieve specific goals, that is, the explicit capabilities that students are expected to develop. We call these capabilities the *objects of learning*. Even in the most open classroom, students' learning should not be accidental but should be the result of conscious attempts on the part of the teacher to bring about the intended learning outcomes. In other words, attention must be paid to the ways in which the objects of learning are dealt with and enacted in the classroom.

Seen in this light, current debates (e.g., concerns about the relative merits of teacher-centered and student-centered instruction) that focus on general aspects, and not on ways of dealing with the specific content of learning, are of limited value both in terms of providing learning opportunities for teachers and in improving student learning. The teaching arrangements (such as whole-class teaching vs. group teaching, and the use of IT in the classroom) should be of concern only if discussed in relation to the specifics of what is taught and learned.

This line of argument parallels what Kilpatrick, Swafford, and Findell (2001) referred to in the context of mathematics education:

> Much debate centers on forms and approaches to teaching: "direct instruction" versus "inquiry," "teacher-centered" versus "student-centered," "traditional" versus "reform." These labels make rhetorical distinctions that often miss the point regarding the quality of instruction. Our review of the research makes plain that the effectiveness of mathematics teaching and learning does not rest on simple labels. Rather, the quality of instruction is a function of teachers' knowledge and use of mathematical content, teachers' attention to and handling of students, and students' engagement in and use of mathematical tasks. (p. 318)

Several recent theories regarding the professional development of teachers also appear to have focused on the different ways of dealing with the object of learning in the classroom. Basing their argument on a study of California elementary school teachers of mathematics, Cohen and Hill (2000) pointed out that teachers' opportunities to learn are a key factor affecting classroom practice, and that such opportunities exist only when teachers are asked to respond deeply to what they are supposed to teach. They found that professional development activities that allowed teachers to learn about the curriculum had a much greater effect on altering teaching practices than those that appeared to be either generic or peripheral to subject matter (Cohen & Hill, 2000). They even suggested that classroom practice was most effectively enhanced by those training activities that gave teachers concrete, topic-specific learning opportunities. Their data also showed that the mathematics achievement of students in schools where teachers were provided with these learning opportunities was considerably higher than in those without such opportunities. They concluded that intervention studies must change what teachers *do* with the curriculum in the classroom in order to affect student learning. What matters, therefore, is the *enacted* object of learning, that is, how the object of learning is actually dealt with in the classroom.

It is in this context that we introduce the idea of the "learning study." The learning study is based on the Japanese style "lesson study," which we feel takes the object of learning as its point of departure, but which also incorporates the methodological concept of the *design experiment* put forward by A. L. Brown (1992) and Collins (1992). We explain these ideas in turn in the following sections.

LESSON STUDY

Stigler and Hiebert (1999) introduced the idea of the lesson study (*jugyou kenkyuu*) in Japan in their book, *The Teaching Gap*. The lesson study, they argued, gives Japanese teachers a model of continuous school-based professional development, which the two researchers see as one of the main reasons for the success of the classroom practice reforms in post-war Japan (and the relatively high achievement rates of Japanese students in international comparison studies). Stigler and Hiebert (1999) explained the rationale of the lesson study as follows:

> The premise behind lesson study is simple: If you want to improve teaching, the most effective place to do so is in the context of a classroom lesson. If you start with lessons, the problem of how to apply research findings in the classroom disappears. The improvements are devised within the classroom in the first place. The challenge now becomes that of identifying the kinds of changes that will improve student learning in the classroom and, once the changes are identified, of sharing this knowledge with other teachers who face similar problems, or share similar goals, in the classroom. (p. 111)

In a typical lesson study, a group of teachers come together and select a topic to be dealt with during one or several "research lessons" (*kenkyuu jugyou*). Members of the group draw on each other's experiences, and together they decide on the intended objects of learning and work out a lesson plan designed to achieve these goals. One teacher will then teach the lesson, while everyone in the group observes. The lesson is then evaluated and the plan revised. Another teacher will then teach the revised lesson with the others observing, and a second round of evaluation and reflection will take place. The research lesson is then documented so that the outcome can be shared with other teachers. According to Stigler and Hiebert (1999), a lesson study is composed of eight steps:

- Defining the problem
- Planning the lesson
- Teaching the lesson
- Evaluating the lesson and reflecting on its effect
- Revising the lesson
- Teaching the revised lesson
- Evaluating and reflecting again
- Sharing the results

DESIGN EXPERIMENTS

As such, the goal of the research lesson is not just to produce an effective lesson, but, through careful planning and evaluation, to ensure that the teachers involved come to realize why and how the lesson works. A lesson study is of course not a controlled experiment in which one factor is allowed to vary while others are kept constant. One would actually question the value and the possibility of a controlled experiment in such complex and confounding environments as those of educational settings. However, as A.L. Brown (1992) and Collins (1992) suggested, it is still worth conducting design experiments in education, especially in classroom research. Although we cannot control all aspects of the environment, argue Brown and Collins, we can still gain considerable insights into the operation of the major variables through systematic intervention and unbiased observations. Conclusions can still be drawn, by comparing the results obtained from different conditions, although we have to interpret those results and guard ourselves against making general claims based on limited observations. The benefits of design experiments are that we will be able to contribute to theory development, and improve practice at the same time.

THE LEARNING STUDY

It was in the spirit of Brown's and Collins' design experiments that we tried to reformulate the Japanese lesson study in the research that we report in the latter part of this chapter. Marton (2001) defined the learning study in the following way:

> A learning study is a systematic attempt to achieve an educational objective and learn from that attempt. It is a design experiment that may or may not be a lesson study. Such a study is a learning study in two senses. First, it aims at bringing learning about, or more correctly, at making learning possible. The students will thus learn, hopefully. Second, those teachers involved try to learn from the literature, from each other, from the students, and not least, from the study itself. (p. 1)

Specifically, in our own research for this book, we wanted to learn the potential value of the theory of variation from these studies. The lesson study is an appropriate model as it allows researchers and teachers to see how the objects of learning are dealt with in the classroom. The learning study differs from the Japanese lesson study model in that our research lessons are based on a theoretical framework of learning—namely, phenomenography (cf. Marton & Booth, 1997), and variation theory—and we wish to find out how well the theory has worked. In this way the learning study is a learning study not in two, but in three senses, as the researchers are supposed to learn from it as well.

The cycle of a learning study comprises the following steps:

1. Choosing and defining a specific set of educational objectives. These are the capabilities or values to be developed during one or several lessons.
2. Finding out the extent to which the students have developed the capabilities or values targeted before the teaching begins.
3. Designing a lesson (or series of lessons) aimed at developing these capabilities or values. The planning work must take into account the existing knowledge of the students, the teachers' prior experiences in dealing with the objects of learning, and the research literature.
4. Teaching the lesson (or lessons) according to the plan.
5. Evaluating the lesson (or lessons) to see the extent to which the students have developed the targeted capabilities or values.
6. Documenting and disseminating the aim, procedures, and results obtained.

In the next three sections, we describe three cycles of a learning study in two separate projects. The first two cycles were conducted within an ongoing research project entitled "Catering for Individual Differences (Building on Variation)," commissioned by the Education Department of Hong Kong Special Administrative Region of the People's Republic of China, while the third cycle consisted of an independent project that employed the theory of variation in designing classroom lessons to help students to learn economics.

CATERING FOR INDIVIDUAL DIFFERENCES (BUILDING ON VARIATION)

The "Catering for Individual Differences (Building on Variation)" project is a 3-year, ongoing research project undertaken by a team of researchers from the Faculty of Education at The University of Hong Kong, and the Hong Kong Institute of Education, with Pong and Lo as principal investigators and Marton as consultant. As there are different ways in which the term *catering for individual differences* can be interpreted, it is therefore important that we explain our understanding of the term and its bearing on the aims of the project. The project members believe that because different people are born with different abilities, characteristics, and orientations, individual differences are a natural phenomenon and are not a problem in themselves. Individual differences only become a problem in the classroom setting, when a teacher has to teach a large group of students the same content. Thus, the project aims at helping teachers to find ways to enable all students—in a typical mixed-ability classroom setting—to learn what is intended by taking into account the students' diverse existing knowledge and understandings.

To achieve this, the project team believes that it is necessary to start with a carefully defined object of learning—that is, the capabilities that students are expected to acquire. For example, if we wish the students to understand a certain phenomenon, it follows that in order to accommodate individual differences, the teacher must first have a deep and thorough understanding of the different possible ways in which the students might understand this phenomenon. Research findings in phenomenography have shown that although students are unique individuals, there are always a limited number of qualitatively different ways in which they understand a particular phenomenon (Marton & Booth, 1997). These different ways of understanding arise mainly because a different set of critical aspects of the phenomenon are discerned.

How do teachers gain access to such knowledge of students' existing understandings? The team believes that teachers can first listen to, and learn from, their students. They can also share their findings with other teachers in the same school. Within the project, experience sharing with other teachers takes place in collaborative groups comprising teachers who teach the same subject at the same level in one school. In this way, individual differences become a resource for the teacher rather than a constraint.

Bearing in mind the various understandings students may bring to the classroom, and having identified the critical aspects of the objects of learning, the group of teachers move on to develop a research lesson that meets those ends.

In developing a research lesson, three aspects of variation are made use of within the project:

Variation in Terms of Students' Understanding of What Is Taught

Students understand that which they are supposed to learn in a limited number of different ways. Our research shows that teachers who pay close attention to such differences (or variations), and who can build on students' prior understanding and experiences, are better able to bring about meaningful learning for their students. Students also learn more effectively when they are made aware of the different ways in which their classmates deal with or understand the same object of learning.

Variation in Teachers' Ways of Dealing With Particular Topics

As a teacher gains experience over the years, he or she will build up a good working knowledge about the different ways in which students deal with particular concepts or phenomena, and will also develop ways of handling these differences. Such knowledge is extremely valuable and should be identified, sharpened, systematically reflected upon, and above all, shared with other teachers.

Variation as a Teaching Method

In previous chapters, we have shown that in any particular lesson there are always things that teachers vary while other things are kept unchanged, and that this pattern of variation—what is varied and what remains unchanged—is of decisive importance in determining how effective the lesson will be. In the "Catering for Individual Differences" project, teachers are encouraged and provided with opportunities to observe, reflect, and share ideas about their own lessons as well as the lessons of other teachers. The aim of this is for the teachers to find optimal patterns of variation for dealing with the intended objects of learning in a lesson, and thus develop more powerful ways of helping their students to learn.

In the first year of the project, two primary schools and a team of about 10 researchers were involved. In each school, two learning study groups were formed, each comprising five teachers. The following table summarizes the background information of the groups (see Table 8.1).

Workshops on the theoretical framework of the project were conducted with the teachers of each school before the learning study. Funding was obtained to allow an extra teacher to be employed in each school, so that each of the 10 teachers involved in the study gained a number of extra free periods, thus enabling them to take part. The meetings were officially scheduled at such times that all the teachers involved were free, and able to attend the meeting.

TABLE 8.1
Background Information of the Learning Study Groups During the First Year of the Project

School	Learning Study Group	Level of Study	Subject	Number of Teachers Participating
A	1	Primary Grade 4	Chinese Language	5
A	2	Primary Grade 4	Mathematics	5
B	3	Primary Grade 1	Mathematics	5
B	4	Primary Grade 4	Mathematics	5

Each of the learning study groups consisted of at least one researcher, a senior research assistant, and all teachers teaching the same subject at the same level in that school. They met once every week for 1 hour to plan the research lessons. The group meetings were audiorecorded, and summary notes were kept of each meeting. Each cycle of the learning study consisted of about 10 meetings, and the whole process was structured according to the six stages described previously. Each research lesson was taught, in turn, by all of the teachers in the group. At least two lessons were videotaped, and then analyzed and discussed in the group. An improved version of the lesson was then developed and written up. The students' performance was also measured before and after the lesson. On average, each group completed two research lessons in the first year. School-based and joint school seminars were also scheduled during the year to facilitate the sharing of experiences among the four groups of teachers. Two of the learning studies are described here. We believe that these studies not only illustrate the concept of the learning study and the use of variation theory, but also *the linguistic constitution of the space of learning* (which is dealt with in chap. 3 of this volume).

A PRIMARY GRADE 4 MATHEMATICS LESSON ON UNITS AND UNITIZING

The following is a learning study that was carried out by a team of five teachers who taught mathematics at the primary Grade 4 level. The entire cycle (from the incubation of ideas, to reflection and evaluation) took a total of nine meetings, which were distributed over a period of 3 months.

The Learning Study Cycle

Choosing the Object of Learning. The first step was to choose a topic. The teachers chose fractions, as they felt that fractions presented some of the most difficult concepts for school children at this level. The second step was to find out why the students had difficulty learning fractions; in other words, what it was about fractions that might be difficult for students.

Understanding What Is Difficult and Critical. The teachers reflected on their own experiences of teaching fractions in the past, and shared these experiences in the team meetings. The following questions were continually raised:

- What is actually learned, when learning about fractions?
- Why is learning fractions difficult?
- What is it that makes learning fractions difficult?
- How can we conceptualize these difficulties?

The university consultant also introduced the teachers to the relevant research literature, in particular Lamon's (1999) book about teaching and

8. TOWARD A PEDAGOGY OF LEARNING 197

learning fractions. Lamon argued that learning fractions constitutes the basis for proportional reasoning, and that the teaching of fractions should have a primary focus on conceptual understanding rather than procedural knowledge. She also pointed out that a critical aspect of fractions that students frequently fail to grasp was *units and unitizing*.

The team then reviewed the students' textbook for pedagogical advice. To their surprise, they found that the textbook not only lacked a formal treatment of units and unitizing, but that its presentation of fractions actually could have contributed to the students' misunderstanding. The chapter on addition of fractions, for example, began with the following diagram (Fig. 8.1), accompanied by a question that asked for a fractional notation of the shaded area:

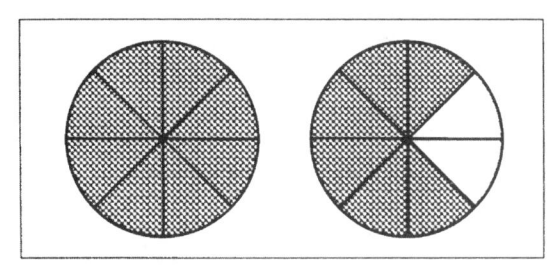

FIG. 8.1. The diagram used in the chapter on addition of fractions. From *Mathematics (Primary 4, First Term)* (1997), p. 49. Copyright © 1997 by Cambridge Publishers Ltd. Reprinted with permission.

Having identified units and unitizing as a problem area, the teachers then noticed that students could have made two perfectly legitimate guesses in response to this question in the textbook (i.e., 14/8 or 14/16), depending on what they understood as one unit. However, the textbook expected only one answer (i.e., 14/8); the tacit assumption in the textbook being that each circle constituted one unit.

At this stage, the teachers were convinced that they should focus on teaching units and unitizing and make this the object of learning of the research lesson. They were also eager to find out what prior knowledge their students would bring to their study of fractions.

Despite the fact that several aspects of fractions had already been taught in primary Grade 3, not all teachers were sure that the students in their classes understood the concepts well. In particular, they felt that the students needed to understand the idea of *equal shares* in fractions, as well as being able to conduct a simple comparison of fractions, before they could understand the idea of *unit*.

Developing a Test. The teachers then designed a test for the students. The purpose was to collect information about the students' ways of thinking about fractions, especially with regard to those aspects that were expected to be difficult. Furthermore, the test was to be used as a pretest to provide the team with a baseline against which the learning outcomes of the research lesson (as measured by the same test) could be compared. The test consisted of three main themes (exemplar questions are shown below):

1. The concept of *equal shares* in fraction, for example,

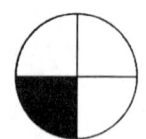

   Question: What fraction of the diagram is shown by the shaded area?

2. The concept of *fraction size* (restricted to the comparison of fractions with either the same denominator or the same numerator, for example,

   Question: Is ½ of a cake (greater than/smaller than/equal to) ¼ of a cake?

3. The concept of a *unit* being referred to by a fraction, for example,

   Question: When 4½ cakes are equally divided among 3 people, how many cakes does each person get? (You may draw diagrams to find the answer.)

The results of the pretest confirmed some of the teachers' speculations, and showed that there were fewer students who had mastered the concept of unit in fractions than those who understood the concept of equal shares, or were capable of comparing simple fractions (see Table 8.2).

Planning the Research Lesson. Informed by the pretest results, the teachers began to plan the lesson. They agreed that there should be some revision of equal shares but decided that this should be taught in a separate lesson prior to the research lesson. The research lesson should begin with comparing fractions but focus mainly on units and unitizing. There were several rounds of lively discussion. The result was a fairly detailed plan that was carefully deliberated and fully discussed.

A. The Lesson Opener—Contextualization

The planned lesson began by establishing a relevance structure (i.e., letting the students view fractions from a point of view that they could immediately experience as meaningful). The students were to discuss the following problem in small groups (see box on p. 200):

TABLE 8.2
The Results of the Pretest

Theme	Question	Freq. of Correct Responses Classes A–E (N = 151)
Equal shares	What fraction of the diagram is shown by the shaded area?	69
	Shade 1/9 of a square.	87
	Shade 1/8 of a circle.	116
	Shade 1/3 of the eggs in the basket.	87
Comparing fractions	1/2 of a cake is (greater than / equal to / smaller than) 1/4 of the same cake	63
	2/4 of a cake is (greater than / equal to / smaller than) 1/2 of the same cake.	58
	2/5 of a kg is (greater than / equal to / smaller than) 4/5 of a kg.	111
	1/2 of an hour is (greater than / equal to / smaller than) 1/200 of an hour.	39
Units and Unitizing	Divide 2 cakes into three equal parts. How many cakes are there in one part?	13
	When 4½ cakes are divided among three persons, how many cakes does each person get?	3
	What fraction of squares is shown by the black squares?	20
	What fraction of the total number of objects is shown by the black squares?	22

> In the yearly Community Chest fund-raising event,
>
> (a) Li Ka Shing, a wealthy man, donated $5 million.
>
> (b) Chan Siu Ming, a student, took out half of what he had saved, and donated $50.
>
> (c) Wong Tai Yung, another student, donated all the $5 that he had.
>
> Questions:
> - Who has donated the most?
> - Who was the most generous?

Hence, the fractions varied from an extremely low value (the case of Li Ka Shing, who is a world famous multibillionaire, well-known to the students) to the highest (Wong Tai Yung's case, i.e., 1, a whole unit). The absolute value varied from very high ($5 million Hong Kong) to very low ($5 Hong Kong). This was to serve as the lesson opener.

B. Dividing Paper Clips

The second part of the lesson plan began by having the students pay attention to two aspects of the fraction—the numerator and the denominator—in a successive manner. For the first activity, the class was divided into five groups. Each group was given a bag of 24 paper clips, and an assigned fraction (ranging from 1/8 to 7/8). Students in each group had to find out how many clips their fraction would represent. The aim of the task was to keep the denominator invariant while the numerator (a dimension of variation) varied. Each group reported their result, and the whole class observed and discussed how the amounts of clips changed as the numerator changed.

The activity was conducted a second time with a new set of fractions (1/2, 1/3, 1/4, 1/6, and 1/8). This time the numerator was deliberately kept constant while the denominator (another dimension of variation) changed. The students were again asked to observe how the number of clips changed with the fractions.

The activity was then conducted a third time with another set of fractions (1/2, 2/3, 3/4, 5/6, and 7/8). The students had to observe the effect as both dimensions of variation (the numerator and denominator) changed simultaneously.

C. Dividing Candies

The lesson then moved on to focus on the unit. In order for students to pay attention to the unit, they had to observe its importance, which necessitated the unit acting as a varying dimension. To do this, the teacher announced another round of dividing-up activities. However, in this round, the groups were given a pack of candies, each of which contained a different amount (12, 18, 24, 36, and 48). Each group had to find out how many candies there were in 1/6 of their pack. In this instance, the size of the pack varied while the fraction remained the same. The teacher then posed the question: Why are the results different when the fraction is the same? The students observed how the number of candies changed with the changing unit.

D. Waffle Cakes

In the next stage, the teacher gave each group a paper disc that represented a round waffle cake. In their groups, the students had to cut out 1/6 of the cake. When they finished, they were given 2 discs, and 1½ discs in turn, with the same task of cutting out 1/6 of the amounts given. They then had to compare the amount of cakes obtained, and see how the size of the unit mattered. The difference between this activity and the previous one was to allow students to see that the concept of *unit* embraces both countable and uncountable amounts.

E. Back to the First Question

At the end of the lesson, the teacher then returned to the two questions about the fund-raising event that were discussed at the beginning of the lesson. The students were to write out their own answers to the questions making use of what they had learned in the lesson.

Questions:
- Who has donated the most?
- Who was the most generous?

Teaching the Lesson and Reflecting on the Results. All five teachers taught their own classes with the same plan. They also tried to observe their colleagues teaching the same lesson, and shared their observations afterward with a view to modifying and improving the plan. Although there were some slight variations when each teacher implemented the lesson plan, the teachers all followed the structure and sequence of activities in a faithful manner.

The same test that was used for the pretest was administered to the students a few days after the lesson had been taught. The assessment items relating to the notion of unit are shown in Table 8.3. The difference between the pretest and posttest results indicates considerable learning gains by the students.

After all of the teachers had taught the lesson, they met on a number of occasions to evaluate the entire process. Although the teachers felt that they had been overambitious and had packed too much information into the double lesson (totaling 80 min.), they were in general quite satisfied with what they had achieved, and were pleased to learn about the students' learning outcomes. Suggestions were made on how to fine-tune the lesson plan with

TABLE 8.3
The Difference Between the Pretest and Posttest Results

Theme	Question	Freq. of Correct Responses Classes A–E (N = 151) Pretest/Posttest (% gain or loss)
Equal shares	What fraction of the diagram is shown by the shaded area?	45.7/68.9 *(+23.2%)
	Shade 1/9 of a square.	57.6/64.9 (+7.3%)
	Shade 1/8 of a circle.	76.8/86.8 *(+10.0%)
	Shade 1/3 of the eggs in the basket.	57.6/67.5 *(+9.9%)
Comparing fractions	1/2 of a cake is (greater than / equal to / smaller than) 1/4 of the same cake.	41.7/50.3 *(+8.6%)
	2/4 of a cake is (greater than / equal to / smaller than) 1/2 of the same cake.	38.4/60.9 *(+22.5%)
	2/5 of a kg is (greater than / equal to / smaller than) 4/5 of a kg.	73.5/81.5 (+8.0%)
	1/2 of an hour is (greater than / equal to / smaller than) 1/200 of an hour.	25.8/45.0 *(+19.2%)
Units and Unitizing	Divide 2 cakes into three equal parts. How many cakes are there in one part?	8.7/4.7 (−4.0%)
	When 4½ cakes are divided among three persons, how many cakes does each person get?	2.0/44.7 *(+42.7%)
	What fraction of squares is shown by the black squares?	13.3/31.3 *(+18.0%)
	What fraction of the total number of objects is shown by the black squares?	14.7/32.0 *(+17.3%)

*A significant change in percentage is observed with $p < 0.05$.

8. TOWARD A PEDAGOGY OF LEARNING   203

more consolidation work at different points in the lesson. The posttest results showed that all the classes obtained substantial gain when compared with the pretest results (see Table 8.4). The effectiveness of the lesson was thus evident.

A PRIMARY GRADE 4 CHINESE LESSON ON TEXT COMPREHENSION

This was another learning study carried out in the first phase of the "Catering for Individual Differences (Building in Variation)" project. Seven meetings, one hour each, were used for the complete cycle.

Stage 1: Choosing a Specific Object of Learning

After much deliberation, the teachers decided to choose chapter 10 of their course book, *A Pencil End,* as the main teaching content. This chapter was chosen for two main reasons: First, according to their teaching schedule, this lesson was to be taught around late November, and so the timing would be about right. Second, the text contained some special features that the teachers considered to be worthwhile for the students to learn. The text was in the form of a story written by a boy who felt that a 2-inch long pencil end was too short to be useful, and so threw it away. He threw the pencil end away three times, and yet each time it reappeared on his desk. Finally he realized that it was his mother who had picked up the pencil and put it back on his desk, hoping that he would use it again and not be wasteful. The boy was then ashamed of his own action and used the pencil to do his homework.

In subsequent meetings, the teachers identified five worthwhile objects of learning:

TABLE 8.4
The Average Scores of Different Classes in the Pretests and Posttests

	Pretest: Average Score	*Posttest: Average Score*	*Both Tests: Total Score*
Class A	6.38	8.78	12
Class B	6.89	9.14	12
Class C	3.77	4.83	12
Class D	3.94	5.31	12
Class E	3.63	4.78	12
Whole class	5.13	6.85	12

1. In the text, the same action (throwing away the pencil end) appeared three times, yet the way in which the sentiment of the boy was conveyed in each case was different. The teachers wished to draw students' attention to the way in which the choice of the verbs matched the actions and the verbal expressions, in order to show escalating feelings of dislike.

2. In the text, there were six words with the "hand" radical [手] or [扌]. These words can be considered to be in the same semantic field as the word *nah* (Cantonese) [拿] (meaning "take"); all the words are associated with some action using the hand. Yet, each word has a slightly different meaning. For example, the word *taih* (Cantonese) [提] has the meaning of "carry, take hold of, or lifting something out"; the word *gim* (Cantonese) [撿] has the meaning of "select and pick up"; *wing/yihng* (Cantonese) [扔] has the meaning of "throw"; *laai* (Cantonese) [拉] has the meaning of "pull"; *jip* (Cantonese) [接] has the meaning of "catch or receive"; *touh* (Cantonese) [掏] has the meaning of "fish out." In written language, depending on the context, it would be more appropriate to use one of these specific words rather than the word "take" [拿] in order to convey more precise meanings and make the written work more elegant. Yet in spoken Cantonese, it would be perfectly acceptable, and in fact more natural, to use the spoken form of "take" [拿], which is *ling* (Cantonese) [拎]. The teachers wished to teach the students how to distinguish the meaning and usage of each of these words. Also, they wanted the students to appreciate that in written language, the use of words has to be more precise in order to bring out the exact meaning to be conveyed.

3. The text showed the different personalities of the boy and his mother. The boy was very impatient and showed his likes and dislikes overtly. The mother was more gentle and subtle. The teachers suggested that the mother's example could show the students how to relate to other people, such as their classmates.

4. In the last paragraph, the mother introduced the idea of conservation. The teachers wished to cultivate in their students an awareness of the environment and a positive attitude toward conservation.

5. It was the policy of the school that the Chinese panel head should specify the learning objectives for each chapter at the beginning of the school term. For this chapter, a number of words and sentence patterns had already been identified as teaching objectives, and these were to be assessed in the examination.

Only two periods had been assigned for the teaching of this chapter, and the teachers felt that there would not be enough time to cover everything that they wished to teach. They admitted that they often had to rush through things superficially, and that there was little time for in-depth treatment. As a result, many students were not able to learn well. This had always been the teachers' problem. After much discussion, they

8. TOWARD A PEDAGOGY OF LEARNING

agreed that for the research lesson, they would try to focus on fewer objects of learning, and deal with each one in greater depth. They decided not to focus on the affective aspects (objects of learning numbers 3 and 4) at this point, because they felt that these ideas should be infiltrated in their lessons throughout the year. Of the three remaining aspects, they felt that the choice of which to focus on should depend on the students' prior experience and knowledge. Therefore, to help them make an informed decision, they decided to wait until they could obtain information about the students from the pretest.

Stage 2: Finding Out the Extent to Which the Students Have Developed the Intended Capabilities

A pretest was administered to all five classes of 148 students. On average, over 85% of students in each class (more than 70% in the weakest class) demonstrated an understanding of the words and sentence patterns specified by the panel head (object of learning number 5), and were able to use these words to fill in appropriately the blanks of a text. Therefore, the teachers decided that it would not be necessary to focus on these aspects in the lesson.

To test the students' understanding of the words with the hand radical, two questions were set. In the first question, three sentences were given. For each sentence, three characters of very similar meaning were provided and the students had to choose the most appropriate one for the particular context. In the second question, students were required to fill in seven blanks to complete a text. Seven words with the hand radical were provided and students had to choose the most appropriate word for each blank. The results of the test showed that students had difficulties distinguishing words with the hand radical. The word that was found to be most difficult for the students was "fish out" [掏]. In the first question, only 10% of the students could use the word "fish out" [掏] appropriately. In the second question, only two students in one class, Class 4C, got all the answers correct. Again, the character "fish out" [掏] was found to be the most difficult, as only 10% of the students used it correctly. Other difficult words were "take" [拿] (20% correct), "carry" [提] (30% correct), and "pick up" [撿] (30% correct). Thus, it became clear that words with the hand radical needed to be given special attention, especially the words "fish out" [掏], "take" [拿], and "carry" [提].

Another question required the students to put two groups of words in order of the strength of feeling expressed. The first group consisted of the words "excited" [興奮], "pleased" [歡喜], and "happy" [快樂]. The second group consisted of the words "angry" [生氣], "discontented" [不滿] and "furious" [憤怒]. Only about 30% of students were able to put the first group of words in the correct order, and about 60% of students were able to put the second group of words in the correct order.

To test whether students were able to match the verbal expressions correctly with the feelings or sentiments expressed, they were asked to match three phrases with three verbal expressions. For example, students had to match the phrase, "Mother said kindly" with "Don't give up, you just have to work harder next time." It was found that about 60% of students could match the phrases with the verbal expressions correctly.

The result of the pretest prompted the teachers to make the decision to focus on the first two objects of learning:

- To be able to appreciate that the choice of verbs should match the actions, and that the verbal expressions should effectively convey sentiments.
- To be able to distinguish the meaning and usage of some words with the hand radical, and to appreciate that in written language, the use of words has to be precise.

Stage 3: Designing a Lesson (Lessons) Aimed to Develop the Intended Capabilities (The Intended Objects of Learning)

The teachers shared their usual methods of teaching a text, which typically included going through the following five stages:

1. Briefly explaining the text as a whole
2. Reading the text aloud
3. Explaining new characters and words
4. Going through the questions at the end of the text and looking at each paragraph in more detail
5. Teaching some of the sentence patterns and special linguistic features in the text.

The teachers in general felt that this routine, which they had been using all along, was sometimes boring, and that it failed to provide a structure that helped the students focus on the objects of learning. They hoped that for the research lesson, they could come up with a better way of structuring the lesson plan in order to help the students focus on the objects of learning by means of suitable variations. It was decided that two lessons would be used for teaching—one for each object of learning. For the purpose of this chapter, only the lesson dealing with the second object of learning—words with the hand radical—is described. The lessons of two classes (Class 4C and Class 4H) were videotaped, and only data from these two classes are used for the analysis.

The Lesson Plan: Teaching Words With the Hand Radical. The lesson plan contained the following essential features, which were aimed at bringing out similarities and differences, contrasts, variation and invariance:

8. TOWARD A PEDAGOGY OF LEARNING 207

1. Students should find all the words showing action that had a similar meaning to "take," and that used the hand radical. Then they should comment on the text after all these words had been replaced with the word "take."
2. Words with the hand radical should be discussed together, to show their similarities and contrast their differences, for example, "drop" [丢] and "throw" [扔]; "pick up" [撿]; "pick up" [拾] and "take" [拿].
3. Variations should be used to help students discern the meaning of the words, for example, using examples and nonexamples. For each pair of words, a sentence was to be used and its structure kept invariant—only the word with the hand radical would be changed. This was intended to enable students to discern the subtle difference in meanings of the different words.

Stage 4: Teaching the Research Lesson (the Enacted Object of Learning)

The Lesson of Class 4C. The teacher first asked the students to find all the words with the same meaning as "take" [拿]. She then pointed out that it was common for the students to take all these words as synonymous, and that they tended to use only the word "take," instead of making use of these different words. She told them that if they always did this, however, the text would become very boring. She used the metaphor of their mother cooking the same dish for every meal; even though it was good to eat at the beginning, it would become boring after a while. The teacher then focused on the five words: "receive" [接], "fish out" [掏], "take" [拿], "carry" [提], and "pick up" [撿]. These were written on the board.

She attended to the words one at a time, always comparing each one with the word "take" [拿]. She used a sentence in which the use of either word was possible. The difference in meaning of the two words was made more prominent by putting them in the same context. By keeping the sentence structure invariant and varying the words, the teacher focused the students' attention on that which varied, that is, the difference in the meaning conveyed by the two sentences because of the difference in meaning of the two words. For example, she dealt with the two words "take" [拿] and "receive" [接] in the following way.

The teacher asked the students to compare the two sentences:

- He *took* the pencil from her hand.
- He *received* the pencil from her hand.

She explained that when the word "received" [接] was used in the second sentence, there was an implication that the one holding the pencil (she) was giving it to the recipient (him). When the word "took" [拿] was used, it had a different implication. The teacher added that the word "took" in the first sentence might give us the feeling that "he" was not very polite because he took without asking, or without being given the pencil in the first place. "Took" in the context of the first sentence means that the actor is "he," and "she" was passive. "Receive" in the context of the second sentence means that the actor is "she," and "he" is the passive recipient.

The teacher dealt with the other words in a similar way.

The Lesson of Class 4H. The teacher first read out loud a piece of text. In this text, the word "take" was used many times, sometimes inappropriately. The teacher asked the students if they noticed which word was used most often. Many students were able to identify the word "take." Then the teacher asked, "What would your teacher think if you wrote a composition with so many "take's?" Many students responded that the teacher would not like it.

The teacher then asked the students to find all the words associated with the action of the hand. Nine words were found. She then explained the meaning of each word, role-played the action conveyed, and analyzed the action of the hand. For each pair of words, she also kept the sentence structure invariant, but changed the verb and asked the students to compare the two resulting sentences. For example, with the words "drop" [丢] and "throw" [扔], she gave the following sentences:

- Don't *drop* banana skins onto the floor.
- Don't *throw* banana skins onto the floor.

She asked some students to come out and act out how they "drop" something, and how they "throw" something. In the subsequent discussion, she focused on the action of the hand—whether the action was large or small, the size of the swing, and the angle made by the arm. Then she said that of the two words that were used to fill in the blank in the same sentence structure, only one of them was correctly used and asked the students to identity the correct one.

She dealt with the rest of the words in pairs and in a similar way. In each case, she focused on the physical movement of the action. For example, she stressed that with the word "carry" [提], the arm should be held straight down.

Finally, the teacher reread the text that she had read out at the beginning of the lesson. This time, the students suggested appropriate words to replace the word "take" in each instance.

The Enacted Object of Learning. We see that both teachers seemed to have taught in very similar ways. However, there was a very important difference in their ways of dealing with the object of learning. With the

8. TOWARD A PEDAGOGY OF LEARNING   209

teacher of Class 4C, the focus was on the subtle difference in meanings of the different words. By keeping the sentence structure invariant and varying the word used, she helped the students to focus on the different meanings of the words. These meanings were made explicit by their relation to the linguistic context, that is, the rest of the sentences. For example the actor versus recipient meaning—implicit in the words "took" versus "receive," respectively—was made explicit by the invariant sentence structure. On the other hand, despite the fact that the teacher of Class 4H also presented two words in the same linguistic context, she focused on the meaning of each word on its own and the action of the hand conveyed by each word. The teacher did not relate the word to the linguistic context to help students discern the differences in meaning. This method of dealing with the meanings of words in a decontextualized manner can create problems for learners of Chinese, as one character may change its meaning when used together with another character (or characters) to form a word or a phrase. For example, when the teacher focused on the meaning of the word "carry" [提], she emphasized that it had the meaning that the arm should be held straight down. This is a correct interpretation if the word is used in the context of "carrying a briefcase/shopping bag," but not correct when it is used in the context of "carrying a lantern," for example, in which case the arm would probably be bent at the elbow.

Stage 5: Finding the Students' Learning Outcomes

Because the object of learning was to help the students to discern the subtle differences in the meaning of the different words associated with the action of the hand, and to be able to use them appropriately, the posttest also tested such a capability in the students. Judging from the enacted object of learning of the two classes (and if the way in which the teacher dealt with the object of learning is influential), it would be expected that the students of Class 4C should perform better than those of Class 4H. This was indeed borne out by the results of the posttest. The questions were the same in both the pretest and the posttest. Table 8.5 shows the results of the question where students were given seven words with the hand radical, and were asked to fill in seven blanks in a text with the appropriate words.

The results of the post-test showed that the students of Class 4C demonstrated significant improvement. In the pretest, only two students were able to choose all seven words correctly, but in the posttest, 17 students got all seven words correct. Of the five words that the teacher attended to, all students in the class were able to fill in three words correctly: "receive" [接], "fish out," [掏], and "carry" [提]. Significant improvement was also found in Class 4H, however the improvement was not as great as in Class 4C. About 10 students got all seven words correct. For the word "fish out" [掏], the relative improvement was about 47% in Class 4H, whereas the improve-

TABLE 8.5
Table to Compare the Results of the Pretest and the Posttest

Filling in the Blanks With the Appropriate Words
Number of Students Correct (Percentage)

	Student number	[1] 撿 pick up	[2] 扔 throw	[3] 接 receive	[4] 拉 pull	[5] 掏 fish out	[6] 拿 take	[7] 提 carry
Class 4C pretest	33	14 (41%)	26 (74%)	24 (68%)	27 (82%)	9 (27%)	14 (42%)	14 (42%)
Class 4C posttest	33	24 (73%)	27 (82%)	33 (100%)	30 (91%)	33 (100%)	32 (97%)	33 (100%)
Relative improvement		54%*	31%	100%*	50%	100%*	95%*	100%*
4H pretest	31	7 (23%)	11 (35%)	9 (29%)	17 (55%)	2 (6%)	9 (29%)	10 (32%)
4H posttest	31	11 (35%)	18 (58%)	22 (71%)	24 (77%)	16 (52%)	18 (58%)	18 (58%)
Relative improvement		51%*	35%*	59%*	49%*	47%*	41%*	38%*

Key: Relative improvement = increase in % ÷ maximum possible increase in %.
*Words that had been specifically dealt with in the lesson by the teacher.

ment was 100% in Class 4C. For the word "carry" [提], the relative improvement in Class 4H was 38% and in Class 4C, it was 100%.

In the question that required students to choose the most appropriate word to be used in a sentence, it was also found that the students in both classes made significant improvement in the understanding of the word "fish out" [掏]. In 4H, the improvement was from 10% to 61% of students getting it correct, whereas in Class 4C, the improvement was again greater, from 21% to 94%.

As we mentioned earlier, these two studies were some of the first studies (carried out within a research project with developmental ambitions) that were based on the particular theory of learning described briefly in chapter 1. Both studies proved to be successful in terms of gains in student outcomes. Furthermore, they showed a phenomenon that was also found in later studies: Although the teachers had agreed on the intended object of learning, the enacted object of learning varied between the groups, and that the results (the lived object of learning) varied accordingly.

Since these studies were carried out, many others have followed (22 by the end of the second year of the project), mostly with results that are very much in line with the results of the two studies described in this chapter. (Reports on other learning studies conducted in this project can be found on the Internet at this address: http://cidv.hku.hk)

The two studies we have just looked at came from a project with a strong emphasis on the enhancement of teachers' professional development. In this way, the aims of the project were close to those of the Japanese lesson study model. The aim of the study described in the following section was primarily to test theoretical conjectures, and thus this study was closer to the idea of the design experiment.

A SECONDARY GRADE 4 ECONOMICS LESSON ON THE INCIDENCE OF A SALES TAX

The aim of this learning study was threefold: to find a powerful way for teachers to help secondary Grade 4 students handle a rather difficult but important economic concept; to evaluate the effectiveness of a learning study in the improvement of teaching and learning (in comparison to the lesson study approach); and to test the tenet of a specific theory of learning (i.e., the theory of variation—that learning to experience something in a certain way is contingent on the pattern of variation in the critical aspects of the object of learning). The investigation also promised to demonstrate that a learning study could be a design experiment (Brown, 1992; Collins, 1992) and serve primarily as a research tool.

The object of learning for this study was the capability of taking into account the notion of the relative elasticity of demand and supply in determining the distribution of a tax burden between buyers and sellers resulting from the introduction of a sales tax. It was envisaged that if students could develop an economic perspective in understanding the topic of the incidence of a sales tax, the different ways in which they were able to understand the economic phenomenon would increase.

The Economic Topic Used in the Study

The economic topic used in this study is "the incidence of a sales tax," taken from the Hong Kong economics curriculum for secondary Grades 4 and 5. When a government levies a sales tax on goods and services, a certain percentage of the cost of our purchase as consumers is paid to the government. At present, Hong Kong does not have a general sales tax, but a limited number of commodities such as tobacco and liquor incur excise duty (i.e., a particular form of sales tax). The Hong Kong government is currently considering a general sales tax, and this has led to heated discussions among the general public. Most people believe that if the general sales tax is introduced, the sellers will transfer the entire tax burden to the buyers, and simply raise the price of the commodities by the amount of sales tax.

The object of learning for this study was the capability of taking into account the notion of the relative elasticity of demand and supply in determining the distribution of a tax burden between buyers and sellers that results from the introduction of a sales tax. It was envisaged that if students could develop an economic perspective in their understanding of the topic of the incidence of a sales tax, the different ways in which they were able to understand the economic phenomenon would increase.

The view that if a general sales tax is introduced, the sellers will transfer the entire tax burden to the buyers by raising the price of the commodities by the amount of sales tax, is not fully supported by economics. Economists argue that instead of making the buyers shoulder the full tax burden in every instance, the distribution of the tax on a particular commodity depends on the relative elasticity of demand and supply of that commodity. According to the law of demand and supply, when prices of a commodity increase, the quantity demanded falls, and the quantity supplied rises. Sellers are willing to supply more of a commodity when they can earn more for what they sell; buyers are less keen on purchasing a commodity when they get less for their money. The effect on prices is therefore not a uniform price increase on all goods.

People need some commodities more than others; water and staple foods are the classic examples. Even when the price of these commodities rises, the quantity demanded will not drop significantly. In other words, the demand is said to be inelastic, or the elasticity of demand is low (the quantity demanded does not change as much as the price). For other commodities such as luxury cars and jewelry, demand is highly susceptible to price change, and the quantity demanded changes more than the change in price. Such demand is said to be elastic, or the elasticity of demand is said to be high.

8. TOWARD A PEDAGOGY OF LEARNING

Based on a commonsense understanding, sellers of commodities with inelastic demand will simply add the newly introduced sales tax to the current prices, and the buyers will then bear the entire tax burden. According to economic analysis, however, when determining the sharing of the tax burden, the seller's condition should also be taken into account. For instance, for staple foods (such as potatoes or rice), people's demand tends to be inelastic, but in the case of an especially good harvest, sellers have piles of unsold stock in hand that they need to sell before the food spoils. The supply is more or less fixed over the period and so is not very sensitive to price changes. In such a case of oversupply, the supply is said to be very inelastic and sellers may need to arrange to absorb part of the sales tax in their price, instead of passing it on to the consumers.

In general, the more elastic the demand and the less elastic the supply, the greater likelihood of the sales tax being absorbed in the price, and so the sellers will share more of the tax burden than the buyers. Conversely, the less elastic the demand and the more elastic the supply, the greater the likelihood of the whole sales tax being added to the previous prices, in which case the buyers will bear the whole tax burden. However, in a situation when both the demand for and the supply of a commodity are elastic or inelastic, we must compare the elasticity of demand and the elasticity of supply. If the elasticity of demand is greater than the elasticity of supply, the buyers have the upper hand, and vice versa. In the case of staple foods, for example, demand is usually more inelastic than supply, so the buyers have to carry a greater part of the tax burden. Overall, the distribution of the tax burden between buyers and sellers is a function of the relative elasticity of demand and supply.

Design of the Study

Two groups, each with five economics teachers, participated in the main study. One of the groups followed the Japanese lesson study model. In this group, the teachers and a researcher (who did not take the lead) discussed—during three preparatory meetings, each of which lasted for around 2 hours—the ways in which the object of learning could best be handled. Drawing on their own experiences and the results of a pilot study in which students' qualitatively different understandings of the incidence of a sales tax were assessed, the group developed a joint lesson plan for a series of four lessons, which were then taught in five different classrooms.

The procedure was basically the same for the other group of teachers, with one major difference. In this group, the researcher actively participated in the discussion, and introduced the theory of variation as a tool for developing a lesson plan to the teachers. Both the lesson plan and the enacted objects of learning demonstrated teachers' understanding of the theory of variation as applied to the particular object of learning. In the following section, this group is referred to as "the learning study group," whereas the first group is referred to as "the lesson study group." The lesson study group served as a reference to reveal the effect of the instructional design based on the theory of variation.

Using the data obtained on teaching and learning, both inter- and intra-group comparisons were conducted in order to explore the relationship between the enacted objects of learning and student understanding. This investigation therefore comprises a learning study and a lesson study, with the primary emphasis being on the comparison between these two studies. A secondary emphasis is on comparisons between classes within each study.

Ten teachers participated in the main study, five in the learning study group and five in the lesson study group. The teachers in the two groups had 8 years and 7.2 average years of teaching experience, respectively. Furthermore, in Hong Kong, secondary school students are divided into five "bands," where Band 1 represents the highest level of academic attainment and Band 5 the lowest. Four of the five classes in the lesson study group comprised Band 1 and 2 students, and one class was of Band 3 students. The learning study group included one Band 1, two Band 2 and two Band 3 classes. Students in the lesson study group were thus classified as having somewhat higher expected attainment. There were altogether 356 students in the age range 16 to 18 years and they all studied economics as a school subject.

All the lessons were videotaped and subsequently analyzed in terms of the enacted objects of learning. After the series of lessons, all 356 students were required to complete a written task, and five students from each class were chosen randomly for interviews. The written tasks and the interviews were to evaluate student understanding of the topic concerned.

Prior to the main study, a pilot study was carried out with two groups, each consisting of two teachers and their students, in order to try out the research design and test the instruments set for evaluating student learning. More importantly, this pilot study attempted to identify the qualitatively different ways in which students made sense of the distribution of tax burden, so as to provide input for the main study. At the end of the pilot study, the participating students' understanding of the topic was probed by asking them to answer the following question in writing:

> In a recent Legislative Council meeting, the proposal to bring in a sales tax to Hong Kong was rejected. A newspaper then conducted interviews with members of the public to canvass opinions on the tax. Most people opposed it. They said that prices would increase by the amount of the tax. Do you agree that prices would increase by the amount of the tax? Why or why not?

Answers from 158 students participating in the pilot study were analyzed in a phenomenographic way in order to reveal their conceptions regarding

8. TOWARD A PEDAGOGY OF LEARNING 215

the incidence of a sales tax. In addition to answering the written question, a subsample of 16 students was interviewed about their understanding of the phenomenon. The analyses of the data from this interview facilitated the analysis of the written data.

The pilot study revealed six qualitatively different ways of conceptualizing the incidence of a sales tax (Conceptions A through F on Table 8.6), and these were used as the basis for the main study. All six conceptions were identifiable in both the written tasks and student interviews, and represent the variation in the ways in which the students experienced the phenomenon.

The set of categories of description described reveal the different understandings among students of the incidence of a sales tax, making up the different conceptions or "ways of seeing." Corresponding to the different referential aspects, which represent different meanings of the incidence of a sales tax, there are different structural aspects, representing what the students discerned and focused on. By comparing the conceptions, the critical features of the conceptions were identified, namely the features that distinguished them from one another.

During the preparatory meetings for the main study, teachers in both groups drew on the findings of the pilot study (i.e., the students' qualitatively different ways of understanding tax incidence), and agreed that the critical aspect of an economic way of understanding was the relative elasticity of demand and supply. They then started to plan a series of lessons around this concept. As regards the intended object of learning, two commonalities and three critical differences between the two groups were identified. In terms of similarities, both groups tried to establish a context for learning this topic by employing current news about the introduction of a general sales tax in Hong Kong, as well as an example of an authentic gasoline bill. This building up of context is in accordance with the principle of building up a relevance structure for students, as espoused by Marton and Booth (1997).

Furthermore, it was found that all teachers had made systematic use of variation; in a sense the intuitive use of variation was a key feature of all the teaching in the study. Both groups introduced variation *sequentially* in the dimension of elasticity of demand and supply. The teachers first varied the elasticity of demand against the invariant elasticity of supply, and then varied the elasticity of supply against the invariant elasticity of demand, in order to direct students' focal awareness toward the effect of such elasticity on the distribution of the tax burden.

However, there were three major differences between the two groups: First, all the teachers in the theory-inspired group sought to find out the ways in which the students understood the phenomenon of the incidence of a sales tax, and use these as the basis for developing their lessons. In contrast, only one teacher in the comparison group attempted to do the same. Second, all the teachers in the theory-inspired group wanted to introduce *si-*

TABLE 8.6
Categories of Description for the Incidence of a Sales Tax

Level of Understanding	Conception	Referential Aspect	Structural Aspect
One	A	Tax is fully borne by buyers, and the tax burden is related to the demand side of the market.	Focused on the demand conditions of the market in which the goods are situated. Variation is brought about by one or more of these factors, such as the nature of the goods.
One	B	Tax is fully borne by buyers, and the tax burden is related to the supply side of the market.	Focused on the supply conditions of the market in which the goods are situated. Variation is brought about by one or more of these factors, such as the market power of the sellers.
One	C	Tax is fully borne by sellers, and the tax burden is related to dimensions other than demand and supply.	Focused on the nonmarket mechanisms of the market in which the goods are situated. Variation is brought about by aspects other than market operation, for example, government intervention, and so on.
Two	D	Tax is shared between buyers and sellers, and the tax burden is related to the demand side of the market.	Focused on the elasticity of demand of the goods. Variation is brought about by changes in demand conditions.
Two	E	Tax is shared between buyers and sellers, and the tax burden is related to the supply side of the market.	Focused on the elasticity of supply of the goods. Variation is brought about by changes in supply conditions.
Three	F	Tax is shared between buyers and sellers, and the tax burden is related to simultaneous interaction between the demand and supply sides of the market.	Focused on the relative elasticity of demand and supply of the goods. Variation is brought about by relative changes in both aspects.

multaneous variation in elasticity of demand and supply, although none of the teachers in the comparison group planned to do so. Third, all the teachers in the theory-inspired group endeavored to introduce the variations in a contextualized manner, and by using the same product (red wine) in every case. In contrast, none of the teachers in the comparison group tried to provide a context for students when dealing with variation in the elasticity of demand and supply, nor did they use the same goods as a context for learning throughout the lessons.

Results of the Study

The key findings of this study can be categorized into three areas: namely, the enacted objects of learning, student learning, and the relationship between the enacted objects of learning and student learning.

The Enacted Objects of Learning

All the teachers, in both the learning study group and lesson study group, focused on the object of learning that had been agreed on, that is, to help students to develop the capability of taking into consideration the relative elasticity of demand and supply when looking at the incidence of a sales tax. The teachers did not begin by thinking about classroom organization; or the teaching arrangements to be used; whether there would be group work or individual study; or whether they would use information technology or not. Instead, they paid great attention to the way in which they should deal with the object of learning in the lessons.

The two commonalities between the two groups that were identified in the intended object of learning (i.e., the building up of a relevance structure for students and the introduction of variation in elasticity of demand and supply in a sequential manner) were also found in the actual enactment of the intended object of learning (i.e., the enacted object of learning). However, of the three critical differences between the two groups that were identified in the intended object of learning, only the second and third critical differences were found in the enacted object of learning. The teachers in the theory-inspired group introduced simultaneous variation and contextualized variation whereas those in the comparison group did not. The first critical difference, which is the solicitation of students' existing understanding of phenomenon, was not found because the students in the theory-inspired group were inhibited by a number of things, including the presence of a camera, an observer, and the use of English as the medium of instruction.

In the intragroup comparison regarding the building up of a relevance structure for students (as shown in Table 8.7), three teachers in the learning study group (Teachers 1, 2, and 3) did not follow the agreed lesson plan, and did not employ the example of an authentic gasoline bill to illustrate how

TABLE 8.7
Comparison Within the Learning Study Group—The Enacted Objects of Learning

	Teacher 1	Teacher 2	Teacher 3	Teacher 4	Teacher 5
Built up relevance structure	Partially effected (Did not use the gasoline bill example)	Partially effected (Did not use the gasoline bill example)	Partially effected (Did not use the gasoline bill example)	Yes	Yes
Revealed variation in the students' ways of understanding	Partially effected	Partially effected (Did not conduct a class survey)	Partially effected	Partially effected	Partially effected (Did not conduct a class survey)
Introduced variation in the dimensions of elasticity of demand and supply in a sequential manner	Yes	Yes	Yes	Yes	Yes
Introduced variation in the critical aspect of relative elasticity of demand and supply in a simultaneous manner	Yes (Did not allow much flexibility for students to vary on their own)	Yes (Did not allow much flexibility for students to vary on their own)	Yes	Yes (Did not allow much flexibility for students to vary on their own)	Yes (Did not allow much flexibility for students to vary on their own)
Contextualization and consistency of contexts	Yes	Yes	Yes	Partially effected (Did not use the case of red wine in the fourth lesson)	Partially effected (Did not use the case of red wine in the fourth lesson)

sales tax appears in daily transactions. Although all of the teachers attempted to reveal the students' different ways of understanding the distribution of the tax burden between buyers and sellers (using the example of a sales tax imposed on red wine), only three of them (Teachers 1, 3, and 4) conducted a minisurvey inviting students to express their views. This part of the lesson plan was not very successful in any of the classes because of the reluctance of students to speak up generally in class.

However, all teachers in the learning study group introduced simultaneous variation in elasticity of demand and supply (although Teacher 3 did it more successfully and with more student contribution than other teachers). With regard to the contextualization and consistency of contexts, all teachers in this group organized their lessons using red wine as the example product. Three of the teachers (Teachers 1, 2, and 3) kept this product invariant throughout all the lessons in order to make the simultaneous variation in elasticity of demand and supply easier to discern, whereas Teacher 4 and Teacher 5 did not use it in the last lesson.

Table 8.8 shows that all teachers in the lesson study group succeeded in carrying out what was stated in the lesson plan, and that some of them introduced additional tasks to enhance the original lesson plan. In order to build up a relevance structure for the students to learn the topic, Teacher 8 further added his own personal experiences of sales tax (from the time when he lived in Canada some years before), and brought in a "giveaway" item from a gasoline station (a box of tissues), which he showed together with the worksheet on the gasoline bill. Teacher 7 designed an extra worksheet in order to help students to acquire the skills to transform numerical data into graph format, and find out the tax burden between buyers and sellers. Finally, when introducing variation in elasticity of demand and supply sequentially, Teacher 9 further included extreme cases that were not covered in the lesson plan, such as perfectly elastic demand, perfectly inelastic demand, perfectly elastic supply and perfectly inelastic supply.

Student Learning (The Lived Object of Learning)

In phenomenography, *learning* is defined as a change in the dynamic state of awareness or the way of experiencing (Pong & Marton, 2001). Hence, the present study describes student learning in accordance with student ways of experiencing the phenomenon or conceptions identified, rather than merely counting the percentage of students who gave the correct words or numbers as answers to questions set in a diagnostic test. Students are said to have shown evidence of learning if they can successfully display advanced and powerful conceptions of the phenomenon in question.

A total of 356 students participated in the main study, in which School A to School E belonged to the learning study group, and School P to School T belonged to the lesson study group. All students were required to complete a

TABLE 8.8
Comparison Within the Lesson Study Group—The Enacted Objects of Learning

	Teacher 6	Teacher 7	Teacher 8	Teacher 9	Teacher 10
Built up relevance structure	Yes	Yes	Yes (Add-on: personal stories about sales tax and giveaways from gasoline station)	Yes	Yes
Revealed variation in the students' ways of understanding	No	No	No	No	Partially effected (Did not conduct a class survey)
Introduced variation in the dimensions of elasticity of demand and supply in a sequential manner	Yes	Yes (Add-on: an extra worksheet on graphical representation of tax incidence)	Yes	Yes (Add-on: discussion on extreme cases)	Yes (Add-on: an extra worksheet on graphical representation of tax incidence)
Introduced variation in the critical aspect of relative elasticity of demand and supply in a simultaneous manner	No	No	No	No	No
Contextualization and consistency of contexts	No	No	No	No	No

8. TOWARD A PEDAGOGY OF LEARNING   **221**

written task at the end of the series of lessons, and five students from each class were chosen randomly to attend an interview on the same day as the last lesson. The data that were collected from these two sources were analyzed, and the ways of experiencing that were identified were then categorized in accordance with the outcome space (which was described in the previous section). The learning outcomes (in terms of the conceptions developed by students) are reported on a group basis, with a comparison made between the learning study group and the lesson study group, as well as between classes within each group.

The major qualitative difference in the understanding of the tax incidence lay in the students' understanding of the simultaneous interaction between the demand and supply side of the market (i.e., the simultaneous relationship between the elasticity of demand and supply). About 73% of the learning study group managed to show this understanding, and manifested Conception F, which took into account the relative elasticity of demand and supply in determining the distribution of the tax burden between buyers and sellers. In the lesson study group, just under 30% of the students reached this level of understanding. The details are shown in Table 8.9.

As regards intragroup variation in the learning study group, there were marked differences in the students' learning outcome among the classes. As we can see in Table 8.10, School C had the best performance with the written task, with 80.0% of the students expressing Conception F in their answers. School A (77.5%) followed, and then School B (72.5%), School D (66.7%), and School E (60.7%).

TABLE 8.9
Distribution of Conceptions for the Written Task

	The Learning Study Group (181 students)		The Lesson Study Group (175 students)	
Group Conception	Occurrence	Percentage	Occurrence	Percentage
A	9	5.0%	19	10.9%
B	4	2.2%	15	8.6%
C	8	4.4%	17	9.7%
D	25	13.8%	66	37.7%
E	4	2.2%	7	4.0%
F	131	72.4%	51	29.1%

Note. Chi-square = 67.553 ($df = 5$; $p < 0.001$). No cells (0.0%) have expected counts of less than 5. The minimum expected count is 5.41.

TABLE 8.10
Distribution of Conceptions Within the Learning Study Group—The Written Task

School Conception	A (40)	B (40)	C (40)	D (33)	E (28)	Total Number of Conceptions
A	1 (2.5%)	2 (5.0%)	2 (5.0%)	2 (6.1%)	2 (7.1%)	9 (5.0%)
B	1 (2.5%)	1 (2.5%)	0 (0.0%)	1 (3.0%)	1 (3.6%)	4 (2.2%)
C	1 (2.5%)	1 (2.5%)	2 (5.0%)	1 (3.0%)	3 (10.7%)	8 (4.4%)
D	5 (12.5%)	6 (15.0%)	4 (10.0%)	6 (18.2%)	4 (14.3%)	25 (13.8%)
E	1 (2.5%)	1 (2.5%)	0 (0.0%)	1 (3.0%)	1 (3.6%)	4 (2.2%)
F	31 (77.5%)	29 (72.5%)	32 (80.0%)	22 (66.7%)	17 (60.7%)	131 (72.4%)

In the lesson study group, as shown in Table 8.11, the percentage of Conception F was similar among the classes, with School T recording the highest score (38.5%), followed by School S (35.3%), School R (33.3%), School Q (20.8%), and School P (20.0%).

The Relationship Between the Enacted Objects of Learning and Student Learning

The differences in the enacted object of learning (as shown by the different patterns of variation made available in the classrooms), were reflected in student learning in terms of the ways of experiencing that were manifested by students after the lessons. The aspects of the phenomenon that students discerned mirrored the pattern of variations, more specifically, the object of learning experienced by the students in the class. As seen in the data on student learning, the students in the learning study group (who were presented with this particular pattern of variation), learned more effectively than those in the lesson study group.

Furthermore, within the learning study group, the differences in students' performance also seemed to coincide with the differences in the pattern of

TABLE 8.11
Distribution of Conceptions Within the Lesson Study Group—
The Written Task

School Conception	P (25)	Q (53)	R (24)	S (34)	T (39)	Total Number of Conceptions
A	4 (16.0%)	5 (9.4%)	4 (14.3%)	3 (8.8%)	3 (7.7%)	19 (10.6%)
B	3 (12.0%)	3 (5.7%)	3 (12.5%)	2 (5.9%)	4 (10.3%)	15 (8.6%)
C	1 (4.0%)	3 (5.7%)	5 (20.8%)	6 (17.6%)	2 (5.1%)	17 (9.7%)
D	12 (48.0%)	29 (54.7%)	3 (12.5%)	8 (23.5%)	14 (35.9%)	66 (37.7%)
E	0 (0.0%)	2 (3.8%)	1 (4.2%)	3 (8.8%)	1 (2.6%)	7 (4.0%)
F	5 (20.0%)	11 (20.8%)	8 (33.3%)	12 (35.3%)	15 (38.5%)	51 (29.1%)

variation made available in each classroom. For instance, Teacher 3 allowed more flexibility for students to introduce simultaneous variation in both elasticity of demand and supply, and at the same time used the context of the red wine throughout all the lessons. In contrast, Teacher 5 did not allow as much flexibility for students to introduce simultaneous variation, and did not keep the product invariant for the last session. It was consequently found that the students taught by Teacher 3 achieved a better understanding of the topic than the students taught by Teacher 5, a finding that might be attributable to the pattern of variation made available in the lessons.

Reflections on the Study

From an analysis of the teaching in terms of the dimensions of variation that were opened up in the lessons—that is, those aspects that were varied simultaneously and those aspects that remained invariant—the pattern of variation critical to the development of an economic understanding of the incidence of a sales tax became apparent. The teachers in the learning study group handled the object of learning in a way that was powerful in enhancing student learning. They did this by focusing on the object of learning and opening up *simultaneous variation* in its critical aspects—that is, they opened up the relative elasticity of demand and supply in a contextualized manner, and deliberately kept the product (red wine) invariant so that students could experience a change in the way that they were aware of the phenomenon in question. This approach will be helpful to teachers dealing with the same object of learning.

In this study, the theory of variation was examined in relation to its efficacy when used to design an effective learning environment. From the data on the teaching methods and the students' learning, the learning study (which built on the theory of variation) was found to be very effective in enhancing learning in the economics classroom, in terms of the possibility for teachers to identify critical aspects related to different ways of understanding and to design the learning situation around these critical aspects. This method was found to considerably enhance the students' understanding of the phenomenon in question, that is, the incidence of a sales tax. The study thus supports the tenet of the theory of variation, that learning to see something in a certain way is a function of experiencing simultaneous variation in critical aspects of the object of learning.

Finally, the findings of the study seem to suggest that the collaboration between teachers in a learning study premised on a specific theory of learning (in this case, the learning study group premised on the theory of variation), is more effective than teachers working together without an explicit theoretical grounding (as in the lesson study group). As we mentioned earlier, more than twice as many students from the learning study group reached a good understanding of the topic of the incidence of a sales tax as students in classes of the lesson study group. This further supports the notion that the learning study was more effective than the lesson study in allowing teachers to improve their teaching, and thereby help students to learn more efficiently.

CONCLUDING REMARKS: LEARNING FROM LEARNING STUDIES

In this chapter, we presented three examples of studies aimed at improving learning from the point of view of the theoretical background briefly introduced in chapter 1, and the descriptive empirical studies presented in chapters 2 through chapter 7. Our basic idea for facilitating more effective learning is thus as follows: Take as the point of departure what it is that the students are expected to learn (the object of learning); find out what makes the difference between the students who have a good grasp, and those who do not; construct a space of learning that makes it possible for all students to have a good grasp of what is to be learned; and finally, analyze the relationship between the space of learning and what happened in the classroom (the enacted object of learning), and the way in which this relationship affected

8. TOWARD A PEDAGOGY OF LEARNING

the learning outcomes (i.e., what the students have achieved). In our view, it is this procedure—which was followed by all the teachers in the three learning studies reported in this chapter—that led to the successful learning outcomes as evidenced by the study findings.

All the studies in this chapter had certain features in common: the same theoretical grounding and systematic evaluation, a focus on the object of learning, and conditions that enabled teachers to work collaboratively.

The first study in this chapter was a clear demonstration of how teachers made use of the theory of variation as a pedagogical tool. However, we saw that even if the teachers had previously agreed on what to do in the classroom, when they carried out the actual lesson, each lesson differed in a number of important respects (as is well demonstrated by the second study reported in this chapter). To the extent that such differences are recognized, they can be seen to account for differences in the learning outcomes (the lived object of learning). In the second study, the better performance of the students in Class 4C over those in Class 4H in the posttest can be attributed to the differences in the enacted objects of learning in the respective lessons. Learning to focus on the critical aspects of the object of learning through the use of an appropriate pattern of variation is not easy, and does not come naturally even to experienced teachers. The third study quoted in this chapter showed that teaching and learning was much more effective when the teachers were guided by the theory of variation.

By creating the conditions for teachers to work together as a team using an action research approach, we enable teachers to learn and develop together. In fact, the benefits go beyond this. The three learning studies show that the process of designing, conducting, and evaluating research lessons benefitted all three parties: the students, the teachers, and the researchers. The students gained a better understanding of the object of learning, the teachers learned how to handle the object of learning in a more effective way, and the researchers gained further insight into the ways in which theory can be translated into practice.

Epilogue

There is a widely held belief today that knowledge is becoming increasingly important in the lives of individuals and in the lives of nations. If this is true, what kind of conclusion can be drawn from the studies reported in this book with regard to facilitating the development of knowledge on individual and collective levels?

The question of promoting the growth of knowledge can, of course, be addressed from political, economic, and social points of view. Our perspective, however, is pedagogical; we are concerned with teaching and learning. Teaching is a human activity involving someone teaching something to someone else. There is someone teaching (a teacher), someone taught (a learner or learners) and something taught (the content). In grammatical terms, the learner is the dative (indirect object), and the content is the accusative (direct object). The failure to focus on both of these two objects at the same time has haunted education for centuries. Focus has, in the main, been on one or the other, but rarely on both at the same time. In one instance, the emphasis has been on the teacher and the learner; in another instance, the emphasis has been on the teacher and the content

Learner-focused education, where the focus is on the learner, and on the ways in which teaching is adjusted to the learner's needs, has very much colored the 20th century movement called "progressivism." The majority of university educationalists in the West probably subscribe to this orientation.

Where the focus is on the content, that is, on the knowledge to be learned, we call this the "traditionalist" approach to education. According to this approach, the most important thing is that the teacher has a good mastery of the content; he or she has to be good at what her students are supposed to become good at. For the traditionalist approach, it is of primary importance that the students are exposed to certain kinds of content;

what is covered in teaching is vital. The "back to basics" movements belong to this school of thought.

In the politics of education, these two orientations—progressivist and traditionalist—have replaced each other in an ever-recurring cycle of pedagogical fashion. This we believe is a major obstacle to improving pedagogical practices. In fact, pedagogical practices will only improve when equal consideration is given to both the learner and the content. The reason why both orientations must be considered together is very simple: There can be no learning without a learner, nor can there be any learning without something learned. We therefore have to focus both on the learner and on the content of learning at the same time.

Let us look at the question "What is to be learned?" In the past, syllabuses were formulated in terms of categories of content. The question of What is to be learned? was answered in terms of different parts of mathematics, history, English, philosophy, and so on (e.g., fractions, second-grade equations, the French Revolution, World War II, irregular verbs, Chuang Tzu, etc.). But what is to be learned is never simply a case of fractions or Chuang Tzu, or anything of the like. What is to be learned is capabilities, that is, what the students are expected to become capable of doing (in the widest sense). For example, being able to express quantities in terms of rational numbers, and carry out arithmetic operations with rational numbers; or having an understanding of Chuang Tzu's view of human existence, and being able to see contemporary phenomena in light of his conception of Taoism.

Such capabilities are what we referred to in this book as the *objects of learning*. The concept of an *object of learning* includes both the learner and the content; it is defined in terms of the content itself (referred to as *the direct object of learning* in chap. 1) and in terms of the learner's way of handling the content (referred to as *the indirect object of learning* in chap. 1). Thus, we cannot talk about the object of learning without referring to the learner and the content at the same time. Our point is that the primary focus of education should be on both the learner and the content, and not on one of them alone. Failure to focus on both will result in lopsided perspectives. Not paying attention to the learners, to how they make sense—or should make sense— of the content, results in an emphasis on just what is covered—or should be covered—by teachers "who know their subject," and not how the content is handled, or should be handled.

Currently, however, content tends to be underplayed in Western educational thinking, resulting in the resurgence of two illusions, albeit in different forms. One illusion is the old dream of finding "the art of teaching all things to all men." This phrase first appeared in the subtitle of Comenius' book *The Great Didactics* in 1657, which is seen as the first systematic attempt to develop a science of teaching. But the dream that we can teach anything to anyone, if only we can find the right method, is probably older than that. It is still very much alive today, although the methods people come up with differ, of course, from time to time. Currently many people are talking about cooperative learning, IT-supported forms of learning, project work, problem-based learning, and so on as the paths to the perfect art of teaching.

However, after reading this book; it should be quite clear that there are specific conditions necessary for learning specific objects of learning. The conditions differ from one object of learning to another, and we have to find out in each particular case what these conditions are. Peer learning, IT support, project work, and problem-based learning may be arrangements for learning that have great potential, but no general approach to instruction can ever ensure that the specific conditions necessary for the learning of specific objects of learning are brought about. In order to do this, we must take the specific objects of learning as our points of departure.

The other illusion is about "generic capabilities." The current line of reasoning goes something like the following: We are facing an exponential growth of knowledge. Widespread use of IT and the Internet around the globe, means that basically all of this knowledge is available to everyone. As we do not know what kind of knowledge our students will need when they grow up, the best thing we can do is to equip them with capabilities for obtaining knowledge instead of equipping them with knowledge. Thus the emphasis is on generic capabilities, such as learning to learn, reading to learn, learning strategies, thinking strategies, cooperative skills, communicative skills, flexibility, creativity, and so on. What is often forgotten is that knowledge is fundamentally ways of seeing the world. Generic capabilities do exist, but not as individual traits, or as a type of intellectual muscle that develops independently from knowledge and content. Generic capabilities are ways of dealing with different topics, content, knowledge; they do not refer to what people have or what they are; they refer to ways in which people act. Generic capabilities are domain specific. The fact that a person possesses the capability of, say, handling words creatively, does not necessarily imply that the person possesses the capability of dealing with numbers, musical or linguistic tones, or economic transactions in the same way. Generic capabilities develop through handling something specific: the mother tongue, calculus, questions about the ecological survival of our planet, and so on.

There seems to be another widely held belief, particularly among educational policymakers, that language is the object of inquiry of linguists, and paying attention to language pedagogically is the responsibility of language teachers only. Discussions about language in the context of education have largely focused on issues of effectiveness and efficiency in attaining language proficiency. We hear concerns expressed by the community about the declining language standards of both learners and teachers, and that something must be done about the language proficiency of language teachers and learners. We seldom hear complaints about the lack of attention paid to language by subject teachers, such as teachers of mathematics, science, and history. Nor do we hear discussions about the effects of the use of language on the learning of mathematical concepts, scientific concepts, and historical concepts, for example. The relationship between language and learning has been narrowly confirmed to language learning.

The exposition of the importance of the role of language in bringing about learning is not something new. Several decades ago, especially in the 1970s, a number of scholars had already drawn attention to the importance of language in education, and had made a strong case for paying attention to language across the curriculum (see, e.g., Barnes, 1976; Barnes, Britton, & Rosen, 1969; Britton, 1970). Particularly influential was the work of Michael Halliday, who showed that when a child learns a language, he or she is not just engaged in one kind of learning, but is learning the foundations of learning itself: Learning is a process of making meaning, and learning language is learning how to mean (see, e.g., Halliday, 1973, 1975, 1978, 1993). Therefore, it was argued, every teacher is a language teacher. At the time, when the language awareness movement was launched in the United Kingdom, language in education was made a compulsory module in teacher education programs (see Hawkins, 1984). The "language across the curriculum" initiative, which is one of the most important moves in education, was unfortunately not sustained (see Hawkins, 1999).

What we have tried to do in this book is to revitalize the discussion about the role of language in learning by showing the critical role that language plays in bringing about the necessary conditions for learning. One necessary condition for bringing about learning is that students are able to focus on the object of learning and discern its critical features. We have demonstrated that language is crucial in structuring students' awareness so that they become focally aware of the critical features of the object of learning, in bringing about simultaneous awareness, both synchronically and diachronically, and in making important conceptual distinctions. We have demonstrated that because language makes meaning, the ability of the students and the teacher to negotiate meaning and to construct meaning collaboratively through language makes qualitative differences in the semantic dimension of the space of learning that is being constituted. Another necessary condition for bringing about learning is that the space of learning is shared by the students and the teacher. We have demonstrated that language plays a critical role in establishing as well as in widening a shared common ground. When the ground on which a specific object of learning is enacted, is not shared, the quality of learning will be adversely affected. We have shown the difference language makes by comparing the classroom discourse of students learning through their mother tongue with that of students learning through a second and weaker language. When students are learning through a language that they can barely use to express themselves, they are inevitably handicapped because they do not have the necessary resources for making meaning. There is a commonly held belief, especially among educational policymakers, that learning through a second language is no more than learning the technical vocabulary in that language. This simplistic view shows a lack of understanding of the role of language in learning.

What we have demonstrated in this book is that there are specific conditions that are necessary for the learning of specific objects of learning. The way in which these objects of learning are handled and the extent to which the necessary conditions are brought about through language in the classroom are of decisive importance for what the students can possibly learn (and what they actually learn).

There are, no doubt, general conditions necessary for learning, such as light, space, exposure, feedback, and a minimum level of activity among the learners. There might also be necessary conditions of learning that are specific to different groups. Some learners may not be able to learn something without sensuous experience, for instance, while others are able to learn the same thing by symbolic means; for some there may be a great difference between actually seeing something and just hearing something described, whereas for others there may not be any difference at all. But we are not talking about necessary conditions for all kinds of learning, or about necessary conditions for specific groups of learners, but about necessary conditions for the learning of specific objects of learning. These conditions have to be discovered for every specific object of learning. Teachers should be engaged in finding out what the specific conditions are in every specific case, and how they can be brought about. When these conditions are discovered, teaching will become a much more powerful and much more professional enterprise.

In the last chapter of this book, we described some teachers engaging in such an enterprise. They came together with specific objects of learning as their point of departure. They did not start with questions about general arrangements and general teaching methods, but asked questions about the specific objects of learning to be dealt with during a lesson or during a sequence of lessons. They also asked questions about the nature of the capabilities they wanted to develop in their students, the necessary conditions for developing these capabilities, how those conditions could be met, and the kind of arrangements and methods that could be used to create these conditions. These teachers did not start with questions about generic attributes; they asked questions about how domain specific generic attributes could be embedded in the specific objects of learning.

We hope that the examples described in this book have succeeded in illustrating what we believe to be the three core elements necessary for dramatically improving learning in schools. The first element is a primary focus on the objects of learning. The second element is a collaborative effort among teachers in planning and enacting the objects of learning in the classroom, as well as reflections on the enactment that are firmly focused on the objects of learning. The third element is powerful theoretical tools that guide this planning, enactment and reflection: a theory of learning and a theory of the role of language in learning. We hope that this book has demonstrated how these three elements together can make a difference in learning.

References

Alexandersson, M. (1994). Focusing teacher consciousness: What do teachers direct their consciousness towards during their teaching? In I. Carlgren, G. Handal, & S. Vaage (Eds.), *Teachers' minds and actions: Research on teachers' thinking and practice* (pp. 139–149). London: Falmer Press.
Barnes, D. (1976). *From communication to curriculum.* Harmondsworth, England: Penguin.
Barnes, D., Britton, J., & Rosen, H. (1969). *Language, the learner and the school.* Harmondsworth, England: Penguin.
Behr, M., Harel, G., Post, T., & Lesh, R. (1993). Rational numbers: Toward a semantic analysis—emphasis on the operator construct. In T. P. Carpenter, E. Fennema, & T. Romberg (Eds.), *Rational numbers. An integration of research* (pp. 13–48). Hillsdale, NJ: Lawrence Erlbaum Associates.
Bereiter, C., & Scardamalia, M. (1993). *Surpassing ourselves. An inquiry into the nature and implications of expertise.* Chicago: Open Court.
Berry, M. (1987). Is teacher an unanalyzed concept? In M. A. K. Halliday & R. Fawcett (Eds.), *New developments in systemic linguistics* (Vol. I., pp. 41–63). London: Francis Pinter.
Biggs, J. B. (1996). Western misperceptions of the Confucian-Heritage Learning Cultural. In D. A. Watkins & J. B. Biggs (Eds.), *The Chinese learner: Cultural, psychological and contextual influences* (pp. 45–67). Hong Kong/Melbourne: Comparative Education Research Center.
Bransford, Y. D., Brown, A. L., & Cocking, R. R. (Eds.). (2000). *How people learn. Brain, mind, experience, and school.* Washington, DC: National Academy Press.
Britton, J. (1970). *Language and experience.* Middlesex, England: Penguin.
Brown, A. L. (1992). Design experiments: Theoretical and methodological challenges in creating complex interventions in classroom settings. *The Journal of the Learning Sciences, 2*(2), 141–178.
Brown, G. A., & Edmondson, R. (1984). Asking questions. In E. C. Wragg (Ed.), *Classroom teaching skills* (pp. 97–120). London: Croom Helm.
Bruner, J. (1987). The transactional self. In J. Bruner & H. Haste (Eds.), *The child's construction of the world* (pp. 81–96). London and New York: Routledge.

Cambridge Publisher Committee. (1997). *Mathematics (primary 4, first term)* [in Chinese]. Hong Kong: Cambridge Publishers Ltd.
Carlsson, B. (1999). *Ecological understanding. A space of variation*. Luleå, Sweden: Luleå University of Technology.
Carpenter, T. P., & Moser, I. M. (1984). The acquisition of addition and subtraction concepts in grades one through three. *Journal for Research in Mathematics Education, 15*, 179–202.
Cestari, M. L. (2001, April 19–21). *The co-production of misunderstandings in mathematics instructional discourse*. Paper presented at I.A.D.A. 2001—Recent Trends in Dialogue Analysis, Göteborg, Sweden.
Chan, S. (2002). *Task-based teaching and learning for ESL young learners*. Unpublished doctoral dissertation, Faculty of Education, The University of Hong Kong.
Chase, W. G., & Simon, H. A. (1973). Perception in chess. *Cognitive Psychology, 4*, 55–81.
Cheng, K. M. (1992). *China educational reform* [in Chinese]. Hong Kong: Commercial Press.
Chik, P. (2002). *Qualitative differences in teaching and learning: A study of six lessons in Chinese language in Hong Kong's primary schools*. Unpublished Master's thesis, The University of Hong Kong.
Cleverley, J. (1985). *The schooling of China*. Sydney, Australia: Allen & Unwin.
Cohen, D. K., & Hill, H. C. (2000). Instructional policy and classroom performance: The mathematics reform in California. *Teachers College Record, 102*(2), 294–343.
Collins, A. (1992). Toward a design science of education. In E. Scanlon & T. O. Shea (Eds.), *New directions in educational technology*. Berlin, Germany: Springer.
Cortazzi, M. (1998). Learning from Asian lessons: Cultural experience and classroom talk. *Education 3 to 13, 26*(2), 42–49.
Cortazzi, M., & Jin, L. (2001). Large classes in China: "Good" teachers and interaction. In D. Watkins & J. B. Biggs (Eds.), *Teaching the Chinese learners: Psychological and pedagogical perspectives* (pp. 115–134). Hong Kong & Australia: CERC & ACER.
De Groot, A. D. (1965). *Thought and choice in chess*. The Hague: Mouton.
Egan, D. E., & Schwartz, B. I. (1979). Chunking in recall of symbolic drawings. *Memory and Cognition, 7*, 149–158.
Ehrlich, K., & Soloway, E. (1984). An empirical investigation of the tacit plan knowledge in programming. In I. Thomas & M. C. Schneider (Eds.), *Human factors in computer systems* (pp. 113–134). Norwood, NJ: Ablex.
Gardner, H. (1989). *To open minds*. New York: Basic Books.
Glaser, R., & Chi, M. T. H. (1988). Overview. In M. T. H. Chi, R. Glaser, & M. I. Farr (Eds.), *The nature of expertise* (pp. xv–xxvii). Hillsdale, NJ: Lawrence Erlbaum Associates.
Gu, L. (1991). *Xuehui Jiaoxue* [Learning to teach]. Beijing, China: People's Education Press.
Gurwich, A. (1964). *The field of consciousness*. Pittsburgh: Duquesne University Press.
Halliday, M. A. K. (1973). *Explorations in the functions of language*. London: Edward Arnold.
Halliday, M. A. K. (1975). *Learning how to mean: Explorations in the development of language*. London: Edward Arnold.
Halliday, M. A. K. (1978). *Language as social semiotic: The social interpretation of language meaning*. London: Edward Arnold.
Halliday, M. A. K. (1993). Towards a language-based theory of learning. *Linguistics and Education, 5*, 93–116.

Halliday, M. A. K., & Matthiessen, C. (1999). *Construing experience through meaning: A language-based approach to cognition.* London: Cassell.

Hawkins, E. (1984). *Awareness of language: An introduction.* Cambridge, England: Cambridge University Press.

Hawkins, E. (1999). Foreign language study and language awareness. *Language Awareness, 8*(3 & 4), 124–142.

Ho, D. Y. F. (1991, June 29–July 2). *Cognitive socialization in Confucian heritage cultures.* Paper presented to Workshop on Continuities and Discontinuities in the Cognitive Socialization of Minority Children, U.S. Department of Health and Human Services, Washington, DC.

Hoare, P. (2003). *Effective teaching of science through English in Hong Kong secondary schools.* Unpublished doctoral dissertation, Faculty of Education, The University of Hong Kong.

Huang, R. (2002). *Mathematics teaching in Hong Kong and Shanghai: A classroom analysis from the perspective of variation.* Unpublished doctoral dissertation, The University of Hong Kong, Hong Kong SAR, China.

Kilpatrick, J., Swafford, J., & Findell, B. (Eds.). (2001). *Adding it up: Helping children learn mathematics.* Washington, DC: National Academy Press.

Ko, P. Y. (2002). *The notion of teaching excellence in the People's Republic of China: The case of Chinese language teachers.* Unpublished doctoral dissertation, Faculty of Education, The University of Hong Kong.

Kwan, T., Ng, F. P., & Chik, P. (2002). Repetition and variation. In F. Marton & P. Morris (Eds.), *What matters? Discovering critical conditions of classroom learning.* Göteborg, Sweden: Acta Universitatis Gothoburgensis.

Lamon, S. J. (1999). *Teaching fractions and ratios for understanding: Essential content knowledge and instructional strategies for teachers.* Mahwah, NJ: Lawrence Erlbaum Associates.

Lee, W. O. (1996). The cultural context for Chinese learners: Conceptions of learning in the Confucian tradition. In D. A. Watkins & J. B. Biggs (Eds.), *The Chinese learner: Cultural, psychological and contextual influences* (pp. 25–42). Hong Kong/Melbourne: Comparative Education Research Center.

Lesgold, A. S. (1988). Problem solving. In R. J. Sternberg & E. E. Smith (Eds.), *The psychology of human thought* (pp. 188–213). New York: Cambridge University Press.

Leung, Y. M. J. (1991). Curriculum development in the People's Republic of China. In C. Marsh & P. Morris (Eds.), *Curriculum development in East Asia* (pp. 61–81). Bristol, England: Falmer Press.

Lo, M. L., & Chik, P. M. (2000, January). *Two faces of progressivism.* Paper presented at 13th International Congress for School Effectiveness and Improvement, HKSAR, China.

Lo, M. L., & Ko, P. Y. (2002). The "enacted" object of learning. In F. Marton & P. Morris (Eds.), *What matters? Discovering critical conditions of learning* (pp. 59–74). Göteborg, Sweden: Acta Universitatis Gothoburgensis.

Lundgren, U. P. (1977). *Model analyses of pedagogical processes.* Lund, Sweden: Gleerup.

Lybeck, L. (1981). *Arkimedes i klassen* [Archimedes in the classroom]. Göteborg, Sweden: Acta Universitatis Gothoburgensis.

Malinowski, B. (1946). The problem of meaning in primitive languages. In C. K. Ogden & I. A. Richards (Eds.), *The meaning of meaning* (8th ed., pp. 296–336). London: Kegan Paul.

Marton, F. (2001). *The learning study*. Unpublished manuscript.
Marton, F., & Booth, S. (1997). *Learning and awareness*. Mahwah, NJ: Lawrence Erlbaum Associates.
Marton, F., & Morris, P. (Eds.). (2002). *What matters? Discovering critical conditions of classroom learning*. Göteborg, Sweden: Acta Universitatis Gothoburgensis.
Miller, G. A. (1956). The magical number seven, plus or minus two. Some limits on our capacity to process information. *Psychological Review, 63*, 81–87.
Mok, I. A. C. (2000, July 23–27). The anatomy of an "open" mathematics lesson. In T. Nakahar & M. Koyma (Eds.), *Proceedings of 24th Conference of the International Group for the Psychology of Mathematics Education*, Hiroshima, Japan.
Mok, I. A. C. (2002). The analysis of an "open" mathematics lesson. In Z. Dai (Ed.), *Open-ended questions: New models in mathematics pedagogy* (in Chinese; pp. 90–105). Shanghai, China: Educational Publishing House.
Mok, I. A. C., Chik, P. M., Ko, P. Y., Kwan, T., Lo, M. L., Marton, F., Ng, F. P., Pang, M. F., & Runesson, U. (1999, December). *Being good at language teaching*. Paper presented at Departmental Conference of the Department of Curriculum Studies, The University of Hong Kong.
Mok, I. A. C., Runesson, U., Tsui, A. B. M., Wong, S. Y., Chik, P., & Pow, S. (2002). Questions and variation. In F. Marton & P. Morris (Eds.), *What matters? Discovering critical conditions of classroom learning*. Göteborg, Sweden: Acta Universitatis Gothoburgensis.
Moxley, S. E. (1979). Schema: The variability of practice hypothesis. *Journal of Motion Behavior, 2*, 65–70.
Mullis, I. V. S., Martin, M. O., Gonzales, E. J., Gregory, K. D., Garden, R. A., O'Connor, K. M., Chrostowski, S. J., & Smith, T. A. (2000). *TIMSS 1999 International Mathematics Report: Findings from IEA's repeat of the Third International Mathematics and Science Study at the eighth grade*. Chestnut Hill, MA: Boston College, Lynch School of Education, The International Study Center.
Neuman, D. (1987). *The origin of arithmetic skills*. Göteborg, Sweden: Acta Universitalis Gothenburgensis.
Ng, F. P., Tsui, A. B. M., & Marton, F. (2001). Two faces of the reed relay. In D. Watkins & J. Biggs (Eds.), *Teaching the Chinese learner* (pp. 135–160). Hong Kong: Comparative Education Research Centre (CERC), The University of Hong Kong.
Ogborn, J., Kress, G., Martins, I., & McGillicuddy, K. (1996). *Explaining science in the classroom*. Philadelphia: Open University Press.
Paine, L. (1990). The teacher as virtuoso: A Chinese model for teaching. *Teachers College Record, 92*(1), 49–81.
Pong, W. Y., & Marton, F. (2001). *Conceptions as ways of being aware of something—accounting for inter- and intra-contextual shifts in the meaning of two economic phenomena*. Unpublished manuscript.
Qian, M. (1985). *The exploration on guided-reading approach on Chinese language* [in Chinese]. Yunan: Yunan People's Publisher.
Runesson, U. (1999). *Variationens pedagogik. Skilda sätt att behandla ett matematiskt innehåll* [The pedagogy of variation. Different ways of handling a mathematical content]. Göteborg, Sweden: Acta Universitatis Gothoburgensis.
Sabers, D. S., Cushing, K. S., & Berliner, D. C. (1991). Differences among teachers in a task characterized by simultaneity, multidimensionality, and immediacy. *American Education Research Journal, 28*, 63–88.
Säljö, R. (1982). *Learning and understanding: A study of differences in constructing meaning from a text*. Göteborg, Sweden: Acta Universitatis Gothoburgensis.

REFERENCES

Sapir, E. (1961). *Culture, language and personality*. Berkeley and Los Angeles: University of California Press.
Seybolt, P. J. (1973). *Revolutionary education in China*. New York: International Arts & Science Press.
Stevenson, H. W., & Stigler, J. W. (1992). *The learning gap*. New York: Summit Books.
Stevenson, W., & Lee, S. (1997). The East Asian version of whole-class teaching. In W. K. Cumming & P. G. Altback (Eds.), *The challenge of Eastern Asian education*. Albany: State University of New York Press.
Stigler, J. W., & Hiebert, J. (1999). *The teaching gap: Best ideas from the world's teachers for improving education in the classroom*. New York: The Free Press.
Svensson, L. (1976). *Study skills and learning*. Göteborg, Sweden: Acta Universitatis Gothoburgensis.
Tsui, A. B. M. (1994). *English conversation*. London: Oxford University Press.
Tsui, A. B. M. (1995). *Introducing classroom interaction*. London: Penguin.
Tsui, A. B. M., Aldred, D., Marton, F., Kan, F., & Runesson, U. (2001). *The medium of instruction and the space of learning*. Unpublished manuscript.
Voigt, J. (1995). Thematic patterns of interaction and socio-mathematical norms. In P. Cobb & H. Bauersfeld (Eds.), *The emergence of mathematical meaning: Interaction in classroom cultures* (pp. 163–201). Hillsdale, NJ: Lawrence Erlbaum Associates.
Vuolab, K. (2000). Such a treasure of knowledge for human survival. In R. Phillipson (Ed.), *Rights to language: Equity, power and education* (pp. 13–16), Mahwah, NJ: Lawrence Erlbaum Associates.
Wells, G. (1986). *The meaning makers: Children learning language and using language to learn*. Portsmouth, NH: Heinemann.
Wells, G. (1999). *Dialogic inquiry*. Cambridge, UK: Cambridge University Press.
Wistedt, I., & Martinsson, M. (1994). *Kvaliteter i elevers tänkande över en oändlig decimalutveckling* [Qualities in how children know about an endlessly repeating decimal]. Report from the Pedagogical Institute of Stockholm University, Sweden.

Author Index

A

Aldred, D., 157
Alexandersson, M., 165

B

Barnes, D., 230
Behr, M., 72
Bereiter, C., 8
Berliner, D. C., 8
Berry, M., 113
Biggs, J. B., 62
Booth, S., 8, 11, 22, 89, 153, 165, 170, 193, 194, 215
Bransford, Y. D., 8
Britton, J., 26, 35, 230
Brown, A. L., 8, 191, 192, 211
Brown, G. A., 128
Bruner, J., 166

C

Carlsson, B., 23
Carpenter, T. P., 14
Cestari, M. L., 32, 33, 34
Chan, S., 141
Chase, W. G., 8
Cheng, K. M., 61
Chi, M. T. H., 8
Chik, P., 13, 43, 91, 121

Chrostowski, S. J., 66
Cleverley, J., 60
Cocking, R. R., 8
Cohen, D. K., 190
Collins, A., 191, 192, 211
Cortazzi, M., 62
Cushing, K. S., 8

D

DeGroot, A. D., 7

E

Edmondson, R., 128
Egan, D. E., 8
Ehrlich, K., 8

F

Findell, B., 190

G

Garden, R. A., 66
Gardner, H., 60
Glaser, R., 8
Gonzales, E. J., 66
Gregory, K. D., 66
Gu, L., 56, 57, 58, 59, 60
Gurwich, A., 19

H

Halliday, M. A. K., 24, 25, 26, 27, 28, 139, 179, 230
Harel, G., 72
Hawkins, E., 230
Hiebert, J., 45, 66, 191
Hill, H. C., 190
Ho, D. Y. F., 62
Hoare, P., 143
Huang, R., 62

J

Jin, L., 62

K

Kan, F., 157
Kilpatrick, J., 190
Ko, P. Y., 10, 46, 91, 167
Kress, G., 117
Kwan, T., 43, 91

L

Lamon, S. J., 196
Lee, S., 61
Lee, W. O., 62
Lesgold, A. S., 8
Lesh, R., 72
Leung, Y. M. J., 60
Lo, M. L., 10, 91, 167
Lundgren, U. P., 128
Lybeck, L., 153

M

Malinowski, B., 27
Martin, M. O., 66
Martins, I., 117
Martinsson, M., 153
Marton, F., 8, 11, 22, 89, 91, 114, 153, 157, 165, 170, 192, 193, 194, 215, 219
Matthiessen, C., 24, 139
McGillicuddy, K., 117
Miller, G. A., 9
Mok, I. A. C., 75, 91, 121
Moser, I. M., 14
Moxley, S. E., 15, 16
Mullis, I. V. S., 66

N

Neuman, D., 7

Ng, F. P., 43, 91, 114

O

O'Connor, K. M., 66
Ogborn, J., 117

P

Paine, L., 61, 62
Pang, M. F., 91
Pong, W. Y., 219
Post, T., 72
Pow, S., 121

Q

Qian, M., 46

R

Rosen, H., 230
Runesson, U., 67, 91, 121, 157

S

Sabers, D. S., 8
Säljö, R., 90
Sapir, E., 27
Scardamalia, M., 8
Schwartz, B. I., 8
Seybolt, P. J., 60
Simon, H. A., 8
Smith, T. A., 66
Soloway, E., 8
Stevenson, H. W., 66, 67
Stevenson, W., 61
Stigler, J. W., 45, 66, 67, 191
Svensson, L., 11, 58, 74
Swafford, J., 190

T

Tsui, A. B. M., 114, 121, 128, 157, 167

V

Viogt, J., 36, 37
Vuolab, K., 28

W

Wells, G., 179, 182
Wistedt, I., 153
Wong, S. Y., 121

Subject Index

A

Awareness, 4, 17–21, 30, 32, 55–56, 63–64, 84, 89, 94, 120, 136–137, 149–150, 153, 165, 168, 170, 172–173, 175, 204, 219, 230
- figure, 30–31
- figure-ground structure of, 19, 30, 170
- focal, 18–19, 30–31, 64, 85, 91, 94, 97, 114–127, 131–137, 142, 149–150, 154, 169, 173, 175, 178, 182, 215
- ground, 30–31, 173
- structure of, 30–31, 136–137, 153, 170–175, 185

C

Chinese lesson, 12, 75, 94–101, 147–156, 176–178, 203–211
- antonyms, 54
- hyponyms, 49
- semantics, 46–56
- synonyms, 51, 55–56

Chinese as a medium of instruction, 114, 117–118, 131–133, 135, 137, 157, 160, 162–163, 169, 179–180, 183–185

Chinese pedagogy, 46, 54

Collaborative construction of meaning, 178–182

Confucian, 62

D

Discernment, 10–14, 20, 63–66, 79–85, 97

E

Economics lesson, 211–224

English lesson, 10, 101–109, 121–127, 131, 137, 141–143, 168–175, 185
- determiner, 30–31, 121, 124–125, 127
- partitives, 102–106, 109
- simple present tense, 167–169, 173
- superlative, 30

English as a medium of instruction, 114, 129, 131, 133, 135, 137, 144, 146, 157, 162–163, 182–184, 217

H

History lessons, 35, 157–162, 179–181, 183–185

Homonyms, 47, 55

Hyponym, 49, 147

L

Language and distinction, 26–30

M

Mathematics lessons, 32–34, 36–37, 62–63, 66–73, 75–84, 86, 91–94, 140–141, 196–203
 division, 74
 division-quotient, 92–93
 quotient, 73
 reflections, 79, 81–85
 rotation, 79, 82
 shrinker, 72
 stretcher, 72
 subtraction, 6, 9

O

Object of learning, 4–8, 22–24, 35, 190, 193, 203–205, 228–230, 232
 enacted, 4–5, 22, 24, 39, 43, 62, 74, 87, 91, 109–110, 127, 137, 165, 184, 191, 207–209, 211, 213–214, 217–219, 222–225
 intended, 4, 22, 43, 45, 62, 86, 90, 110, 127, 131, 137, 167, 170, 189, 191, 195, 205–207, 211, 215, 217
 lived, 5, 22, 38, 90–91, 137, 162, 165, 211, 219–222, 225

P

Part, 6–7, 9, 11–14, 18–19, 24, 36–39, 44–45, 58, 69, 71, 74–75, 89–91, 95–98, 107, 109–110
Part–part relationships, 37, 90–91
Part–whole relationships, 7, 13, 89–91, 94, 96–98, 103–105, 109
Pedagogy, 3, 35–40
Phenomenography, 193–194, 219

Physics lessons, 117–121, 128–136, 169–170
 reed relay, 114–121
Presuppositions, 117, 166, 178

Q

Question, 113–136
 blank-filling, 124, 128, 130, 132, 136
 closed, 127–128, 133–134, 136
 funneling, 128
 open, 127–130, 132–134, 136, 159, 180
 piloting, 128

S

Science Lesson—neutralization, 143–146
Simultaneity, 17–20
 diachronic, 17–18, 20
 synchronic, 18, 89, 97
Space of learning, 20–24, 39, 127–136
 linguistic constitution, 24–31
 semantic, 31–32, 139–146
 shared, 32–35, 170–184
Space of variation, *see* Variation

T

TIMSS, 66

V

Variation, 11, 14–17, 21, 37, 39, 43–46, 54–62, 65, 73–74, 85, 193–196, 207, 213, 215–216, 223
 contextual, 84–85, 140–146, 217
 space of, 65, 73